Assessing the Landscape of Taiwan and Korean Studies in Comparison

Brill Series in Taiwan Studies

Series Editors

Niki Alsford, *University of Central Lancashire*
Mark Harrison, *University of Tasmania*

VOLUME 1

The titles published in this series are listed at *brill.com/bsts*

Assessing the Landscape of Taiwan and Korean Studies in Comparison

Edited by

J. Bruce Jacobs†
Niki J.P. Alsford
Sojin Lim

BRILL

LEIDEN | BOSTON

Library of Congress Cataloging-in-Publication Data

Names: Jacobs, J. Bruce, editor. | Alsford, Niki J. P., editor. | Lim, Sojin, editor.
Title: Assessing the landscape of Taiwan and Korean studies in comparison /
    edited by J. Bruce Jacobs, Niki J.P. Alsford, Sojin Lim.
Description: Leiden ; Boston : Brill, [2021] | Series: Brill series in Taiwan
    studies, 2589-3939 ; volume 1 | Includes bibliographical references and index. |
    Summary: "In Assessing the Landscape of Taiwan and Korean Studies in
    Comparison, the chapters offer a reflection on the state of the field of Taiwan
    and Korean Studies. The volume not just identifies their similarities, but
    also reflects on their differences. Both have national identities formed in
    a colonial period. The surrender of Japan in 1945 ignited the light of
    independence for Korea, but this would be ideologically split within five
    years. For Taiwan, that end forced it into a born-again form of nationalism
    with the arrival of the Chinese Nationalists"– Provided by publisher.
Identifiers: LCCN 2021006684 | ISBN 9789004461307 (hardback) |
    ISBN 9789004461314 (ebook)
Subjects: LCSH: Taiwan–Study and teaching (Higher) | Korea (South)–
    Study and teaching (Higher)
Classification: LCC DS799.48 .A77 2021 | DDC 951.24905071/1–dc23
LC record available at https://lccn.loc.gov/2021006684

Typeface for the Latin, Greek, and Cyrillic scripts: "Brill". See and download: brill.com/brill-typeface.

ISSN 2589-3939
ISBN 978-90-04-46130-7 (hardback)
ISBN 978-90-04-46131-4 (e-book)

Printed by Printforce, United Kingdom

"My heart joined the Thousand, for my friend stopped running today": A Tribute to J. Bruce Jacobs

On 24 November 2019, J. Bruce Jacobs became tired and passed away. I was fortunate to have had a brief conversation with him earlier the previous week. I spoke mainly with Jung-Sim, his wife, but was able to exchange a few words with Bruce over the speakerphone. In situations such as this, one never truly knows what to say. I wish I had said more.

In June 2018, during the workshop that inspired this volume, Bruce and I strolled along the banks of the River Ribble in Preston, the city of the University of Central Lancashire in the UK. We had decided that the second day of the workshop should take place at Brockholes, a nature reserve a few miles outside the city. The weather was uncharacteristically gorgeous and the gamble to host an evening's barbeque truly paid off. As Bruce and I chatted – both shop and personal – I was joyed to hear an upbeat tone in Bruce's voice once again. It was not long after the workshop ended and the weather closed in, as it does in the north of England, that Bruce called to tell me the news that his cancer had returned. I was numb. We both knew in our silences that this would be Bruce's last project. The unspoken aspect of it filled me with dread that it might not be completed in time. This fear was realized in November 2019.

For the title of this tribute page, I have chosen a quote from Richard Adams' masterpiece *Watership Down*, as I see it fitting in so many ways. I hail from the south and I recall the undulating hills of the South Downs – the backdrop to Adams' tales – so vividly. That walk on a beautiful June morning, with the explosion of wildlife, the sounds and sights of the Lancashire countryside in June, was so characteristically similar.

Bruce was indisputably a Hazel-rah character. He was both brave and intelligent. He earned the respect of the academic community because his authority and leadership rested on courage and his readiness to utilize the skills of others for the good of the 'warren'. Throughout his life, Bruce was willing to sacrifice for what he believed in.

Bruce heard and listened to the 'Black Rabbit of Inle' and left for the 'great Owsla' at the age of 76, but his larger-than-life persona and trademark stubbornness will not be forgotten. He will be remembered for his contagious smile, sparkling blue eyes, gentle heart and amazing sense of humor.

He took tremendous pride in his work and always told you the truth, even if it was not what you wanted to hear. He was generous to a fault, a bunny-rabbit at heart, and yet he sugar-coated absolutely nothing. As Winston Churchill would have put it if he had had the honor of meeting him, "he was a riddle, wrapped in a mystery, inside an enigma."

Quite a teller of tales, Bruce's elaborate stories were often punctuated with that emblematic smile.

He will be greatly missed and fondly remembered by many.

Years from now, the children of the 'warren' will gather at our annual conferences and hear the great tales of Bruce Jacobs-rah.

My greatest honor is that I knew him. I conversed and debated with him. What I know today, and what I will pass onto the generations to come, is because I was able to stand on the shoulders of giants.

Bruce will forever be a giant in this field of study. Yet my heart still aches that Sojin and I must complete this edited volume without him.

Bruce Jacobs, we thank you, 謝謝你! 감사합니다!

Niki J.P. Alsford
2020

Contents

Figures and Tables

Figures

Tables

Notes on Contributors

Niki J.P. Alsford

is Professor in Asia Pacific Studies and Head of Asia Pacific Institutes at the University of Central Lancashire, as well as Director of the Institute for the Study of the Asia Pacific, Co-Director of the International Institute of Korean Studies and the Northern Institute of Taiwan Studies, and Chair of the Centre for Austronesian Studies. He is also Research Associate at the Centre of Taiwan Studies at School of Oriental and African Studies (SOAS), University of London and Research Fellow at the Ewha Institute of Unification Studies at Ewha Womans University in Seoul. He received his PhD in Modern East Asian History from SOAS. As a historical anthropologist, his research focuses on Taiwan comparative ethno-histories. Chief among these is an engagement with Austronesian migration and the historical anthropology of the maritime Asia Pacific region. In addition to this, he works on developmental anthropology in North Korea and climate anthropology in the case of the Pacific. He is author of *Transitions to Modernity in Taiwan: The Spirit of 1895* and the *Cession of Formosa to Japan*, published by Routledge in 2017. He is book series editor for the Taiwan series at BRILL and the Korean series at Routledge.

Evan Dawley

is Associate Professor of History at Goucher College. He completed his PhD in History at Harvard University. His first monograph, *Becoming Taiwanese: Ethnogenesis in a Colonial City, 1880s-1950s*, was published in 2019 by the Harvard Asia Center Press. He has co-edited *The Decade of the Great War: Japan and the Wider World in the 1910s* (Brill, 2014). His new research explores the ongoing creation of Chinese identities in the context of international relations between the ROC and other governments around communities of overseas Chinese, from the 1920s to the 1970s.

Moises de Souza

is Lecturer (Assistant Professor) in Asia Pacific Studies at the School of Humanities, Language and Global Studies, University of Central Lancashire, and Chair of the Northern England Policy Centre for the Asia Pacific (NEPCAP). He is also researcher in Asia Studies at the International Relations Research Center of the University of São Paulo (NUPRI-GEASIA), and deputy-director of the South China Sea Think Tank (SCSSTT).

Dafydd Fell

is Reader (Professor) in Comparative Politics with special reference to Taiwan at the Department of Politics and International Studies of SOAS, University of London. He is also the Director of the SOAS Centre of Taiwan Studies. In 2004 he helped establish the European Association of Taiwan Studies. He has published numerous articles on political parties and electioneering in Taiwan. His first book was *Party Politics in Taiwan* (Routledge, 2005), which analyzed party change in the first fifteen years of multi-party competition. His second book was *Government and Politics in Taiwan* (Routledge, 2011) and the second edition was published in early 2018. He co-edited *Migration to and from Taiwan* (Routledge, 2013) and his next edited volume, *Social Movements in Taiwan under Ma Ying-jeou* (Routledge) was published in 2017. His most recent co-edited book was *Taiwan Studies Revisited*, published in 2019. He is also the book series editor for the Routledge Research on Taiwan Series.

Fabricio A. Fonseca

is Assistant Professor at the College of International Affairs, Tamkang University, Taiwan. He holds a PhD in Asia-Pacific Studies, with a specialization in International Political Economy, from National Chengchi University (NCCU), and a MA degree in China Studies from El Colegio de México. His research interests include China-US relations, China-Latin America relations, and comparative politics between East Asia and Latin America. His works have been presented and published in conferences, books and journals in Asia, Latin America and Europe.

J. Bruce Jacobs†

was Professor of Asian Languages and Studies at Monash University in Melbourne, Australia. He also studied as a postgraduate student in the History Research Institute of National Taiwan University and has been an Exchange Scholar and a Concurrent Professor at Nanjing University. He published many books, research articles and book chapters as well as newspaper columns on Taiwan and China, including Democratising Taiwan (BRILL, 2012) and The Kaohsiung Incident in Taiwan and Memoirs of a Foreign Big Beard (BRILL, 2016).

Young-Im Lee

is Assistant Professor of Political Science at California State University, Sacramento. Her main research areas are gender in legislative and presidential elections in South Korea and Taiwan. Her research has appeared in *Electoral*

Studies, Politics & Gender, Feminist Media Studies, and *The Washington Post,* among other outlets.

Sojin Lim

is Senior Lecturer (Associate Professor), Course Leader for both MA North Korean Studies and MA Asia Pacific Studies, and Co-Director of the International Institute of Korean Studies (IKSU) at the University of Central Lancashire. She works as Co-Editor of the *Routledge Research on Korea* series and is also Research Fellow at the Ewha Institute of Unification Studies at Ewha Womans University. Prior to joining UCLan, she worked for aid agencies as a senior research fellow with hands-on field experiences. She obtained both BA and MA degrees from Ewha Womans University, South Korea, and her PhD from the Institute for Development Policy and Management (IDPM) at the University of Manchester, UK. Her research interests lie in development studies, area studies, public policy, and political economy, with cases of North Korea, South Korea and the Pacific islands. She frequently discusses changes in North Korea and in the Korea Peninsula in media interviews, such as appearing on BBC.

Michael J. Seth

is Professor of History at James Madison University. There he teaches East Asian and world history. Seth is the author of *Education Fever: Society, Politics and the Pursuit of Schooling in South Korea* (2002), *A Concise History of Korea* (third edition, 2020), *North Korea: A History* (2018), *Korea: A Very Short Introduction* (2020) and editor of *The Routledge Handbook of Modern Korean History* (2016).

Nataša Visočnik

is Assistant Professor at the Department of Asian Studies, University of Ljubljana, Slovenia after she gained her PhD at the Department of Ethnology and Cultural Anthropology at University of Ljubljana. Her research is focused on identity issues in Japan and South Korea, including identity processes, minority questions and marginality; but she also deals with religious and women's issues, and she has done some research on anthropology of body, dance and space. In her recent research, she focuses on Zainichi Koreans in Japan and on 'diaspora at home', studying Zainichi Koreans moving and living in Korea, as well as doing research and fieldwork as a research fellow at University of Kyoto in Japan and Seoul National University in South Korea. She is also a member of a project called East Asian Collections, where she is working on the East Asian collections in Slovene museums, and she is a managing editor of the journal *Asian Studies* at the Faculty of Arts, University of Ljubljana.

CHAPTER 1

Introduction

Comparing Taiwan and Korea

J. Bruce Jacobs†

When I was a postgraduate student half a century ago, the field of Comparative Politics was starting to become mainstream in political science. Unlike the natural scientist, the social scientist and historian can rarely conduct and replicate controlled experiments to see what happens when certain key variables change. Thus, we cannot "rerun history" to see what would have happened had some variable been different. In addition, the tremendous complexity of every culture ensures that analyses must confront numerous—and often contradictory—explanations. The comparative approach provides the social scientist and historian with one means to overcome these difficulties: if two or more situations have similarities, then attempts to explain differences can focus on the variables which differ.[1]

I do not wish to evaluate Comparative Politics as a field, though I remember many books which neglected "facts" as they pronounced on theory and I also remember "famous" books which were very poorly written and virtually unintelligible. However, I do believe that comparison is useful in providing insights into the social sciences and history.

Early on, I was drawn more to what I called "intra-cultural" comparison rather than the more common "cross-cultural" comparison.[2] Presumably, when two states or societies share many characteristics, the number of differences will be fewer. Thus, I was quite drawn to comparisons between China, Taiwan and even Hong Kong, Singapore and overseas Chinese communities and argued that comparisons could be made across space, time and level.[3] I felt that such comparisons could provide insights into several topics like lineages, surname groups, frontiers and migration.[4] Such an emphasis on comparing China and Taiwan worked during the dictatorships of Chiang Kai-shek and

---

1   J. Bruce Jacobs, "Chinese Studies, Cross-Cultural Studies and Taiwan," *Pacific Affairs* 54, no. 4 (Winter 1981–82), 688.
2   Jacobs, "Chinese Studies, Cross-Cultural Studies and Taiwan."
3   Jacobs, "Chinese Studies, Cross-Cultural Studies and Taiwan," 689.
4   Jacobs, "Chinese Studies, Cross-Cultural Studies and Taiwan," 698.

Chiang Ching-kuo as well as Mao Zedong and Deng Xiaoping. One could make many comparisons including the nature of the Chinese Communist Party (CCP) and Chinese Nationalist (Kuomintang, KMT) dictatorships.[5] However, the KMT colonial dictatorship misleads many scholars about the nature of Taiwan's history and culture. Today, after Taiwan has democratized for three decades and although Taiwan has had a large migration of people from China over the past four centuries, we know that Taiwan is different from China both in culture[6] and identity.[7] In addition, there are huge differences in scale: China is a great power, while Taiwan is a middle power. Thus, comparisons between China and Taiwan often make serious mistakes.[8]

One of the most stimulating cross-cultural comparisons has been between Taiwan and Ireland. Both are islands on the opposite ends of the Eurasian landmass. Both have suffered harsh colonialism and many deaths from colonial oppression. Both have had immigration and emigration, and both have emigrant communities living overseas. In both, language issues have played at least some role. In recent years both have succeeded economically and moved from being peasant societies to quite industrialized and hi-tech economies. Both have also democratized.

The main comparison between Ireland and Taiwan occurred in a volume entitled *Taiwan and Ireland in Comparative Perspective* edited by Fang-Long Shih and John McNeill Scott and published as a special issue of the journal *Taiwan in Comparative Perspective*.[9] Seven of the eight substantial articles focus on both Taiwan and Ireland looking at subjectivity and national narrations,[10] how Lin Hsien-tang appears to have learned from the Irish Home

---

5   J. Bruce Jacobs, "Paradoxes in the politics of Taiwan: Lessons for comparative politics," *Politics* XIII, no. 2 (November 1978), 239–247.

6   David C. Schak, *Civility and Its Development: The Experiences of China and Taiwan* (Hong Kong: Hong Kong University Press, 2018).

7   J. Bruce Jacobs and Peter Kang, eds., *Changing Taiwanese Identities* (London and New York: Routledge, 2018).

8   A recent case where such a comparison has failed is Mikael Mattlin, *Politicized Society: The Long Shadow of Taiwan's One-Party Legacy* (Copenhagen: NIAS Press, 2011). My review and Mattlin's response is available at J. Bruce Jacobs, "[Review Article]," *China Review International* 19, no. 3 (2014), 367–381. I would like to thank Mikael Mattlin for coming up to me at a conference in London in 2015. We had a very friendly discussion and we now have a much better mutual understanding.

9   Fang-Long Shih and John McNeill Scott, eds., *Taiwan and Ireland in Comparative Perspective*. Published as a special issue of *Taiwan in Comparative Perspective*, 4 (2012).

10   Fang-Long Shih, "Taiwan's Subjectivity and National Narrations: Towards a Comparative Perspective with Ireland," *Taiwan in Comparative Perspective* 4 (2012), 6–33.

Rule movement,[11] cinema,[12] working-class theatre,[13] Taiwanese and Irish communities in the United States (US),[14] developmental immigration,[15] and language movements.[16] As would be expected, the contributions are uneven, but the effort is fabulous and even the book reviews often compare Ireland and Taiwan. Sadly, I have not been able to find further publications making comparisons between Taiwan and Ireland.

Taiwan and Korea also make an excellent pairing for comparison and I devote the rest of this introduction to this comparison.

1   Comparing Taiwan and Korea: Geography

Taiwan and Korea do share some geographical features. Taiwan is an island, while Korea is a peninsula. Both have few flat areas with mountains accounting for 80 percent of the two land masses. The highest mountain in Taiwan is Yushan (Jade Mountain) which rises 3,952 meters above sea level. Taiwan also has 164 separate mountains 3,000 meters and higher. The highest mountain in Korea is Mt. Paektu (Baekdu), on the border with Manchuria, which rises 2,744 meters. In South Korea, the highest mountain is Mt. Halla, on Cheju (Jeju) Island, which reaches 1,950 meters. Thus, agriculture, though prosperous in both places, has limitations. The closeness of the sea to both places means that both have had substantial shipping and trade.

Both places are also middling in size and population. Korea has a total area of 219,020 square kilometers, with South Korea accounting for 100,210 square kilometers. Taiwan has an area of 36,193 square kilometers. The population for Korea totals 76.8 million with 51.2 million in the South and 25.6 million in the North, while Taiwan's population totals 23.5 million.

---

11   Fu-San Huang, Sam Huang, and Conor Mulvagh, "Lin Hsien-Tang's Taiwanese Home Rule Movement as Inspired by the Irish Model," *Taiwan in Comparative Perspective* 4 (2012), 65–88.

12   Ming-Yeh T. Rawnsley, "Cinema, Identity, and Resistance: Comparative Perspectives on *A City of Sadness* and *The Wind that Shakes the Barley*," *Taiwan in Comparative Perspective* 4 (2012), 89–107.

13   Wei H. Kao, "Voices from Two Theatrical Others: Labour Issues in the Theatres of Ireland and Taiwan," *Taiwan in Comparative Perspective* 4 (2012), 108–127.

14   Pei-Te Lien and Jeanette Yih Harvie, "The Political Incorporation of Taiwanese Americans and Irish Americans Compared," *Taiwan in Comparative Perspective* 4 (2012), 128–153.

15   Bryan Fanning, "Developmental Immigration in the Republic of Ireland and Taiwan," *Taiwan in Comparative Perspective* 4 (2012), 154–175.

16   Khin-Huann Li and Liam Mac Mathúna, "A Comparative Study of Language Movements in Taiwan and Ireland," *Taiwan in Comparative Perspective* 4 (2012), 176–188.

2   Comparing Korea and Taiwan: Pre-17th Century History

Until the arrival of the Dutch in 1623–1624, Taiwan was inhabited by indigenous Austronesian peoples, the ancestors of today's aborigines, who never united the island politically. Archaeological evidence traces the presence of these peoples in Taiwan back at least 6,000 years. These peoples had substantial trade with Southeast Asia, but not with China, going back at least 2,500 years.[17] They never developed states. The tribes varied considerably. Some were very egalitarian; others had rigid social structures. Some were matrilineal while others were patrilineal. Evidence suggests that Taiwan's indigenous peoples were quite healthy.

From the 4th century CE, Korea had five aspects which contrast significantly from Taiwan. First, Korea had states—kingdoms—which until the 20th century remained independent even though they often had tributary relationships with Mongol and Manchu tribes. Under the Mongols, Koreans called themselves a "Son-in-law Nation" (pumaguk, bumaguk) as the kings married Mongol princesses. Their successors were of course sons-in-law of the Mongol rulers.

Second, Koreans often fought for their independence and at least twice suffered horrendous devastation. The Koryŏ (Goryeo) (935–1392) court sought refuge on tiny Kanghwa (Ganghwa) island off the west coast of Korea, but the Mongols laid waste to the countryside of the Korean mainland. Later Korean accounts recorded: "The fields were covered with the bones of the dead; the dead were so many that they could not be counted ... [wherever the Mongol army passed] the inhabitants were all burned out, so that not even dogs and chickens remained."[18] In addition, the Mongols took over 200,000 prisoners.

The Japanese invaded Korea in 1592 and 1597. The destruction of Korea was again horrendous. Farmland production was reduced to only about 30 percent of its previous capacity. In a poem entitled "Song of Great Peace," the Korean poet Pak Il-lo (Bak Inro) wrote:

> Higher than mountains
> The bones pile up in the fields,

---

17   J. Bruce Jacobs, "A History of Pre-Invasion Taiwan," *Taiwan Historical Research* 23, no. 4 (December 2016), 5–9.

18   Michael J. Seth, *A Concise History of Korea From the Neolithic Period through the Nineteenth Century* (Lanham, Md et al: Rowman & Littlefield, 2006), Vol. I, 107.

> Vast cities and great towns
> Became the burrows of wolves and foxes.[19]

As proof of their success, the Japanese commanders sent 38,000 Korean and Chinese ears back to Japan. These were pickled and buried in Kyoto in what became known as the "Mound of Ears."[20]

Third, Koreans maintained a rigidly hierarchical society over the centuries. We can divide Chosŏn (Joseon) (1392–1910) society into four broad social categories. On top were the *yangban*, who had status and wealth. (Sometimes, they were called *sadaebu*, a term that comes from the Chinese *shidafu* 士大夫 meaning scholar-official). *Yangban* totally dominated Chosŏn society virtually monopolizing all official roles. They comprised less than 10 percent of society.

The second group, the petty functionaries called the "middle people" (*chung-in, jungin*), included professionals like medical people, science specialists, and foreign language specialists. They also accounted for less than 10 percent of society.

The third group, the "good people" (*yangmin*) or "commoners" (*sangin*), included farmers, craftsmen, fishermen and merchants. They accounted for perhaps 80 percent of the population.

The fourth group, the *ch'ŏnmin* (*cheonmin*) or "low born" or "inferior people," included butchers, gravediggers, those involved in tanning and leatherwork, morticians, and entertainers. Slaves were also included in this group. In 1650, all common prostitutes became slaves. Nahm suggests that there were 400,000 slaves in Korea in the early Chosŏn, but that this declined to 190,000 in 1655.[21] Government slavery was abolished in 1801, but domestic slavery continued up until 1894.

The fourth characteristic of pre-modern Korea relates to belief systems. Buddhism entered Korea during the Three Kingdoms period (4th–7th centuries CE) and remained predominate until the founding of the Chosŏn Dynasty in 1392 when Zhu Xi's Neo-Confucianism came to the fore. This change was not absolute, however, as Buddhism remained important during the Chosŏn Dynasty and Neo-Confucianism also existed before the Chosŏn Dynasty.

Finally, with Neo-Confucianism dominating from the founding of the Chosŏn Dynasty, the status of women declined considerably compared to

---

19   Andrew C. Nahm, *Korea: Tradition and Transformation: A History of the Korean People* (Elizabeth, NJ and Seoul: Hollym, 1988), 124–125.
20   Seth, *Concise*, 142.
21   Andrew C. Nahm, *Korea: Tradition and Transformation: A History of the Korean People* (Elizabeth, NJ and Seoul: Hollym, 1988), 101.

men. At least at higher social levels, women who were widowed were no longer permitted to remarry and women could no longer freely mix with men. In 1402, women were forbidden to ride horses, something which had been popular among higher-class women during the Koryŏ dynasty. Later in the Chosŏn dynasty, women could only go out on the streets during curfew hours for men. In addition, even people's houses became segregated by gender with an inner section for women and an outer section for men.

3   Comparing Korea and Taiwan: Histories of the 17th to 19th Centuries

With the arrival of the Dutch in 1623–1624, Taiwan's history entered a new stage. A series of six separate colonial governments of rule by outsiders dominated Taiwan for 364 years. These were (i) the Dutch (1624–1662), (ii) the Spanish (1626–1642), who ruled in north Taiwan simultaneously with the Dutch, (iii) the Zheng 鄭 family (1662–1683), (iv) the Manchus (1683–1895), (v) the Japanese (1895–1945), and the authoritarian Chinese Nationalist regime (KMT) (1945–1988). Of these, the Manchu regime lasted by far the longest.

A few things need to be made clear about the Manchu period in Taiwan. First, the Manchu empire was not Chinese. It was twice the size of the Ming empire and it ruled in diverse ways.[22] China was a colony of the Manchu empire and the Chinese clearly resented Manchu rule. Second, Manchu rule in Taiwan varied over time and differed in different places. The main Manchu control originated in the southwest (following Dutch and Zheng rule) and then proceeded north. However, right to the end of Manchu rule in Taiwan, the Manchus never controlled the aboriginal areas in the mountains. Third, ethnicity played an important part in Taiwan's politics and society under the Manchus,[23] though Harry Lamley demonstrates that a new sense of Taiwan identity began to replace the local ethnic identities beginning in the 1860s.[24] John Shepherd's magisterial work remains the key book in English on this period.[25]

---

22   Justin Tighe, *Constructing Suiyuan: The Politics of Northwestern Territory and Development in Early Twentieth-Century China* (Leiden and Boston: Brill, 2005), 21.

23   J. Bruce Jacobs, "Taiwan's Colonial Experiences and the Development of Ethnic Identities: Some Hypotheses," *Taiwan in Comparative Perspective* 5 (July 2014), 47–59.

24   Harry J. Lamley, "Subethnic Rivalry in the Ch'ing Period," in *The Anthropology of Taiwanese Society*, ed. Emily M Ahern and Hill Gates (Stanford: Stanford University Press, 1981), 312.

25   John Robert Shepherd, *Statecraft and Political Economy on the Taiwan Frontier, 1600–1800* (Stanford: Stanford University Press, 1993).

Although the Manchus ruled much of Taiwan directly, they ruled Korea indirectly and made Korea a tributary state. During the war between the Ming and the Manchus, the Manchus invaded northern Korea in 1627 and forced the Chosŏn government to declare neutrality. Since the Korean court did not honor this promise, the Manchus invaded again in 1636 and forced the Koreans to accept a tributary relationship with the Manchus. The Manchus came to power in China in 1644 and Korea remained a vassal of the Manchus until 1894.

One difference this subordination to the Manchus made related to writing. Before the Manchus forced the Koreans into the tributary relationship, the seals of the Korean kings only had Chinese script. Afterward, they contained Manchu script as well. But they never contained *hangul,* the Korean alphabet.

The Chosŏn dynasty staggered on until the first decade of the 20th century. It made some efforts at reform to deal with the West and the Japanese, but, by and large, these were not successful. Korea became the object of competition between the Manchus and the Japanese. Then, the Russians and Americans also got involved. This all resulted in Korea becoming a Japanese colony from 1905 (informally) or 1910 (formally) until Japan's defeat in World War II in 1945.[26]

4   Comparing Korea and Taiwan during the Japanese Colonial Periods

When we get to the Japanese colonial periods in Taiwan (1895–1945) and Korea (1905/1910–1945), the number of similarities between the two countries increases considerably and comparative analysis becomes more fruitful. Among Asian countries, Japan modernized in a planned, determined manner. As part of this process, Japan wanted to establish a colonial empire to demonstrate to the European colonial powers that Japan had reached their level and was their equal.

From 1895 to 1914, Japan gained five colonies, though in terms of area, population, and economic strength Taiwan and Korea were the two key colonies.[27]

---

26   There is quite a large literature on Korea during the Manchu period, but I am far from an expert on this subject.

27   The five colonies were: Taiwan (Formosa), The Kwantung Peninsula in north China/ Manchuria (Kantōshū), the southern half of Sakhalin Island (Karafuto), Korea (Chōsen), and Micronesia (Nan'yō). Manchukuo 滿洲國 (taken September 18, 1931) was technically ruled as an independent state, not as part of the Japanese empire. Thus, Manchukuo had its own citizens who carried Manchukuo passports. Under Japanese colonial rule, citizens of Taiwan and Korea were actually citizens of Japan, even if they were second-class citizens.

In terms of area, Taiwan was 9.5 percent of the size of Japan, while Korea was 58.5 percent of Japan's size. In terms of population using 1935 figures, Taiwan had 7.5 percent of Japan's population while Korea had 33.1 percent.

How did Japan annex Taiwan and Korea? Japan had occupied Taiwan briefly in 1874 but withdrew under Western threats. However, despite this history, research on the role of Taiwan in the Manchu-Japanese War of 1894–1895[28] suggests:

> Japan did not have a long-range plan for the annexation of Taiwan. It is even doubtful that the notion of annexation ever entered the minds of Premier Ito Hirobumi and Foreign Minister Mutsu Munemitsu at the time of the outbreak of the war. Korea, not Taiwan, was the basic issue of the war in 1894; it was only after China's [sic] defeat had become a fore-gone conclusion that the Japanese leaders began to entertain the notion of annexing the island as a prize of victory ... Japan's interest in Taiwan was revived because of the war; it was not the reason she went to war.[29]

Taiwan (including the Pescadores Islands or Penghu) became part of Japan as a result of the Treaty of Shimonoseki, dated April 17, 1895, which ended the Manchu-Japan War.

Japan annexed Korea in two stages. Japan defeated Russia in the Russo-Japanese War, which ended with the Treaty of Portsmouth, dated September 5, 1905.[30] Article II of the Portsmouth Treaty accepted Japanese paramountcy in Korea:

> The Imperial Russian Government, acknowledging that Japan possesses in Korea paramount political, military and economic interests engages neither to obstruct nor interfere with measures for guidance, protection

---

28   In English, the 1894–1895 War is usually called the Sino-Japanese War. However, this is not correct as the war was between Japan and the Manchu Empire. In many documents from the late 19th century, the term "Great Qing" 大清 was often incorrectly translated into English as "China." At this time, China was not a sovereign country; rather it was a colony of the Manchu Empire. This distinction is important if we are to understand the history correctly.

29   Edward I-te Chen, "Japan's Decision to Annex Taiwan: A Study of Ito-Mutsu Diplomacy, 1894–95," *The Journal of Asian Studies* XXXVII, no. 1 (1977), 61–62.

30   American President Theodore Roosevelt won the 1906 Nobel Peace Prize—the sixth such prize—for helping to negotiate this peace treaty. The text of the Treaty of Portsmouth is available at "Treaty of Portsmouth," https://wwi.lib.byu.edu/index.php/Treaty_of_Portsmouth, accessed December 30, 2018.

and control which the Imperial Government of Japan may find necessary to take in Korea ...

Formal annexation took five more years. On August 22, 1910, Japan and Korea, which Japan dominated, signed a treaty, which was called a "Treaty of Annexation."[31] In the "Proclamation" at the beginning, this treaty said:

> The Governments of Japan and Korea ... have, with the approval of His Majesty the Emperor of Japan and His Majesty the Emperor of Korea, concluded ... a treaty providing for complete annexation of Korea to the Empire of Japan. By virtue of that important act, which shall take effect on its promulgation on August 29, 1910, the Imperial Government of Japan shall undertake the entire government and administration of Korea ...

The first two articles of this Treaty are:

> Article 1. His Majesty the Emperor of Korea makes the complete and permanent cession to His Majesty the Emperor of Japan of all rights of sovereignty over the whole of Korea.
>
> Article 2. His Majesty the Emperor of Japan accepts the cession mentioned in the preceding article and consents to the complete annexation of Korea to the Empire of Japan.

So, Korea too formally became part of the Japanese Empire.

The Japanese stressed how their first colony, Taiwan, was to be a model colony. In fact, the Taiwanese resisted the Japanese invasion following the Treaty of Shimonoseki and the Japanese severely repressed the Taiwanese. A Japanese source says that up to 1902 the Japanese killed more than 32,000 Taiwanese or 1 percent of the population.[32] Repression continued after the consolidation of the takeover. Resistance, such as the 1915 Ta-pa-ni uprising in Southern Taiwan, led to well over a thousand deaths.[33] In the decade from 1905 to 1914,

---

31   The text of the Treaty is available at "Treaty of Annexation," http://international.ucla.edu/institute/article/18447, accessed December 30, 2018.

32   Kiyoshi Ito, *History of Taiwan*, trans. Walter Chen (Taibei: Qianwei, 2004), 138–139.

33   Paul R. Katz, *When Valleys Turned Blood Red: The Ta-pa-ni Incident in Colonial Taiwan* (Honolulu: University of Hawai'i Press, 2005), 1–2.

the Japanese killed 150,000 Korean militiamen.[34] In both Taiwan and Korea, this repression continued up to 1920 when a series of reforms took place.

There were several reasons why the reforms took place in 1920. First, towards the end of World War I, on January 8, 1918, US President Woodrow Wilson gave an important speech to the US Congress, often called the "Fourteen Points."[35] In the conclusion, President Wilson said:

> In regard to these essential rectifications of wrong and assertions of right we feel ourselves to be intimate partners of all the governments and peoples associated together against the Imperialists. We cannot be separated in interest or divided in purpose. We stand together until the end.

These ideas of self-determination and the equality of all peoples struck colonized peoples like wildfire.

Second, in Korea, a series of demonstrations began which became known as the March First Movement (1919), and during which Koreans proclaimed their independence.[36] During the three months from March to May 1919, the Japanese killed 7,509 Koreans, wounded 15,961, and arrested a further 47,948 in an attempt to suppress the demonstrations.[37] According to official figures, which are too low, in just the month of March 1919 there were over 500 demonstrations with 587,641 participants and 553 people killed. The March First movement was brutally suppressed, but it inspired both the Korean and Taiwanese peoples.

Third, Japan too was entering a liberal phase, that of Taisho democracy. In September 1918, Hara Kei (also known as Hara Takashi) became prime minister, a position he held until he was assassinated in November 1921. In both Korea and Taiwan, there was some liberalization. However, Koreans and Taiwanese were still second-class citizens in their own countries. Japanese migrants to Korea and Taiwan had privileged positions in both societies. In Taiwan, there were a series of social movements, but in fact these only gained momentum

---

34   Kim Sam-ung, *Ilche nun Chosŏn ul olmana mangchyossulkka* [*How much Japan destroyed Korea*] (Seoul: Saram kwa Saram, 1998), 36.

35   For the text of President Wilson's speech, see Woodrow Wilson, "Fourteen Points," http://avalon.law.yale.edu/20th_century/wilson14.asp, accessed December 30, 2018.

36   For the classic account of the March 1st Movement, see Frank Baldwin, "Participatory Anti-Imperialism: The 1919 Independence Movement," *Journal of Korean Studies* 1 (1979), 123–162.

37   Kim Sam-ung, *Ilche nun Chosŏn*, 73. For the same figures, except one thousand fewer arrested, see Kim Chin-bong, *Samil undongsa yongu* [*Research into the history of the March First Movement*] (Seoul: Kukhak Charyowon, 2000), 39.

when liberal Japanese led these movements from Japan and publications came into Taiwan from Japan. Attempts to publish in Taiwan were censored by the colonial government.[38]

Both Taiwan and Korea were run with very strong police systems. In both places, police used the Japanese model of police getting to know a small area very well. The police systems in Korea and Taiwan remained under Japanese colonial control, but in both places, Taiwanese and Koreans did hold some inferior police positions.

Japanese education was important in both Taiwan and Korea, but Taiwanese and Koreans remained second-class citizens. The best education was reserved for Japanese in both colonies. Only much later did a very few Taiwanese and Koreans win access to the special schools set up for Japanese.

Taiwan and Korea each had one university dominated by Japanese staff and students. The roles of Taiwanese and Koreans were small and subordinate. Taiwanese and Koreans certainly did not have leadership positions in administration, research or teaching.

In both places, however, basic education became reasonably widespread. In Taiwan, in 1943 about 71.3 percent of school-age children were in primary school (80.9 percent of the boys and 60.9 percent of the girls).[39] In Korea, by 1940, about half of the school-age children were in primary school.[40] We can get some idea of the impact of this education if we look at the populations of Taiwan and Korea that could speak and read reasonably fluent Japanese: in 1942, the figure is 62 percent in Taiwan and 20 percent in Korea.[41]

In both Korea and Taiwan, the Japanese conducted cadastral surveys to establish who owned the land and who could be taxed. In fact, in both

---

38 For example, *Taiwan Seinen (Taiwan Youth)* was published as a monthly in Japan starting in July 1920. Later it became a daily newspaper. It was only published in Taiwan beginning in 1932 and was repressed in 1937. According to Edward Chen, it was the only Taiwan voice permitted to publish in Taiwan, Edward I-te Chen, "Formosan Political Movements Under Japanese Colonial Rule, 1914–1937," *The Journal of Asian Studies* XXXI, no. 3 (1972), 481–482.

39 *Taiwan sheng wushiyi nian lai tongji tiyao* 臺灣省五十一年來統計提要 [*Statistical Abstract of Taiwan Province for the Past Fifty-One Years*], ed. . (Taipei: Statistical Office of the Taiwan Provincial Administration Agency 臺灣省行政長官公署統計室編印; reprint ed. Taipei: Guting shuwu 古亭書屋, 1946 [1969]), 1241.

40 E. Patricia Tsurumi, "Colonial Education in Korea and Taiwan," in *The Japanese Colonial Empire, 1895–1945*, ed. Ramon H. Myers and Mark R. Peattie (Princeton, NJ: Princeton University Press, 1984), 305.

41 Edward I-te Chen, "The Attempt to Integrate the Empire: Legal Perspectives," in *The Japanese Colonial Empire, 1895–1945*, ed. Ramon H. Myers and Mark R. Peattie (Princeton, NJ: Princeton University Press, 1984), 242, n. 3.

Taiwan and Korea, the Japanese took over a lot of land. Koreans complain that with the cadastral surveys the rates of tenancy increased and that Korean landlords, as well as new Japanese landlords, benefitted. Taiwanese farmers too became poorer as Japanese companies such as sugar companies took over land.

Both Taiwan and Korea became "granaries" for Japan. In the words of Samuel Ho, both Taiwan and Korea "became agricultural appendages of Japan."[42] This was a mixed blessing. Japan conducted considerable research into both seeds (this was a beginning of the Green Revolution) and into agricultural techniques. In both Taiwan and Korea improved techniques were widely taught and implemented. Thus, the standard of living in both places went up even as both were exploited by Japan.

In both places considerable public health measures were implemented. In semi-tropical Taiwan, malaria was eliminated. In both Taiwan and Korea, disease rates were lowered, local people were trained as doctors and other health professionals, and hygiene improved. Japanese dominated, but Taiwanese and Koreans benefitted.

Clearly, in the mid-1930s the conservatives and the military regained power in Japan. This led to considerable repression in Taiwan and Korea. In Taiwan, from 1919 civilian governors-general had been appointed. Now, all appointees again came from the military. Taiwanese and Koreans were drafted into the military while other Taiwanese and Koreans were forced to work for the war machine. This led to a decline in economic conditions. A study of height in Taiwan suggests that "the sustained rise in average heights indicate considerable health and welfare return to Taiwanese from colonial economic development ... [But] Our finding of stagnation in the upward trend in average height in the 1930s is striking evidence of the negative impact of the late phase of Japanese colonialism."[43]

In summary, being a member of the Japanese empire was no special privilege for Taiwanese and Koreans. During the war, when the Japanese set up military brothels for their soldiers, they kidnapped Korean, Taiwanese and women from elsewhere who were forced to work in these brothels. Korean women accounted for over 80 percent of the total. These sorts of "privileges" were not sought by the colonial subjects.

---

42   Samuel Pao-San Ho, "Colonialism and Development: Korea, Taiwan, and Kwantung," in *The Japanese Colonial Empire, 1895–1945*, ed. Ramon H. Myers and Mark R. Peattie (Princeton, NJ: Princeton University Press, 1984), 350.

43   Stephen L. Morgan and Shiyung Liu, "Was Japanese Colonialism Good for the Welfare of Taiwanese? Stature and the Standard of Living," *The China Quarterly*, no. 192 (2007), 1016.

There are some other comparisons which I have drawn from an excellent article by Edward I-te Chen.[44] First, governors-general in Korea all came from the military. From 1919–1936, civilians were appointed as governor-general in Taiwan.[45] Second, the percentage of Japanese as a proportion of the total population was much higher in Taiwan, where it was 6.0 percent in 1942, compared to 2.8 percent in Korea.[46] Perhaps because of this difference in Japanese migrants to the two colonies, no native Taiwanese rose above the position of county head, while Koreans occupied many senior positions in the Government-General and in the provincial governments.[47] Third, the Japanese used force for different purposes in the two colonies. In Taiwan, force was used to "eliminate active resistance," a goal achieved by 1919. In Korea, Japan "decided to relax control somewhat in the hope that the Koreans might be reconciled to 'autonomy' and abandon their demand for independence."[48] There are also other reasons for differences in the colonial experiences of Taiwan and Korea. For example, the lack of a Taiwan state prior to 1950 contrasts with the long-term Kingdoms of Korea through several centuries and dynasties.

Some scholars have tentatively suggested one other possibility for difference: that the Japanese Navy controlled the colonial government in Taiwan while the Japanese Army controlled the colonial government in Korea. However, both generals and admirals were appointed governors-general in both Taiwan and Korea,[49] a fact which makes this hypothesis unlikely.

In sum, the Japanese colonial empire resembled the European colonial empires. The colonial subjects were treated as inferiors. In an analysis of European colonial empires, Albert Memmi wrote:

> Racism appears then, not as an incidental detail, but as a consubstantial part of colonialism. It is the highest expression of the colonial system

---

44   Edward I-te Chen, "Japanese Colonialism in Korea and Formosa: A Comparison of the Systems of Political Control," *Harvard Journal of Asiatic Studies* 30 (1970), 126–158.

45   Chen, "Japanese Colonialism in Korea and Formosa," 129–131.

46   Chen, "Japanese Colonialism in Korea and Formosa," 144, n. 35.

47   Chen, "Japanese Colonialism in Korea and Formosa," 134.

48   Chen, "Japanese Colonialism in Korea and Formosa," 158. Of course, in Taiwan the important aboriginal Musha uprising of October 1930 was an exception that killed more than 200 Japanese including the provincial governor. Thousands of Taiwanese aborigines were killed in retaliation. See George H. Kerr, *Formosa: Licensed Revolution and the Home Rule Movement 1895–1945* (Honolulu: The University Press of Hawaii, 1974), 151–154. A useful, extended analysis is Leo T.S. Ching, *Become "Japanese": Colonial Taiwan and the Politics of Identity Formation* (Berkeley, Los Angeles and London: University of California Press, 2001), 133–173.

49   Chen, "Japanese Colonialism in Korea and Formosa," 129–131.

and one of the most significant features of the colonialist. Not only does it establish a fundamental discrimination between colonizer and colonized, a sine qua non of colonial life, but it also lays the foundation for the immutability of this life.[50]

It is noteworthy that scholars have also applied this quote to the Japanese empire.[51] Like the Japanese empire, the European empires too were basically torn apart by World War II. Those that survived World War II were all gone by the 1950s and 1960s as Woodrow Wilson's ideas on the equality of peoples and their rights to self-determination finally took root.

5   Comparing the Dictatorships in Taiwan and South Korea, 1945–1988

Both the Taiwanese and Korean peoples faced dictatorships following the surrender of Japan in 1945 and the dismantling of the Japanese colonial governments. Yet the nature of these dictatorships was very different. South Koreans faced Korean dictatorships.[52] Here, the chapter covers mostly South Korea in the postwar period. From 1961 until the start of democratization in early 1988, South Korea's dictatorships were all military governments. In contrast, the government of Chiang Kai-shek and his son Chiang Ching-kuo can best be described as colonial.[53] The Chiangs treated Taiwanese as second-class citizens and Mainlanders, who had come to Taiwan with Chiang Kai-shek in 1949, completely dominated government. In addition, although both Chiangs had strong military backgrounds, they created a civilian-led dictatorship in which the military were kept under civilian (and party) control. Generals who appeared to gain too much independent power, such as Sun Li-jen, were arrested.[54] Thus, the South Korean and Taiwan postwar dictatorships differed in important ways.

---

50   Albert Memmi, *The colonizer and the colonized* (New York: The Orion Press, 1965), 74.

51   Carter J. Eckert et al., *Korea Old and New: A History* (Seoul: Ilchokak Publishers for the Korea Institute, Harvard University, 1990), 319.

52   Some would argue that the government of Prime Minister Chang Myŏn (Jang Myeon), which lasted only eight months until the coup of Park Chung-hee on 16 May 1961, was democratic. This was the only cabinet-led government in postwar Korea.

53   For six similarities between the Japanese colonial government and the Chiang governments, see J. Bruce Jacobs, "Whither Taiwanization? The Colonization, Democratization and Taiwanization of Taiwan," *Japanese Journal of Political Science* 14, no. 4 (2013), 573–575.

54   J. Bruce Jacobs, *Democratizing Taiwan* (Leiden and Boston: Brill, 2012), 35.

6   Comparing Two Key Events in Democratization: the Kaohsiung Incident and the Kwangju Massacre

During the dictatorships in South Korea and Taiwan, democratic movements worked to promote democratic reform. Each country had a major event at a similar time in their struggle for democracy. The Kaohsiung Incident of December 10, 1979 led to the arrest of many leaders of the democratic movement. The Kwangju (Gwangju) Massacre of May 18–27, 1980 led to many arrests and the deaths of hundreds of demonstrators, killed by the military government of Chun Doo-hwan (Jeon Duhwan). There were also significant differences between the two events.[55]

The Kaohsiung Incident was one of a series of demonstrations led by Taiwan's democrats and more demonstrations were planned. The ruling Kuomintang (Nationalist Party) was meeting at the same time and more than fifty hours after the demonstration, decided to arrest all of the leaders and many others. The newspapers at the time claimed that the demonstrators had been involved in "violence," but in fact no one was killed, and no one was seriously injured. The arrested leaders were convicted in several trials and most were imprisoned for several years. Ironically, the imprisonment of the democratic leaders helped elect wives and other relatives of the imprisoned. Later, under democratization, many of the democratic leaders and their lawyers became prominent and won.

The Kwangju Massacre, on the other hand, was one of a series of demonstrations held in various parts of South Korea. Thus, while the Kaohsiung Incident was led by "national" democratic leaders, the Kwangju demonstrations were led by "local" democratic leaders. The important prior events to these demonstrations were the assassination of Park Chung-hee (Bak Jeonghui) on October 26, 1979 by his Korean CIA chief, Kim Chae-gyu (Gim Jaegyu), and the seizure of power by General Chun Doo-hwan on December 12, 1979. On May 17, 1980, Chun Doo-hwan extended martial law to the whole of South Korea and sent troops to many cities including Seoul, Pusan (Busan), Taegu (Daegu), Taejon (Daejeon), Chonju (Jeonju) and Kwangju. These troops, armed with combat equipment rather than riot control gear, immediately occupied Chonnam (Jeonnam) National University in Kwangju and severely beat many students.

---

55   This analysis draws upon J. Bruce Jacobs, "Two Key Events in the Democratisation of Taiwan and South Korea: The Kaohsiung Incident and the Kwangju Uprising," *International Review of Korea Studies* 8(1) (2011), 29–56. For a more detailed analysis of the Kaohsiung Incident, see J. Bruce Jacobs, *The Kaohsiung Incident in Taiwan and Memoirs of a Foreign Big Beard* (Leiden and Boston: Brill, 2016).

On May 27 at 5 AM the military attacked demonstrators near the Provincial Government. The death toll was very high with an official count of 191 killed. The American Ambassador to South Korea, William H. Gleysteen, had said that 1,000 were killed, though he later wrote: "our estimate at the time was that between 200 (the government's claim) and 1,000 people lost their lives."[56] In addition, the military buried people killed outside Kwangju in agricultural fields. Thousands were also injured. Unlike the prominence of the Taiwan "national" democratic leaders after democratization, only two of the twelve surviving members of the Kwangju Struggle Committee served at the national level with one serving two terms and another serving one term in the National Assembly. The Kwangju Massacre remained as a "birth defect" that "continued to plague Chun Doo Hwan throughout his rule."[57]

7   Comparing Democratization in Taiwan and South Korea

In Asia, only four countries have consolidated democratic political systems: India, Japan, South Korea and Taiwan. Of these, Taiwan and South Korea are the only two "third-wave" democracies, both beginning their democratizations in about 1988. I would argue that the Japanese colonial period made three significant contributions to the later democratization of both countries.[58] First, the strong Japanese colonial bureaucratic rule established patterns of administration that the postwar governments were able to use, thus enhancing their efficacy. Second, the Japanese colonial experience increased national consciousness among all sectors of both societies. Finally, the Japanese colonial experience advanced both countries economically, socially, and educationally.

Both postwar dictatorships implemented some similar strategies of economic development beginning with import substitution industrialization and shifting to export-oriented industrialization in the 1960s. Thus, from 1976 to 1991, Taiwan's exports always exceeded 40 percent of gross national product (GNP) while in South Korea exports during 1976–1981 ranged from 24 to

56   William H. Gleysteen, *Massive Entanglement, Marginal Influence: Carter and Korea in Crisis* (Washington, DC: Brookings, 1999), 131.

57   Jung-kwan Cho, "The Kwangju Uprising as a Vehicle of Democratization: a Comparative Perspective," in *Contentious Kwangju: The May 18 Uprising in Korea's Past and Present*, ed. Gi-Wook Shin and Kyung-Moon Hwang (Lanham, Boulder, New York, Oxford: Rowman & Littlefield, 2003), 73.

58   Much of the analysis in this section draws upon J. Bruce Jacobs, "Taiwan and South Korea: Comparing East Asia's Two 'Third-Wave' Democracies," *Issues & Studies* 43, np. 4 (December 2007), 227–260.

31 percent of GNP. A key difference is that small and medium industries domi-nated in Taiwan, while Park Chung-hee established huge interlocking *chaebol* such as Hyundai, Samsung and Lotte, which he forced to obey the government.

Both countries also achieved considerable social mobility as people moved from the farm to the city and moved from agriculture to industry. Both coun-tries moved towards greater equality in income and both emphasized the importance of education and greatly facilitated the education of the two pop-ulations. Dictators in both countries promoted Confucianism in order to main-tain discipline in their societies, but Confucianism also emphasizes education and it has many proto-democratic ideas.[59] Both countries also had many lead-ers and cabinet ministers who had studied in democratic countries and which may have liberalized their thought. Nevertheless, as noted earlier, the postwar dictatorships differed considerably in the two countries.

In a sense, both democratic movements had some luck. In Taiwan, Chiang Ching-kuo's vice-president, Lee Teng-hui, succeeded as president when Chiang died. He did not play the expected figurehead role and fought to make his pres-idency powerful and democratic. In South Korea, General Roh Tae-woo (No Taeu), who had worked with Chun Doo-hwan, succeeded as party president and began to implement more democratic procedures including the freeing of political prisoners.

I have argued that Taiwan and South Korea shared seven factors that facili-tated democratization, but that Taiwan had an additional three factors which South Korea lacked:

1. Administrative, economic, social, and educational development under the Japanese.
2. Relatively high educational levels under Japan and the postwar authori-tarian governments.
3. Electoral experience under the Japanese and postwar authoritarian regimes.
4. Increasing economic prosperity with increasing equality.
5. Links between government and opposition.
6. American political pressure.
7. The fall of President Marcos in 1986, which frightened authoritarian rul-ers in much of Asia.

The three additional attributes that Taiwan had, which facilitated democrati-zation, were:

---

59   J. Bruce Jacobs, "Democracy and China," *Economic and Political Weekly* (Bombay) XXVI, no. 33 (17 August 1991), 1906.

1.   There were some "liberals" among the top leadership.
2.   The democratic opposition was nonviolent.
3.   Taiwan had popular associations which engaged in proto-interest group
     activity.[60]

There is one additional difference that deserves mention. In South Korea, about 30 percent of the population is Christian (Protestant and Catholic), the second-highest proportion in Asia after the Philippines. These Christians were quite supportive of democratization during the postwar authoritarian periods. Taiwan has far fewer Christians (5–6 percent) and, except for the Presbyterians, most of these Christian groups were supportive of the Chiang Kai-shek and Chiang Chiang-kuo dictatorships.

Both countries have dual leadership with a president and a prime minister and many debates about the relative power of the two offices. Both elect the president through popular elections. Both have a unicameral legislature. Both have had several transfers of power. In South Korea, geographic origin is an important political fault line. In Taiwan, the main fault line has been ethnicity, though this sometimes reflects in a geographical fault line as well. Both countries have attempted impeachment of the president, though the only successful impeachment was of Park Geun-hye (Bak Geunhye) (the daughter of military dictator Park Chung-hee) in 2017. Citizens of both countries firmly support their democratization and neither country is likely to return to authoritarianism.

8   Three Recent Books Comparing South Korea and Taiwan

Three relatively recent books that have used a comparison between Taiwan and South Korea. Joseph Wong compares the implementation of health insurance in the two countries as they democratized and draws many useful lessons.[61] Jong-Sung You compares Taiwan, South Korea and the Philippines looking at democracy, inequality and corruption, with the last as the dependent variable.[62] You challenges such concepts as the "developmental state" and finds that democracies have less corruption than authoritarian states. In another important point, You argues that Confucianism did not contribute to the meritocratic

---

60   Jacobs, "Paradoxes," 243–244.
61   Joseph Wong, *Healthy Democracies: Welfare Politics in Taiwan and South Korea* (Ithaca and London: Cornell University Press, 2004).
62   Jong-sung You, *Democracy, Inequality and Corruption: Korea, Taiwan and the Philippines Compared* (Cambridge: Cambridge University Press, 2015).

principles in the bureaucracies of Taiwan and South Korea. Rather, he argues, land reform played a much more important role.[63]

In a much more problematic book, Sheena Chestnut Greitens believes "autocrats face a 'coercive dilemma'" in which they must design their internal security apparatus to deal with a popular threat *or* to "coup-proof" against other elite rivals. Her theory has two major variables for security agencies, fragmentation versus unity in structure and socially exclusive versus socially inclusive in recruitment. With these variables, she draws many conclusions with an emphasis on Taiwan and South Korea as well as the Philippines.[64] The problem is that she gets many of the "facts" of the situations in Taiwan and South Korea wrong.

For example, Greitens argues that after huge fragmentation and social exclusivity in recruitment, the Taiwan government created a unitary and socially inclusive security apparatus. Before the reforms, in 1950, Greitens expresses shock that Taiwan had thirteen security agencies in many cities in 1950.[65] However, in 1980, during my own three months of constant involuntary contact with Taiwan's security agencies, I discovered Taiwan had virtually the same number of competing security agencies (fragmentation) and that at higher levels these agencies were socially exclusive having only Mainlanders as leaders. Mark Pratt, who at the time was the US Government expert on Taiwan's security agencies, immediately and without hesitation named eleven.[66] It also seems clear that different security agencies had responsibility for different defendants in the Kaohsiung Incident trials and even though a higher level coordinated this work, the different cultures affected the ways in which defendants were treated including at least one who was physically tortured.[67]

Greitens also greatly lowers the numbers of those killed in the February 28, 1947 Democratic Movement by relying on an early book with many methodological problems.[68] Thus, she says the resultant deaths totaled 6,000 to

63   For my review of You, see J. Bruce Jacobs, "Review of Jong-Sung You, *Democracy, Inequality and Corruption: Korea, Taiwan and the Philippines Compared* (Cambridge: Cambridge University Press, 2015," *The China Journal*, no. 76 (July 2016), 159–161.

64   Sheena Chestnut Greitens, *Dictators and their Secret Police: Coercive Institutions and State Violence* (Cambridge: Cambridge University Press, 2016), 292–293.

65   Greitens, *Dictators*, 84, 193.

66   Jacobs, *Kaohsiung Incident*, 142.

67   Jacobs, *Kaohsiung Incident*, 29–30, 65. Lin I-hsiung was clearly physically tortured by the agency responsible for his interrogation. Other defendants suffered sleep deprivation, but no physical torture.

68   Lai Tse-han, Ramon H. Myers, and Wei Wou, *A Tragic Beginning: The Taiwan Uprising of February 28, 1947* (Stanford: Stanford University Press, 1991). For my review, see J. Bruce Jacobs, "Review of Lai Tse-han, Ramon H. Myers, Wei Wou, A Tragic Beginning: The

10,000[69] when most estimates are considerably higher. Many of her errors come from underestimating the importance of the KMT's Central Reform Commission (1950–1952) which completely rebuilt the KMT as well as many institutions in Taiwan. Thus, Chen Li-fu was forced into exile in the US and Chen Kuo-fu was already dying of tuberculosis when he was permitted to live in Taiwan. Greitens does not understand this history.[70]

Greitens also gets South Korea wrong. She repeatedly states that Park Chung-hee was much more violent than Chun Doo-hwan, but her own writing undercuts this statement. Thus, she gives Park responsibility for the Kwangju Massacre deaths even though Park had been assassinated and Chun had taken over through a coup several months before the Kwangju Massacre occurred in May 1980.[71]

For a specialist in dictators, Greitens seems to have little appreciation for democracy. Thus, she states, "Ching-kuo's eventual legacy would be to set Taiwan on a course toward liberal democracy ..."[72] Even worse, she repeatedly refers to Park Chung-hee as "democratically elected," a strange characterization since, as she says, he came to power through a military coup.[73]

Greitens seems burdened by her "theory" of how autocrats operate. A much simpler explanation for the declines in violence in Taiwan and South Korea under both Chiang Kai-shek and Park Chung-hee is that both had demonstrated to their populations that they had consolidated power and that any demonstration would be met with violence. This strikes me as a much more persuasive argument than her variables of fragmentation versus unity in structure and socially exclusive versus socially inclusive in recruitment.

9   The Chapters

The practice of writing a draft chapter is a familiar process to many. As the three editors of this volume embarked on their journey in June 2018 each person was tasked with their own role. Bruce began writing up the introduction.

Taiwan Uprising of February 28, 1947 (Stanford: Stanford University Press, 1991)." *Bulletin of the School of Oriental and African Studies* LVI, no. Part 1 (1993), 181–182.

69   Greitens, *Dictators*, 187.
70   Greitens, *Dictators*, 88.
71   Greitens, *Dictators*, 237–262.
72   Greitens, *Dictators*, 93. This is not correct, see J. Bruce Jacobs, "Myth and Reality in Taiwan's Democratisation," *Asian Studies Review* 43, no. 1 (2019).
73   Greitens, *Dictators*, 14, 68, 141, 149.

He used his keynote speech as the premise for the chapter that you just read. After completing it, we sent it for review, he made his changes and it ended up in the shared 'completed' file. It was not until recently that Sojin and I began to put the final chapters together. At the very point that you are now reading, we came across the following editorial message:

> This section will introduce the various chapters. If my cancer wins first, this will have to be done by Niki or Sojin, possibly writing their own preface and deleting this section.

As written in the tribute, I wish this had simply been deleted by the person that originally typed it. Alas, I find myself sat at my desk thinking about how to put these last few paragraphs together. The marrying of the book is important. The essence of this volume is to assess the landscape of Taiwan and Korean studies. Its purpose was to identify not just their similarities within the field of study but also their differences. Both have national identities that were formed in a Japanese colonial period. There was one Japanese empire, but not one Japanese experience. The surrender of Japan in 1945 ignited the light of independence for Korea, but this would be ideologically split within five years. For Taiwan, that end forced it into a born-again form of nationalism with the arrival of the KMT.

The Wilsonian rhetoric of self-determination in January 1918 and the Paris Peace Conference exactly a year later would become global flashpoints of calls for change. The following period witnessed the Irish War of Independence (1919–21), the Egyptian Revolution (November 1918-July 1919), the Jallianwala Bagh Massacre (April 13, 1919), March 1st Movement, South Korea (1919), and May 4th Movement, China (1919) among others. The emergence of a popular nationalism that was shaped by transnational identities forms the base of Michael J. Seth's chapter on Korean Colonial Cosmopolitanism. Evan Dawley, in the following chapter, follows this by looking at how interactions with Japanese imperialism altered the face and consciousness of the people of Taiwan. Moises L. Souza and Fabricio A. Fonseca in their chapter on decolonization, democratization, and pragmatism argue that national identity is cut from the fabric of historical international events. For Korea and Taiwan, these were the Japanese colonization, the Second World War, the Chinese Civil War and the Korean War and its subsequent divide.

Both Korea and Taiwan were clearly crafted by similar fabric. Not the same piece of cloth, but similar. Niki J.P. Alsford and Nataša Visočnik use new religious movements (Tzu-Chi and the Unification Church) as examples of how in the absence of state-led welfare it was up to grassroots-level organizations to provide aid. This chapter serves as a useful comparison in how both South Korea and Taiwan, although similar in socio-historical contexts, differ politically and religiously. This is then followed by Young-Im Lee who explores the similarities and differences between Taiwan and South Korea's only elected female presidents. She identifies how neither Park Geun-hye nor Tsai Ing-wen identified themselves as feminists despite both being 'trailblazers' in male-dominated politics. What is more, she argues that both had used positive stereotypes to garner public support, but equally demonstrated just how different they were not just in their personal backgrounds, but also within the politics that they governed.

The final chapter in this volume, written by Sojin Lim and Dafydd Fell, details how we can use the similarities and differences between Korea and Taiwan studies in our teaching and our research. Both places provide useful foundations for exploring the wider region through the prism of area studies. Sojin highlights the successes of Korean Studies at the University of Central Lancashire (UCLan) and Dafydd on Taiwan Studies at the School of Oriental & African Studies (SOAS), the University of London.

Niki J.P. Alsford
June 2020

10   Conclusion

The comparison between Taiwan and Korea clearly has much potential for drawing attention to particular aspects of the two countries, thus increasing our understanding of both places. I hope that readers learn much from the various chapters in this book.

11   Acknowledgement

I wish to express appreciation to Ms Jung-Sim Kim, Korean Studies Librarian at Monash University, for her considerable assistance obtaining and interpreting Korean-language materials.

References

Baldwin, Frank. "Participatory Anti-Imperialism: The 1919 Independence Movement." *Journal of Korean Studies* 1 (1979): 123–162.

Chen, Edward I-te. "The Attempt to Integrate the Empire: Legal Perspectives." In The *Japanese Colonial Empire, 1895–1945*, edited by Ramon H. Myers and Mark R. Peattie. 240–275. Princeton, NJ: Princeton University Press, 1984.

Chen, Edward I-te. "Formosan Political Movements under Japanese Colonial Rule, 1914–1937." *The Journal of Asian Studies* XXXI, no. 3 (May 1972): 477–497.

Chen, Edward I-te. "Japan's Decision to Annex Taiwan: A Study of Ito-Mutsu Diplomacy, 1894–95." *The Journal of Asian Studies* XXXVII, no. 1 (November 1977 1977): 61–72.

Chen, Edward I-te. "Japanese Colonialism in Korea and Formosa: A Comparison of the Systems of Political Control." *Harvard Journal of Asiatic Studies* 30 (1970): 126–158.

Ching, Leo T.S. *Become "Japanese": Colonial Taiwan and the Politics of Identity Formation.* Berkeley, Los Angeles and London: University of California Press, 2001.

Cho, Jung-kwan. "The Kwangju Uprising as a Vehicle of Democratization: A Comparative Perspective." In *Contentious Kwangju: The May 18 Uprising in Korea's Past and Present*, edited by Gi-Wook Shin and Kyung-Moon Hwang. 67–85. Lanham, Boulder, New York, Oxford: Rowman & Littlefield, 2003.

Eckert, Carter J., Kai-baik Lee, Young Ick Lew, Michael Robinson, and Edward W. Wagner. *Korea Old and New: A History*. Seoul: Ilchokak Publishers for the Korea Institute, Harvard University, 1990.

Fanning, Bryan. "Developmental Immigration in the Republic of Ireland and Taiwan." *Taiwan in Comparative Perspective* 4 (2012): 154–175.

Gleysteen, William H. *Massive Entanglement, Marginal Influence: Carter and Korea in Crisis*. Washington, DC: Brookings, 1999.

Greitens, Sheena Chestnut. *Dictators and Their Secret Police: Coercive Institutions and State Violence*. Cambridge: Cambridge University Press, 2016.

Ho, Samuel Pao-San. "Colonialism and Development: Korea, Taiwan, and Kwantung." In *The Japanese Colonial Empire, 1895–1945*, edited by Ramon H. Myers and Mark R. Peattie. 347–398. Princeton, NJ: Princeton University Press, 1984.

Huang, Fu-San, Sam Huang, and Conor Mulvagh. "Lin Hsien-Tang's Taiwanese Home Rule Movement as Inspired by the Irish Model." *Taiwan in Comparative Perspective* 4 (2012): 65–88.

Ito, Kiyoshi. *History of Taiwan* [in Chinese and English, Japanese original on enclosed CD]. Translated by Walter Chen. Taibei: Qianwei, 2004.

Jacobs, J. Bruce. "Chinese Studies, Cross-Cultural Studies and Taiwan." *Pacific Affairs* 54, no. 4 (Winter 1981–82): 688–698.

Jacobs, J. Bruce. "Democracy and China." *Economic and Political Weekly* (Bombay) XXVI, no. 33 (17 August 1991): 1905–1906.

Jacobs, J. Bruce. *Democratizing Taiwan*. Leiden and Boston: Brill, 2012.

Jacobs, J. Bruce. "A History of Pre-Invasion Taiwan." *Taiwan Historical Research* 23, no. 4 (December 2016): 1–38.

Jacobs, J. Bruce. *The Kaohsiung Incident in Taiwan and Memoirs of a Foreign Big Beard.* Leiden and Boston: Brill, 2016.

Jacobs, J. Bruce. "Myth and Reality in Taiwan's Democratization." *Asian Studies Review* 43, no. 1 (2019).

Jacobs, J. Bruce. "Paradoxes in the Politics of Taiwan: Lessons for Comparative Politics." *Politics* XIII, no. 2 (November 1978): 239–247.

Jacobs, J. Bruce. " Review of Anne-Marie Brady (ed.), Looking North, Looking South: China, Taiwan, and the South Pacific (New Jersey et al: World Scientific, 2010), Wei-chin Lee (ed.), Taiwan's Politics in the 21st Century: Changes and Challenges (New Jersey et al: World Scientific, 2010) and Mikael Mattlin, Politicized Society: The Long Shadow of Taiwan's One-Party Legacy (Copenhagen: NIAS." *China Review International* 19, no. 3 (2012): 367–381.

Jacobs, J. Bruce. "Review of Jong-Sung You, Democracy, Inequality and Corruption: Korea, Taiwan and the Philippines Compared (Cambridge: Cambridge University Press, 2015." *The China Journal* 76 (July 2016): 159–161.

Jacobs, J. Bruce. "Review of Lai Tse-Han, Ramon H. Myers, Wei Wou, a Tragic Beginning: The Taiwan Uprising of February 28, 1947 (Stanford: Stanford University Press, 1991)." *Bulletin of the School of Oriental and African Studies LVI* Part 1 (1993): 181–182.

Jacobs, J. Bruce. "Taiwan and South Korea: Comparing East Asia's Two 'Third-Wave' Democracies." *Issues & Studies* 43, no. 4 (December 2007): 227–260.

Jacobs, J. Bruce. "Taiwan's Colonial Experiences and the Development of Ethnic Identities: Some Hypotheses." *Taiwan in Comparative Perspective* 5 (July 2014): 47–59.

Jacobs, J. Bruce. "Two Key Events in the Democratization of Taiwan and South Korea: The Kaohsiung Incident and the Kwangju Uprising." *International Review of Korea Studies* 8, no. 1 (2011): 29–56.

Jacobs, J. Bruce. "Whither Taiwanization? The Colonization, Democratization and Taiwanization of Taiwan." *Japanese Journal of Political Science* 14, no. 1 (December 2013): 567–586.

Jacobs, J. Bruce, and Peter Kang, eds. *Changing Taiwanese Identities.* London and New York: Routledge, 2018.

Kao, Wei H. "Voices from Two Theatrical Others: Labor Issues in the Theatres of Ireland and Taiwan." *Taiwan in Comparative Perspective* 4 (2012): 108–127.

Katz, Paul R. *When Valleys Turned Blood Red: The Ta-Pa-Ni Incident in Colonial Taiwan.* Honolulu: University of Hawai'i Press, 2005.

Kerr, George H. *Formosa: Licensed Revolution and the Home Rule Movement 1895–1945.* Honolulu: The University Press of Hawaii, 1974.

Kim Chin-bong. *Samil Undongsa Yongu* [Research into the History of the March First Movement]. Seoul: Kukhak Charyowon, 2000.

Kim Sam-ung. *Ilche Nun Chosŏn Ul Olmana Mangchyossulkka* [How Much Japan Destroyed Korea]. Seoul: Saram kwa Saram, 1998.

Lai Tse-han, Ramon H. Myers, and Wei Wou. *A Tragic Beginning: The Taiwan Uprising of February 28, 1947*. Stanford: Stanford University Press, 1991.

Lai, Tse-han, Ramon H. Myers, and Wou Wei. *A Tragic Beginning: The Taiwan Uprising of February 28, 1947*. Stanford: Stanford University Press, 1991.

Lamley, Harry J. "Subethnic Rivalry in the Ch'ing Period." In *The Anthropology of Taiwanese Society*, edited by Emily M Ahern and Hill Gates. 282–318. Stanford: Stanford University Press, 1981.

Li, Khin-Huann, and Liam Mac Mathúna. "A Comparative Study of Language Movements in Taiwan and Ireland." *Taiwan in Comparative Perspective* 4 (2012): 176–188.

Lien, Pei-Te, and Jeanette Yih Harvie. "The Political Incorporation of Taiwanese Americans and Irish Americans Compared." *Taiwan in Comparative Perspective* 4 (2012): 128–153.

Mattlin, Mikael. *Politicized Society: The Long Shadow of Taiwan's One-Party Legacy*. Copenhagen: NIAS Press, 2011.

Memmi, Albert. *The Colonizer and the Colonized*. New York: The Orion Press, 1965.

Morgan, Stephen L., and Shiyung Liu. "Was Japanese Colonialism Good for the Welfare of Taiwanese? Stature and the Standard of Living." *The China Quarterly* 192 (2007): 990–1017.

Nahm, Andrew C. *Korea: Tradition and Transformation: A History of the Korean People*. Elizabeth, NJ and Seoul: Hollym, 1988.

Rawnsley, Ming-Yeh T. "Cinema, Identity, and Resistance: Comparative Perspectives on a City of Sadness and the Wind That Shakes the Barley." *Taiwan in Comparative Perspective* 4 (2012): 89–107.

Schak, David C. *Civility and Its Development: The Experiences of China and Taiwan*. Hong Kong: Hong Kong University Press, 2018.

Seth, Michael J. *A Concise History of Korea from the Neolithic Period through the Nineteenth Century*. Lanham, Md et al: Rowman & Littlefield, 2006.

Shepherd, John Robert. *Statecraft and Political Economy on the Taiwan Frontier, 1600–1800*. Stanford: Stanford University Press, 1993. Stanford: Stanford University Press, 1993.

Shih, Fang-Long. "Taiwan's Subjectivity and National Narrations: Towards a Comparative Perspective with Ireland." *Taiwan in Comparative Perspective* 4 (2012): 6–33.

Shih, Fang-Long, and John McNeill Scott, eds. "Taiwan and Ireland in Comparative Perspective." Published as Special Issue of Taiwan in *Comparative Perspective* 4 (2012).

Taiwan Sheng Wushiyi Nian Lai Tongji Tiyao 臺灣省五十一年來統計提要 [*Statistical Abstract of Taiwan Province for the Past Fifty-One Years*]. Taipei: Statistical Office of

the Taiwan Provincial Administration Agency 臺灣省行政長官公署統計室編印;
reprint ed. Taipei: Guting shuwu 古亭書屋, 1946 [1969].

Tighe, Justin. *Constructing Suiyuan: The Politics of Northwestern Territory and Development in Early Twentieth-Century China*. Leiden and Boston: Brill, 2005.

Tsurumi, E. Patricia. "Colonial Education in Korea and Taiwan." In *The Japanese Colonial Empire, 1895–1945*, edited by Ramon H. Myers and Mark R. Peattie. 275–311. Princeton, NJ: Princeton University Press, 1984.

Wong, Joseph. *Healthy Democracies: Welfare Politics in Taiwan and South Korea*. Ithaca and London: Cornell University Press, 2004.

You, Jong-sung. *Democracy, Inequality and Corruption: Korea, Taiwan and the Philippines Compared*. Cambridge: Cambridge University Press, 2015.

CHAPTER 2

Korean Colonial Cosmopolitanism

Michael J. Seth

1   Korean Colonial Cosmopolitans

Colonial Korea saw the emergence of a small modern middle class that identified with the world of modernity, in fact, prided itself in being part of a larger community of civilized progressive humanity.[1] This middle class consisted mainly of professionals such as teachers, doctors, accountants, bankers and civil servants in the colonial bureaucracy. And they included journalists, writers, artists and some members of the rural landowning aristocracy that moved into the modernizing cities and towns. They wore Western-style clothes, sent their children to modern schools, and read newspapers, magazines and modern literature by foreign writers in translation or by Korean writers such as Yi Kwang-su. Their backgrounds were diverse. Some came from the old aristocratic yangban class, some from the class of clerks and specialists called the *chungin*, and many came from peasant or other commoner backgrounds. This class identified with all foreign things, a fact that is reflected in their consumer trends in which they were concerned to follow the latest fashions and innovations from Europe and America as well as Japan.[2] Writers, musicians, artists and dancers such as Ch'oe Sŭnghŭi (1911–1969) introduced modern, international culture. Publications such as the newspapers *Dong-a Ilbo* and *Chosŏn Ilbo* kept their readers informed of international news and cultural developments. Periodicals such as *Kaebyŏk* (Creation) and the short-lived, but significant, woman's journals *Sin yŏja* (New Woman) and *Yŏja kye* (Woman's World) connected political and social discourse with the intellectual and cultural currents from New York, London, Paris and Tokyo.

What most of these modern Koreans had in common was their education. They attended one of the new state or private schools with modern curricula. Quite a few were educated in Protestant missionary schools, and a number

---

1   Modernity is variously defined; here it means what Koreans called "civilized and enlightened," that is keeping up with what they perceived as the most civilized societies.
2   Min Hyun Jeong, "New Women and Modern Girls: Consuming Foreign Goods in Colonial Korea," *Journal of Historical Research in Marketing* 5, no. 4 (Fall 2013): 494–520.

© MICHAEL J. SETH, 2021 | DOI:10.1163/9789004461314_003

had studied in Japan. A smaller number were educated in Europe or America. Members of this new middle class were urban, cosmopolitan and open to new ideas.

Although colonial cosmopolitanism as a conscious identification with the international community was mainly confined to the elite, ordinary Koreans were being exposed to the international culture. A new mass vernacular literature emerged after 1920 including popular novels influenced by Western culture. Western movies became popular, Western music, and new hybrid popular culture emerged mixing traditional Korean, Japanese and Western forms. However, most Koreans in the colonial period were poor, rural and illiterate, without exposure to the new world of ideas. The new cosmopolitan middle class was modest in size, accounting at the most for five to 10 percent of the population. But from the 1920s they provided the economic and cultural leadership of colonial Korea.

2   Koreans and Their Place in the World before 1910

The cosmopolitanism of this new colonial class grew out of the historical experiences of the Korean people. Prior to the late 19th century, Koreans shared a collective identification with the state and with Korean culture and society. They, especially the educated elite, also identified with the larger Sino-centric world of East Asia. Beyond East Asia, they had very limited contact and little direct connection. The yangban elite of Korea followed intellectual and cultural trends in China and wrote in classical Chinese, the same language as the elite in China. Connections to other parts of the world were limited and were on the margins of Korean consciousness. There was some trade with Southeast Asia, and India was known as the home of Buddhism. Contact with the West only began with encounters with the Jesuit mission in Beijing in the seventeenth and eighteenth centuries. Some Korean scholars were impressed by the learned Jesuits and a few using Chinese translations studied European mathematics, science, geography and medicine.[3] In the late 18th century, a small number of Koreans converted to Catholicism as a result of the meetings with the Jesuits. In the 19th century, the Christian community in Korea grew into the tens of thousands, small but large enough to bring about three government-sponsored persecutions.

---

3   Donald Baker, "Cloudy Images: Korean Knowledge of the West from 1520–1800: *B.C. Asian Review* 3, no. 4 (1990): 51–73.

Korea's sense of the world before 1876 was reflected in the Ch'ŏnhado (world beneath the heavens) maps that became popular in the 18th century. These depicted a square land mass under a circular sky. China was in the center, Korea next to it and Japan to the east of Korea. In the central land mass with China, there were Southeast Asia plus India and Arabia. Beyond this, there was an outer ring containing exotic lands with names such as "land of the hairy people."[4] The maps based on centuries-long Sinitic concepts of geography suggested a society with little awareness of the emerging global system. Yet, even these showed some Western influence such as the adaptation of European style grid lines indicating longitude and latitude.[5]

This world view was shattered quickly with the intrusion of the Western imperialist powers in East Asia in the mid-19th century. Koreans watched in alarm while China suffered a humiliating defeat by the British in the Opium War, 1839–1842. This was followed by the American opening of Japan to trade and diplomacy in 1854, a second European war with China that led to a brief Anglo-French occupation of Beijing in 1860, and Russia's annexation of Chinese territory that same year. The last gave Russia a short border with Korea. Then Tokyo, following the Western example, used modern gunboats in 1876 to force Korea to open its ports to unrestricted trade with Japan. It was Japan's "opening of Korea" by gunboat in 1876 that finally forced Koreans to confront the new emerging, Western-dominated global order. Korea established relations with the United States (US) in 1882. Trade and diplomatic relations with other Western powers soon followed.

Koreans both inside and outside the government were quick to grasp the need to learn from outside powers and to make major changes in order to survive and flourish in the new world they were facing. In the 1880s, the Korean government sent fact-finding missions to China, Japan, and the US. At the same time, American missionaries as well as European merchants and diplomats entered Korea, further exposing Koreans to the wider world. Considering the country's previous isolation, it is surprising how quickly many educated Koreans accepted the need to learn from abroad. Efforts at carrying out an indigenous modernization, however, were complicated and at the time hampered by the interference of China, Russia and Japan into Korean affairs. Each competed for control of the peninsula until Japan defeated Russia in the Russo-Japanese War in 1905 and established a paramount position.

---

4   John Rennie Short, *Korea: A Cartographic History* (Chicago: University of Chicago Press, 2012), 86–88.
5   Short, 88.

Their abrupt entry into the new age of modern imperialism forced Koreans to grapple with their identity, with their place in the world. Koreans had been proud to be one of the most enlightened and civilized societies. The collapse of their Sino-centric international order forced Koreans to reexamine the standards by which they judged societies and their rank in the emerging international order. The educated elite of society were quick to accept a new vision of the world as an international community of states. For many, the Western nations of Europe and North America now represented the center of civilization. And for many, Japan represented a model of how an Asian people with a similar culture could learn from the West and modernize its society. However, Korea's attempt at an autonomous modernization was terminated when the Japanese took over, first as a protectorate in 1905 then annexing Korea and making it a colony in 1910.

3   Japan's Colonial Rule in Korea

Colonial cosmopolitanism was shaped by the peculiar nature of Korea's colonial experience. In many ways, Japan's administration of Korea was typical of Asian and African peoples in the age of imperialism. As with other colonies, economic development was directed toward the needs and interests of the imperial government rather than the people it ruled. Tokyo regarded Korea as a market for its manufacturers and a source of primary products for the homeland. Following the 1918 Tokyo rice riots, the colonial government emphasized the production of rice for Japan. Korea was seen, at least initially, as a supplier of primary products to the metropolitan center. Koreans were treated as inferior subjects; their traditions were often denigrated, and they were excluded from positions of authority. Korea's subordinate rule in the Empire was reflected in education. Under the education law of 1911, education for Koreans was limited to basic levels and vocational training, in effect, to provide semi-skilled labor for the Japanese Empire. Nonetheless, some embraced the new opportunities that were made available and accepted the claim by the Japanese that they were bringing progress and enlightenment. Many Koreans were active agents, not just passive victims, of the colonial administration serving as police and holding minor positions in the bureaucracy. Some became admirers of the Japanese culture and took pride in being part of the great, rising Japanese Empire. Others resisted, some violently, some more passively. Several thousand became exiles and plotted the overthrow of the colonial rule from abroad. These mixed reactions to colonial rule were typical as well.

In other ways, however, Korea's colonial experience was unusual. Unlike many colonial subjects, such as the people of Indochina, India or West Africa who were ruled by a distant and alien nation, Koreans were governed by a more familiar, culturally related neighbor. Although warrior-dominated Japan had a very different social system than Korea, it shared the traditions of Buddhism, Confucianism and a long history of borrowing from China. Therefore, the cultural gap between the two people was much narrower than between most Asian or African colonies and their imperial masters. But Korea also had a history of Japanese aggression, including the late 16th century invasion and attempted conquest contributing to the distrust and tensions between the two peoples.

Furthermore, Korea's colonial experience was unusual in its intensive and intrusive nature. Europeans often ruled indirectly working with local African chiefs, or rajas or emirs, but in Korea, all authority was concentrated in the centralized Japanese administration. To administer the country, the Government-General had about 10,000 officials in 1910. This grew dramatically to 87,552 in 1937 of whom 52,270 were Japanese and 35,282 were Koreans. There were over 60,000 policemen by the 1930s, the majority were Japanese; over half of the colony's schoolteachers were Japanese. If all members of the military, state, and semi-government banks and companies are included, about 246,000 Japanese served the colonial state.[6] This was about the same number of British in India which had more than fifteen times the population, and ten times as many French in Vietnam, a colony with a similar population to Korea.[7] While an Indian or African peasant might only rarely encounter a British or French colonial official, ordinary Koreans encountered them every day – the Japanese school teacher, the village policeman, the postal clerk. The police were particularly intrusive with the power to judge and sentence Koreans for minor offenses, to collect taxes, to oversee local irrigation works, even to inspect businesses and homes to see that health and other government regulations were being enforced.

Japan constructed a top-down administration with all officials, police and military directly answerable to the governor-general, always a Japanese military man appointed by Tokyo. Koreans served mainly at the lower ranks of the bureaucracy and were excluded from any meaningful participation in decision-making. Attempts by Tokyo to attract Japanese farmers and other settlers to Korea were not very successful, yet because of the large number of people from

---

6   Andrew J. Gradjanzev, *Modern Korea* (New York: Institute of Pacific Relations, 1944), 75–76; Nahm, 226–227.

7   Bruce Cumings, *Origins of the Korean War*, Vol.1 (Princeton, NJ: Princeton University Press, 1981), 46.

the homeland employed by the state and by semi-state institutions such as banks, many Japanese lived in the colony. By 1940 there were almost three-quarters of a million Japanese residents in Korea amounting to 3.2 percent of the population.[8] They made up as much as a quarter of the urban population. Each city had its Japanese sections with its residences, shops, and entertainment districts. These were invariably more modern with better sanitation and other infrastructure.

Korea's geopolitical situation also made its colonial experience different. The Japanese saw the peninsula as occupying a strategic position – first as protecting the homeland from foreign invasion, and second, as a springboard for advancing into Manchuria and the Chinese mainland. This led to another peculiar feature of colonial Korea, its high level of industrialization. In 1920, the Japanese government began to encourage investment by Japanese companies in Korea, which were flush with funds from the wartime boom. Large-scale industrialization, however, began after 1931 when the Japanese took over Manchuria, creating a puppet state the following year. Korea was now targeted by Tokyo for development as part of a larger project for building a great industrial empire in northeast Asia. All of Japan's major *zaibatsu* (industrial-financial conglomerates) invested in Korea. One, Noguchi, was entirely based in Korea. Most industrial development was concentrated in the northern region which had rich deposits of iron, coal, tungsten and other minerals and considerable hydro-electric potential which the authorities developed. Large iron and steel industries were established; the Nippon Chisso plant in the northeast city of Hŭngnam was one of the world's largest chemical complexes. By 1945 Korea, was perhaps the world's most industrialized colony.

Korea also had considerably higher infrastructure development than most colonies including an extensive rail network. This infrastructure, as with its industry, was created as a result of Korea's strategic location in the empire; in other words, it was constructed to serve the needs of the metropolitan center. For example, by 1940, the colony had as many miles of track as China, a country with twenty times its size in area and population.[9] But it was designed to ship goods to the ports for export to Japan, and perhaps more importantly, to facilitate the movement of Japanese troops within Korea and after 1931 to Manchuria. From the mid-1920s to the early 1940s, the urban population more than doubled as a percentage of the total; Seoul grew nearly four times from somewhat over 300,000 to 1.1 million.[10] Modern education expanded, much of it by private schools and a modern urban middle class emerged. However, Korea remained mostly rural and agricultural; and the majority of the adult population had no formal education.

Another peculiar feature of Japan's rule was its assimilationist policy. Other colonial powers, especially the French, had sought to promote cultural integration among elements of the educated elite, but Japan conducted a massive, if inconsistent, attempt to forcibly assimilate the entire population into Japanese culture. Officially, the policy was based on the fiction that the two peoples were originally one but had become separated. The Japanese had progressed, and the Koreans had stagnated. It was now the duty of Tokyo to reunite the Koreans and absorb them into Japanese society. But this policy, which meant trying to erase Korean culture and identify was contradicted by the practices of carefully segregating Koreans and Japanese, building different schools, dividing cites into separate neighborhoods, and of treating Koreans as an inferior people with a subordinate role in the Empire.

4   Korean Nationalism and the Nationalist Movement

Korea was unusual among colonies in its ethnic homogeneity, and with its history of more than a millennium as a state with territorially stable boundaries. Few countries could match that sense of unity and continuity. Koreans, although they were a part of an East Asian cultural tradition along with China, Japan and Vietnam, had a language unrelated to any other, their own alphabet, style of clothing, domestic architecture, and distinctive customs. But prior to 1910, Korea had been a dynastic state, not a modern state with modern concepts of national sovereignty. Nor did the general population participate in governing the state. They had a cultural, ethnic identity but not yet a national one. Only at the end of the dynasty did ideas of nation and nation-state, imported from the West, often via Japanese translations, become part of the intellectual discourse.

This ethnic homogeneity associated with a long existing state explains the unusual speed with which nationalism emerged as a powerful emotional force among the Korean people during colonial period. At the start of colonial rule in 1910, the concepts of nation and nation-state were still largely confined

---

10   Soon-won Park, "Colonial Industrial Growth and the Emergence of the Korean Working Class," in *Colonial Modernity in Korea*, Gi-wook Shin and Michael Robinson, eds. (Cambridge, MA: Harvard University Press, 1999), 128–60, 133.

to small circles of thinkers and people who had been educated abroad or in Western run mission schools. By 1945, most Koreans had come to see themselves as members of a Korean nation. The Korean nationalism which emerged was in good part a reaction to Japanese domination. It also was influenced by Japan's own version of nationalism with its strong ethnic-racial character. Modern nationalist sentiment and nationalist movements emerged in almost all of the colonies during the first half of the 20th century in the form of anti-colonialism. In most colonies, nationalism was a means of integrating diverse ethnic, religious and other groups into a single community based on the colonial territory. In Korea, this process was not necessary. In fact, Korea has been considered by John Duncan and other scholars as an example of a proto-nationalist society with many of the elements of nationalism already in place before the late 19th century.[11] For that reason, nationalism was able to quickly become a popular and powerful force.

The emergence of nationalism among the educated elite manifested itself in the years just prior to Korea's loss of sovereignty. As Andre Schmid has pointed out, in the years after 1895, the new journals, newspapers and various educational associations were starting to create a community of educated Koreans who argued over how to protect the nation, and after 1905, how to revive it.[12] The Independence Club, active from 1896–1898, was an early manifestation of this new conceptualization of Korea as a nation among a world of nation-states. Historians and political thinkers such as Pak Ŭn-sik (1859–1923) and Sin Ch'ae-ho (1880–1936) were re-examining Korea's place in the world and what it meant to be Korean. In 1908, the young Sin published an especially important essay "A New Reading of History" (*Toksa Sillon*) which borrowed the concept of "folk" (Korean: *minjok*) from Japanese and Chinese writers and placed it at the center of history.[13] The history of Korea became the history of a Korean people with their unique cultural tradition. Other scholars were standardizing and promoting the Korean alphabet *han'gŭl* which was becoming a symbol of a modern, national identity.

Nationalism in colonial Korea was a part of colonial cosmopolitanism since it was linked with being associated with the international community of nations. This is seen in the first great outburst of Korean nationalism, the March First

---

11   John Duncan, "Elements of Proto-nationalism John Duncan, Proto-Nationalism in Pre-modern Korea," in *Perspectives on Korea*, Sang-Oak Lee and Duk-soo Park, editors (Sydney: Wild Peony Press, 1998), 191–211.

12   Andre Schmid, *Korea Between Empires, 1895–1919* (New York: Columbia University Press, 2002), 65–75.

13   Schmid, 181–192.

Movement of 1919, which was inspired by the Treaty of Versailles and Woodrow Wilson's Fourteen Points, in particular his principle of self-determination. It excited colonial elites throughout the world. In late February representatives from groups of Protestants, Buddhists and the indigenous Chŏndogyo religion decided to issue a declaration of independence, as a kind of peaceful protest statement in a park in Seoul. What happened instead was largely spontaneous mass protests involving hundreds of thousands of Koreans in every province in 90 percent of its counties and cities.[14] Although mostly peaceful, it was violently suppressed by the Japanese; several thousand were killed, thousands arrested. As historian Michael Shin has pointed out "the March First Movement marked the transformation of nationalism from a project of elite intellectuals into a social movement with the rise of the masses as a political force."[15]

Taken by surprise, an embarrassed Japanese government changed its colonial policy toward a more liberal one in the 1920s. Upon, annexing Korea in 1910, the colonial authorities had closed most Korean newspapers and publications, as well as many private schools. But in the wake of the March First Movement, they allowed newspapers and journals in vernacular Korean, as well as a number of private organizations that promoted Korean culture. In this limited space, there was a great flowering of Korean literature, political thought, and historical studies. This decade of the 1920s marked the growth of Korean nationalism a project still led by the educated elite of society. It also saw the full emergence of a new middle class that increasingly identified trans-national communities. Just what kind of regional or global communities Koreans identified with shaped the nature of Korean nationalism and eventually post-liberation Korea.

5   Identifying with East Asia and the Japanese Empire

Among the many competing forms of trans-national identity that emerged was identification with East Asia and with the Japanese Empire. While Koreans had long seen themselves as part of a Sino-centric, Confucian world, the concept of "East Asia" (*Tonga*) was an imported one from the West. As a result of their encounter with Western ideas Korean intellectuals toward the late 19th century began to think of the world as divided by races and by an "East and West." They began identifying as "Easterners" and as "Asians." Some, such

---

14   Michael D. Shin, *Korean National Identity under Japanese Colonial Rule: Yi Gwangsu and the March First Movement of 1919* (London: Routledge, 2018), 2.

15   Shin, 210.

as late 19th century reformer Kim Ok-kyun, identified Korea as being, along with China and Japan, one of the three Asian *hwa* (cultures or societies) that had to unite against Europe and America. This idea of East Asia was not just a cultural identity but a racial one, as the East Asians formed the yellow races. These racial views, new to Korea, were also borrowed from the West. To express them Korean intellectuals used neologisms coined by the Japanese to translate terms such as "race" and "volk."

A number of Koreans in the early 20th century embraced this new identity in the form of Pan-Asianism (*asia yŏndaeron* "theory of Asian solidarity"), an idea developed by some Japanese thinkers that all the peoples of the Pacific Rim of Asia should cooperate in challenging the dominance of the West, and that Japan should lead them in this effort.[16] Pan-Asianism was influenced by social Darwinism, especially its German form that saw history as a struggle for survival among the races.[17] In Korea, Social Darwinism was referred to as *yakyuk kangsik* (the weak are meat, the strong eat) and lent urgency to the reform of Korea lest it fall prey to stronger societies.[18] This was interpreted both in cultural and racial terms. At the start of the colonial rule, Pan-Asianism was perhaps at least as influential among Korean thinkers as Korean nationalism. But during the 1910s and especially after the March First Movement of 1919, it lost out in the competition with Korean national identity. There were always limits to identification with other Asians. In fact, Korean intellectuals often looked down on the Chinese and well as other Asians. Even in the peak of Pan-Asianist popularity Korean writers and publications often portrayed the Chinese as an inferior, backward people, projecting on them the same stereotypes that the Japanese had of Koreans. These negative views of China and the Chinese were reinforced by a shared resentment over the presence of Chinese merchants, resentment that led to anti-Chinese riots in 1931.[19] After 1931, with the expansion of the Japanese Empire, Pan-Asianism was promoted by the colonial regime and was revived and held by some Koreans.

Pan-Asianism remained inseparable from its association with Japanese imperialism. But an attempt to be both Korean and a member of the Empire was made problematic by Japan's colonial policy of assimilation. The colonial

---

16   Shin, 33.

17   Gi-Wook Shin, *Ethnic Nationalism in Korea: Genealogy, Politics, and Legacy* (Stanford, Cal: Stanford University Press, 2006), 22.

18   Vladimir Tikhonov, *Social Darwinism and Nationalism in Korea: The Beginning (1880s-1910s): "Survival" as an Ideology of Korean Modernity* (Leiden, Neth: Brill, 2010), passim.

19   Vladimir Tikhonov, *Modern Korea and its Others: Perceptions of the Neighboring Countries and Korean Identity* (New York: Routledge, 2018), 130.

administration promoted the idea that Koreans and Japanese were racially the same people, not in terms of being members of an Asian yellow race, but of a "national" race or a *minjok* (Japanese: *minzoku*). Japan and Korea were originally the same people who became separated centuries earlier. Japan had gone on to progress while Korea had stagnated. The colonial occupation was reuniting the two again. Yet the colonial regime was ambiguous about this policy, insisting that Koreans were now Japanese but also maintaining their distinct identity and status as subordinate and inferior subjects. Thus, the Korean attempt to be both Korean and cosmopolitan ran into the Japanese theoretical aim of absorbing the Korean people into the Japanese race and culture.[20]

From 1920 to 1931, the so-called colonial "culture policy" permitted Korean newspapers and periodicals to be published, and for Koreans to form various social and cultural associations. There were in effect two educational systems, one for Koreans and one for Japanese residents. Japanese was a required language in all schools, but Korean schools carried out instruction in Korean. The policy was "separate but equal" education. Korean businessmen had their own separate chamber of commerce apart from that of the Japanese.[21] At the same, time there was an effort to encourage Koreans to see themselves as members of a greater Japan and adopt Japanese language and customs. This policy changed with the Japanese expansion into China after 1931. From then on, there was greater pressure for Koreans to assimilate into Japanese culture and the colonial authorities imposed greater restrictions on Korean activities. Koreans were encouraged to participate in ceremonies at Shinto shrines and Korean schools began with ritual bowings in the direction of the imperial palace. Greater emphasis was placed on Japanese language in all schools.

This change accelerated under Governor-General, Minami Jirō (1936–1942), who pledged to end discrimination and promote reconciliation between Japan and Korea under the slogans "Japan and Korea as one body" (*Nai-Sen ittai*) and "harmony between Japan and Korea" (*Nissen yūwa*). All Koreans were required to register at Shinto shrines, even though this was an alien religion to all Koreans and especially offensive to Christians. The authorities required students and government employees to attend Shinto ceremonies. Then in late 1939, the government issued the Name Order, which set in motion the process by which Koreans were to change their names to Japanese ones. Generally, this

---

20   Mark E. Caprio "the Politics of Assimilation: Koreans into Japanese," in Michael J Seth, editor, *Routledge Handbook of Modern Korean History"* (London: Routledge, 2016): 111–123, 111.

21   See Carter Eckert, *Offspring of Empire: The Koch'ang Kims and the Origins of Korean Capitalism* (Seattle: University of Washington Press, 1991).

was done by having people select Chinese characters that could either be the same or similar to their names, but pronounced in a Japanese way, or they could select entirely new names. From 1940, all government employees, families with children in school, and others affiliated with the state were more or less pressured to adopt new Japanese names. Eventually, about 84 percent of Koreans complied and adopted new names.[22] In a society where ancient family lineage was prized, this loss of names was a particular humiliation. Korean-language newspapers were ordered closed in 1940; except for the Korean edition of the official government daily, all remaining twelve newspapers were in Japanese. By the early 1940s, the publication of all Korean books ceased. Korean language use in schools was extremely restricted after 1938, and by 1943, students could be punished for speaking Korean at school.

Yet, Koreans were not Japanese. All public documents, school records, and job applications listed the original family name as well as the place of birth and the clan. Official reports made a clear distinction between "peninsular" people and "homeland" Japanese. Japanese leaders themselves had no clear, consistent idea of exactly what the relationship between Koreans and Japanese was. There was some debate among Japanese political leaders as to whether Koreans could be allowed to participate directly in the Japanese government. From 1921 the House of Representatives, or Diet, introduced resolutions calling for extending the franchise to Koreans and allowing Korean representation in parliament. Some Koreans actively campaigned for the franchise. In the 1920s, the writer Ch'oe Rin led a home-rule movement demanding that the political rights guaranteed to Japanese people in their 1889 constitution be extended to Korea.[23] A number of pro-Japanese associations flourished in the 1930s; in 1937 Minami created the National Association of Koreans to unite them. A resolution in 1939 and another in 1940 to grant the franchise to Koreans passed, but both were vetoed by the cabinet. Only in December 1944 did Tokyo approve of Korean (and Taiwanese) representation in the Diet, which was to begin in 1946.

Koreans, however, were far from assimilated into Japanese culture. They lived apart from Japanese people. Towns divided Japanese and Korean neighbors.[24] Most Koreans could not speak Japanese, did not have any social interaction with Japanese, or identify with Japan. One Japanese source in 1943 stated

22   Caprio, 115–116.
23   Michael E. Robinson, *Cultural Nationalism in Colonial Korea, 1920–1925* (Seattle: University of Washington Press, 1988), 144.
24   E. Taylor Atkins, "Colonial Modernity" in Michael J Seth, editor, *Routledge Handbook of Modern Korean History* (London: Routledge, 2016): 124–140, 132.

that 23 percent of Koreans comprehended Japanese, 12 percent without difficulties.[25] Some Koreans may have genuinely been attracted to Japanese culture.
Among the small professional class, there were many who enjoyed Japanese
literature, films, and music and enjoyed the opportunity to visit Tokyo. Yet
assimilation failed. Japanese and Koreans remained two separate peoples who
did not mix socially. By the early 1940s, out of some 750,000 Japanese living in
Korea, most of them men, fewer than 1,000 were married to Koreans.[26] Rather
than leading to assimilation, the presence of a privileged alien minority in this
historically homogeneous society, and the clumsy and inconsistent efforts at
erasing their culture, created a strong collective sense of ethnic and national
identity among Koreans of all social classes.

6   Identifying with the Western-Centered Global Community

Unlike the Pan-Asian or Imperial Japanese cosmopolitanism, identifying with
the Western-centered global community proved more compatible with identifying with a Korean nation. Both Korea and Japan looked to the West in the
late 19th century as the new standard of civilization. Since Japan pioneered
in modernization it was a natural model to learn how to become modern,
enlightened and civilized (and the terms were often interchangeable). But
many Koreans had always looked directly to Europe and North America for
inspiration. Under colonial rule, many intellectuals and members of the rising "modern" middle class saw the West as a model that could enable them to
assert their autonomy from Japan. As members of this Western-based world
order, Koreans could take their place as part of the community of nation-states
without pressure to assimilate into another society.

This was especially true of Christians, a group disproportionally represented among moderate nationalists. With their ties to Western missions and
the uneasy relations with the non-Christian Japanese and their Shinto shrines
and emperor worship, they were especially open to Western concepts of
modernity. Protestant missionaries arriving in the late 19th century built many
schools and hospitals to attract Koreans. Very quickly, many Koreans saw these
new mission schools as opportunities to gain access to modern education
and successfully navigate the new modern world. Many became Christian. In
fact, Korea was the one place in Asia where missionaries had great success in

---

25   Gradjanzev, 269.
26   Gradjanzev, 270.

making converts. At the start of colonial rule, there were about 200,000 Korean Christians or about 1.5 percent of the population.[27] Most converts came from lower-class rural families but there was a significant number of officials, politicians and intellectuals drawn to Christianity. With their modern education, their English language skills and exposure to Western culture they played a role in the modern leadership of Korea considerably greater than their modest numbers might suggest. The greatest concentrations of Christians was in Pyongyang, the center of a 1907 religious movement known as the Great Revival. During colonial times, Christians became leaders in national affairs, but Christian communities were active in civic life throughout the country. Buddhists, long excluded from public affairs and lacking the links with the international community, were less active in colonial politics and intellectual discourse. However, recent research suggests that Buddhist leaders shared a sense of being part of a trans-national community.[28]

The colonial administration had an uneasy relationship with the Korean Christian foreign missionary communities. With their separate schools and church networks, they potentially formed an organizational base for opposition to the colonial regime. Their very ties with the global Christian world and the foreign missionary community made them potential obstacles in Japan's effort at imposing control over the Korean population. Colonial authorities saw the churches as centers for pro-Western, anti-Japanese nationalist activities. At the start of colonial rule, in 1911, Japanese rounded up a number of Korean Christian leaders in the so-called "105 Incident" (named for the 105 Koreans placed on trial) in which Christians were arrested for allegedly conspiring against the colonial regime. The incident drew unfavorable publicity in the Western press that pointed out the flimsy evidence that was brought against the defendants. An embarrassed government released the Christian leaders, but it continued to try to restrict their activities. In 1915, the Regulations on Private Schools ordered Christian schools to revise their curricula to that of the state-sponsored schools and to limit religious instructions. The same year Regulations on Religious Propaganda issued registration requirements for Christian pastors and leaders.[29] Yet Christianity continued to grow. In 1937, there were 281,000 Presbyterians, 110,000 Catholics, 55,000 Methodists and

---

27   Kenneth Wells. *New God, New Nation: Protestants and Self-Reconstruction Nationalism in Korea, 1896–1937* (Honolulu: University of Hawaii Press, 1990), 32–33.

28   See Hwansoo Ilmee Kim, *The Korean Buddhist Empire: A Transnational History, 1910–1945* (Cambridge, Mass: Harvard University Press, 2018).

29   Kyung Moon Hwang. *Rationalizing Korea: The rise of the Modern State, 1894–1945* (Berkeley, Cal.: University of California Press, 2016), 162.

30,000 members of other denominations.[30] While constituting only 3 percent of the total population, they made a much more sizeable percentage of the cosmopolitan middle class and held influence in Korean society far beyond their numbers. Increasingly Korean Christians were becoming the spokespeople for Korean national interests.[31] Christians took leading roles in modernizing education and using it as a means to identify with the West. Prominent among this group were Paek Nak-chun, son of a farmer who attended Christian schools and spent twelve years studying in the US, earning a PhD from Princeton; O Chŏn-sŏk son of a Protestant who graduated from Teachers College, Columbia University, and Kim Hwal-lan (Helen Kim) who became a leader in women's education.[32] However, in the 1930s, the state imposed compulsory Shinto worship, expelled most of the foreign missions, and increased pressure on all Koreans to cooperate with the colonial regime. These measures weakened the ability of the Christian community to play a leadership role in the colony.

Korea's middle class was inspired by the Western liberal ideals articulated by President Wilson at the end of World War I. When at the Versailles peace settlement, the principle of national self-determination was proclaimed, members of Korea's intellectual, and modernizing middle class, took action to join their hopes for independence to the new liberal world order. Their views were reinforced by what they learned of anti-colonial movements such as Philippines and India. Gandhi, in particular, was an inspiration. Cho Man-sik (1882–1950) a Presbyterian elder who studied at Waseda University in Japan, became an admirer of Gandhi's non-violent, noncooperation nationalist movement in British India.[33] He organized the Society for the Promotion of Korean Production in early 1923 to encourage Koreans to buy locally made products and boycott Japanese goods. It was not just a Christian movement, but joined by the globally conscious middle-class including Buddhist and Chŏndogyo leaders, who were impressed by both the effectiveness of Gandhi's movement and the favorable attention it received in the international press.

The Korean Production Movement 1923–1924, as the campaign was called, failed for a number of reasons: the colonial state offered subsidies for Korean businessmen, Japanese businesses lowered prices, and Korean manufacturers could not meet the demand for their products that the boycott created.

---

30   Todd A. Henry, *Assimilating Seoul: Japanese Rule and the Politics of Public Space in Colonial Korea, 1910–1945* (Berkeley, Cal.: University of California Press, 2014), 203.
31   Todd, 34.
32   Donald K. Adams, "Education in Korea, 1945–1955," PhD diss, University of Connecticut, 1956.
33   Robinson, 95, 97.

Another movement popular among the middle class was for the establishment of a modern Korean university. A Society for the Establishment of a
National University launched fundraising efforts but was undermined when
the Japanese established Keijō (Seoul) National University in 1926. These
movements made little progress and the momentum of the nationalist movement went to more radical nationalists influenced by socialism. Nonetheless,
a major segment of the Korean middle class continued to identify with the
liberal democratic nations of the West. And in the 1930s, some became influenced by European fascism, seeing it as another model of modernization and
national self-fulfillment.

7   Identifying with the International Struggle of the Masses

While many Koreans who identified with the international community did so
primarily with the middle-class Western world, others identified with the international struggle of the masses, many becoming socialists, Marxist-Socialists,
and anarchists. While cosmopolitan in the sense that they saw themselves as
part of a global movement, almost all were radical nationalists equally linking
the liberation of the nation with the liberation of the people from exploitation
by landlords and elites

   Not all Koreans identifying with the global struggle of the masses became
communists, but the communists were the largest and best-organized radical nationalists. When Korean intellectuals became aware of socialism, they
began to identify their efforts to regain the country's liberation from Japan
with the international struggle of the masses against oppression. This new
form of transnational identity emerged with powerful force after the Bolshevik
Revolution of 1917, Lenin's denunciation of imperialism, and the offers of the
new Bolshevik regime in Russia to provide assistance in organizing resistance
to colonial oppression. Korean intellectuals proved to be highly receptive to
socialist ideas. In socialism, they found an explanation for the country's weak-
ness, its poverty and its victimization under the hands of the Japanese. And
they were able to place their struggle in the context of an international, universal movement. Many young Koreans were quick to respond to the appeal
of joining an international socialist movement. When Lenin called an international conference of the Toilers of the Far East in Moscow in 1922, Koreans
were the largest group to attend.[34]

---

34   Robert Scalapino and Chong-sik Lee, *Communism in Korea Part I*. (Berkeley, Cal: University
      of California Press, 1973), 149.

Koreans first encountered communism abroad. In Siberia, which had several hundred thousand Koreans as part of a migration that began after 1860 became an early center of communism. Koreans there organized the first political group to adopt communism when the resistance fighter Yi Tong-hwi organized a Korean People's Socialist Party in Khabarovsk, Siberia in June 1919. Shortly afterward, he went to Shanghai to participate in the Korean Provisional Government, becoming its prime minister. While in Shanghai, he formed the Koryŏ Communist party in May 1920. At about this same time Yi organized the Korean People's Socialist Party Nam Man-ch'un formed a Korean section of the Bolshevik Party in the Siberian city of Irkutsk. The two communist groups became rivals. The Irkutsk communists were critical of Yi Tong-hwi with his *ŭibyŏng* (righteous army) and Christian past, regarding him as not a true communist but simply a nationalist who was taking advantage of Soviet assistance. On June 27, 1921, the Irkutsk Koreans with Soviet forces attacked Yi's forces at Alekseyevsk in Siberia in what was called the "Free City Incident," killing and capturing hundreds of them. Although Moscow tried to patch things up, the two groups remained rivals. The Irkutsk faction became part of the Bolsheviks with their own Korean regiments in the Red Army. In the 1930s, Stalin, becoming distrustful of the loyalty of the Koreans, disbanded these regiments and purged Korean army cadres. The Korean community in the Soviet Union no longer played an active role in the nationalist movement but they would be important in the creation of the North Korean state after 1945.

Meanwhile, Korean students in Japan became increasingly interested in Marxism-Leninism and organized communist circles in the early 1920s. They formed their own communist party, sometimes with the assistance of the illegal Japanese Communist Party. Upon returning to Korea, they established study clubs, youth organizations, and labor and tenant farmer unions. Thus, led by students from Japan, an internal communist movement in Korea began. Like the radicals outside of Korea, radicals in Korea split into rival groups. Two such groups were the Saturday Society (T'oyohoe) formed in 1923 and the Tuesday Society (Hwayohoe) formed in 1924. Local communists in Seoul competed with the returned students, the latter, generally possessing a more sophisticated understanding of Marxism, looked down on locally organized groups. In April 1925, youthful leftists established the Korean Communist Party, the first party within Korea. Seven months later the colonial authorities carried out a mass arrest of its members. Others created a new party in 1926 which again resulted in mass arrests in June of that year. Nonetheless, the persistent young radicals formed a third and then a fourth party, the latter of which saw its leadership arrested in 1928. In the face of relentless repression by the colonial authorities, it became extremely difficult for Korean communists to operate even underground, especially under the new tighter police regulation enforced from 1926. Besides Japanese arrests, the domestic communists faced criticism from the Comintern, the communist international in Moscow.[35]

Despite their organizational failures, many Korean intellectuals openly rejected the liberalism of moderate nationalists, seeing it as both a rationale for self-interest and cooperation with the Japanese. While many moderate nationalists admired Gandhi, others pointed to the fact that India was still under British rule. Furthermore, they believed that socialism, not liberalism, was the international trend. In an anonymous article in the journal *Kaebyŏk* in 1924, the author argued that the liberal tradition might have been seen as the wave of the future, but in fact, the future was socialism. Socialism, he stated, was "cosmopolitanizing" the Korean intellectual community but it was based on "scientific methods and principles of social development" and would unite Korean intellectuals "with a wider community of intellectuals in colonies around the world."[36] The ideas and language of radical socialism had spread widely among educated young people. In 1926, when the last Korean ruler Emperor Sunjong, who had been forced to abdicate sixteen years earlier, died, it sparked a number of anti-Japanese demonstrations in what became known as the June Tenth Movement. The colonial authorities were better prepared and able to contain them, but it was still a large-scale anti-colonial movement. It differed from the March First Movement in that communists rather than Christians and members of the Chŏndogyo were the principal organizers. Instead of appealing to the Western powers as those leaders of the March First Movement did, the organizers of the June Tenth Movement appealed to the masses to bring about revolution. To the extent that they looked outside of Korea for assistance and inspiration, it was to the Soviet Union and the international socialist movement.[37] The influence of the leftist nationalists appeared again in 1929 when a student strike against their Japanese administrators in the southwest city of Kwangju spread to 194 schools and involved 54,000 students in a nationwide anti-Japanese movement. Students distributed pamphlets with slogans such as "Down with Imperialism" and "Long Live the Proletarian Revolution."[38]

35   Chong-sik Lee, *The Korean Workers' Party: A Short History* (Stanford, Cal: Stanford University Press, 1978), 20–29.
36   Robinson, 145–147.
37   Michael Shin, 212.
38   Nahm, 286–88.

Although Marxists in theory base their struggle on the proletariat, in Korea their struggle was a movement of the cosmopolitan middle class of students, intellectuals and political activists. They were drawn from the same background as the moderate nationalist leadership, in fact, some came from Christian backgrounds. Several Christian leaders of the Korean Products Promotion Society became socialists or Marxists.[39] Kim Il-sung, for example, the future leader of North Korea, came from a middle-class Christian home in Pyongyang. The lack of working-class representation drew criticism from the Comintern in Moscow. At the end of 1928, in the "December Thesis" the Comintern admonished the Korean communists for their isolation from the proletariat movement. This was a reasonable charge, since the domestic Korean communists were primarily circles of young intellectuals with limited ties to the proletariat. In fact, most Korean communists lacked party discipline, did not always understand Marxist doctrine and made less than impressive efforts to organize the working class.[40]

Working-class Koreans were slower in developing a broader "proletarian consciousness." Korea's industrial workforce was small but grew at an accelerated rate after 1930. But the large labor force was divided between unskilled rural migrants who worked irregularly in mines, on construction projects and in the informal economy. They were mostly illiterate and only semi-urbanized. A smaller group of skilled industrial workers who emerged in the 1920s and 1930s were often active in labor strikes and unrest. Contributing to their small numbers was the proximity to Japan which made it easy for Japanese companies operating in the colony to import skilled labor from the homeland, a practice encouraged by the regime. Technical training for Koreans was largely neglected. However, with the rapid industrialization in the 1930s, imported workers could not meet the demand and the colonial regime increased technical training and companies hired more Koreans.[41] The number of Korean factory workers increased from 99,000 in 1933 to 390,000 in 1943.[42] Yet, Korean factory workers still had low levels of education and, in any case, the wartime conditions made any kind of political activism difficult.

For the most part, the leftist movement in Korea had little connection with the communist movements in exile. Thousands of Koreans became members of the Chinese Communist Party. Some, like Kim Chŏng, accompanied Mao Zedong on his Long March 1934–1935. He was joined by Kim Tu-bong,

---

39 Hwang, 163.
40 Robinson, 114–115.
41 Park, 146–149.
42 Park, 140.

a distinguished linguist who along with another Korean exile Ch'oe Ch'ang-ik, formed the Korean Independence League. In the mountains of southern Manchuria, several thousand guerillas fought under the Chinese Communist Party, the most notable of these being Kim Il-sung, the future leader of North Korea. The willingness of thousands of Koreans to join with the Chinese communists in the common struggle against not only Japan but with the Chinese Nationalist Guomindang was part of the powerful sense that they were in a transnational struggle.

While identification with the masses was associated with Marxism, it was not an exclusively Marxist concept. Many Korean intellectuals were attracted to anarchism, especially after 1919. In much the same way as the Marxists, they saw anarchism as a way of identifying Korea's loss of sovereignty and its backward status as part of a universal process. Koreans encountered anarchism mainly in intellectual circles in Shanghai and Tokyo. It placed their efforts to liberate Korea from colonial rule as part of a broader effort of liberating the masses of the world from the tyranny of capitalism and the capitalist state. Thus, anarchists identified with the global community of oppressed masses.[43] Anarchist groups were mainly active abroad, but they had many intellectual adherents in Korea.

8   Competing Cosmopolitan Identities and the Legacy for Postwar Korea

The competing cosmopolitan identities of Koreans during colonial rule were important in shaping the history of postwar Korea. Korean nationalism was divided by its cosmopolitan orientations, identifying with either the capitalist West or with the international movement of the masses. When the US and the Soviet Union effectively partitioned the peninsula into two occupation zones, they constructed states based on these differences in orientations. For South Koreans, the US and its capitalist and democratic allies became the standards for modernization and progressive development. The influence of the US was profound in popular culture, education, and eventually in political orientation. Emulation of the US and the democratic West (as well as democratic Japan) was a major, if not decisive, factor in the country's successful transition to a liberal democratic society. Christians continued to play a role in South Korea as

43   Dongyoun Hwang, *Anarchism in Korea: Independence, Transnationalism, and the Question of National Development, 1919–1984* (Albany, NY: SUNY Press, 2016), 1–7.

agents of modernization and as links with the global West beyond their numbers. And Christian numbers expanded – from 5 percent of the population in
1945 to over a quarter of the population by the 1990s.

The socialist cosmopolitanism of the colonial era continued as the basis for
North Korea's understanding of its place in the world. It was the conceptual
framework for the geopolitical orientation of the North Korean state toward
the Soviet Union, the People's Republic of China and their socialist allies.
Despite its fierce ethno-nationalism, identification with the global movement
of the proletariat was a central element of the ideology of the Democratic
People's Republic of Korea until the 1990s when following the end of the Cold
War it took a more inward, ultra-nationalist turn. However, not only in North
Korea but also in South Korea, the social-anarchists and the Marxists influ-
ences remained strong among the intellectuals and students, as well as some
labor activists. South Korea's *minjung* movement which identified the struggle
of the masses in a broader sense than simply the Marxist proletariat, grew out
of colonial proletarian cosmopolitanism and was an important factor in the
democratization of the Republic of Korea in the 1980s.

The crushing defeat of Japan in the Second World War, the collapse of its
empire and its reduction to a military-political client state of the US discred-
ited the idea of a united East Asia under the leadership of Tokyo. The ideological division of East Asia into communist and anti-communist spheres undermined whatever lingering Pan-Asian ideas remained. However, both North and
South Korea were profoundly influenced by their Japanese Imperial legacy.
Both states promoted a blood and soil ethnic nationalism, strongly echoing
that of Japan. Both adopted the authoritarian state-led model of economic
development. North Korea's cult of the ruling Kim family drew on the imagery
and vocabulary as well as the example of the Japanese cult of the imperial
family.

In the 1960s, under President Park Chung-hee, a former officer in the
Imperial Army, South Korea again followed the Japanese model of economic
development and opened its economy to Japanese trade and investment. South
Korea followed Tokyo's state-assisted development path with close cooperation between the huge conglomerates called *chaebŏl*, a Korean pronunciation
of the characters for *zaibatsu*. In its entertainment, its business culture and
its educational system, South Korea has often patterned itself, intentionally or
not, after Japan. Japan remained a usable model of modernity. However, historical and political tensions between the two countries remain.

Thus, colonial cosmopolitanism provided the framework for Korean identification with the larger world and the place of their society in it. And it is a key
to understanding the historical trajectories of the two Koreas after 1945.

References

Adams, Donald K. *Education in Korea*. 1945–1955, PhD diss, University of Connecticut, 1956.

Atkins, E. Taylor. "Colonial Modernity," in Michael J Seth, editor. *Routledge Handbook of Modern Korean History*." London: Routledge, 2016, 124–140.

Baker, Donald. "Cloudy Images: Korean Knowledge of the West from 1520–1800: *B.C. Asian Review* 3, no. 4 (1990): 51–73.

Caprio, Mark E. "The Politics of Assimilation: Koreans into Japanese," in Michael J Seth, editor. *Routledge Handbook of Modern Korean History*." London: Routledge, 2016, 111–123.

Cumings, Bruce. *Origins of the Korean War* Vol.1. Princeton, NJ: Princeton University Press, 1981.

Duncan, John, "Elements of Proto-nationalism in Pre-modern Korea," in Sang-Oak Lee and Duk-soo Park, editors. *Perspectives on Korea*. Sydney: Wild Peony Press, 1998, 191–211.

Eckert, Carter. *Offspring of Empire: The Koch'ang Kims and the Origins of Korean Capitalism*. Seattle: University of Washington Press, 1991.

Gradjanzev, Andrew J. Modern Korea New York: Institute of Pacific Relations, 1944.

Henry, Todd A. *Assimilating Seoul: Japanese Rule and the Politics of Public Space in Colonial Korea, 1910–1945*. Berkeley, Cal.: University of California Press, 2014.

Hwang, Dongyoun. *Anarchism in Korea: Independence, Transnationalism, and the Question of National Development, 1919–1984*. Albany, NY: SUNY Press, 2016.

Hwang, Kyung Moon. *Rationalizing Korea: The Rise of the Modern State, 1894–1945*. Berkeley, Cal.: University of California Press, 2016.

Jeong, Min Hyun. "New Women and Modern Girls: Consuming Foreign Goods in Colonial Korea," *Journal of Historical Research in Marketing* 5, no. 4 (Fall 2013): 494–520.

Kim, Hwansoo Ilmee. *The Korean Buddhist Empire: A Transnational History, 1910–1945*. Cambridge, Mass: Harvard University Press, 2018.

Lee, Chong-sik. *The Korean Workers' Party: A Short History*. Stanford, Cal: Stanford University Press, 1978.

Nahm, Andrew. *Korea: Tradition and Transformation*. Elizabeth, NJ: Hollym International, 1988.

Park, Soon-won. "Colonial Industrial Growth and the Emergence of the Korean Working Class," in, Gi-wook Shin and Michael Robinson, eds. Colonial Modernity in Korea. Cambridge, Mass: Harvard University Press, 1999, 128–60.

Robinson, Michael E. *Cultural Nationalism in Colonial Korea, 1920–1925*. Seattle: University of Washington Press, 1988.

Scalapino, Robert and Chong-sik Lee. *Communism in Korea Part I.* Berkeley, Cal: University of California Press, 1973.

Schmid, Andre. *Korea Between Empires, 1895–1919.* New York: Columbia University Press, 2002.

Shin, Gi-Wook. *Ethnic Nationalism in Korea: Genealogy, Politics, and Legacy.* Stanford, Cal: Stanford University Press, 2006.

Shin, Michael D. *Korean National Identity under Japanese Colonial Rule: Yi Gwangsu and the March First Movement of 1919.* London: Routledge, 2018.

Short, John Rennie. *Korea: A Cartographic History.* Chicago: University of Chicago Press, 2012.

Tikhonov, Vladimir. *Modern Korea and its Others: Perceptions of the Neighboring Countries and Korean Identity.* New York: Routledge, 2018.

Tikhonov, Vladimir. *Social Darwinism and Nationalism in Korea: The Beginning (1880s-1910s): "Survival" as an Ideology of Korean Modernity.* Leiden, Neth: Brill, 2010.

Wells, Kenneth. *New God, New Nation: Protestants and Self-Reconstruction Nationalism in Korea, 1896–1937.* Honolulu: University of Hawaii Press, 1990.

CHAPTER 3

Taiwan in Transformation

The Japanese Colonial Era

Evan Dawley

The Taiwan of August 1945 was vastly different from the Taiwan of May 1895. That contrast meant, on one level, that Taiwan had experienced, in the interim, processes of modernization and globalization that were common to much of the world. However, these broad similarities obscure the specificities of the island's transformations and the particularities that made this an era of utmost importance for the production of autonomous Taiwanese identities. Although more attention has been devoted to the post-1945 period, it was the interactions between the peoples of Taiwan and the machinery and discourses of Japanese colonialism that fundamentally altered both the face of Taiwan and the consciousness of many of its residents. On the surface were administrative and physical infrastructures that reorganized the lived environment and relations between the state and the people; the attempted unification of Taiwan via the closure of a long-standing frontier between settlers and indigenous communities; educational and other institutions that aimed at the creation of new subjects loyal to Japan and its Emperor; and economic and social policies that facilitated a dramatic socio-economic transition. These changes, most of which were concentrated in Taiwan's expanding urban centers, provided the framework within which the island's residents created new identities and many of the non-indigenes emerged from five decades of Japanese rule with a sense of themselves as Taiwanese. When Taiwan became a part of the Republic of China at the end of this period, the legacies of Japanese colonization meant that it did not easily fit within its new country, an incongruity that continues to have profound implications up to the present day. This essay will examine these multi-layered transformations in order to better understand Taiwan as an autonomous socio-political entity.

Taiwan's autonomy is a fraught reality, a condition that has influenced the historical perspectives that scholars have taken on Taiwan. The practical advocacy of an independent Taiwanese nation-state has been a dangerous proposition since the short-lived Republic of Taiwan in 1895, which might be reflected in the fact that the study of Taiwan's history has been and often remains subsumed within that of other states, be it Qing China, imperial

Japan, or Republican China. During the past two decades, however, there has been an increasing tendency to examine Taiwan's history in its own right, and this essay joins that movement and summarizes much of it. This scholarship generally presents history in the national mode and when it addresses issues of identity, the emphasis has been upon the origins, evolution, and manifestations of Taiwanese nationalism. The present work draws from that foundation, and it also argues that the study of an autonomous Taiwan does not need to depend upon a national history, but rather should explore other identities and processes within narratives that center Taiwan and the Taiwanese.

1   The Qing Transformation

When Taiwan became a formal colony of the Japanese Empire in June 1895, it was not a blank slate upon which the Japanese regime could write itself. Long the home of vibrant indigenous communities, it had spent two centuries as a part of the Qing Empire, absorbing settlers from the coastal regions of Fujian and Guangdong provinces who implanted their social structures and practices even as the government attempted to control their movements. These three groups—indigenous, Chinese settlers, Qing officials—interacted to produce complex, often conflictual, processes of assimilation, Sinicization, and localization.

After deciding to retain control of this so-called "ball of mud" following the defeat of its long-standing antagonist, the regime of the half-Japanese Zheng Chenggong (Koxinga) and his successors, the Qing court wanted to ensure that Taiwan would become a defensive shield and a producer rather than consumer of imperial resources. Beginning with Kangxi, Qing emperors placed restrictions on which of their subjects could migrate to Taiwan and where they could reside. Long-standing prohibitions on the emigration of women meant that the great majority of Chinese settlers were men. Moreover, the Qing state established a formal guard line beyond which these Han (mostly Hokkien) and Hakka were not allowed to settle. This movable line demarcated a frontier between settler society on the coastal plains and indigenous groups in the hills and mountains, and a conceptual distinction between plains indigenous (*pingpuzu*, also known as *shufan* or "cooked indigenous") and mountain indigenous (*gaoshanzu*, also known as *shengfan* or "raw indigenous"). Qing rulers also tried to limit the impact of Chinese settlement through a complex series of land-ownership arrangements that, in theory, left underlying land rights in the hands of indigenous owners.

These restrictionist policies left substantial numbers of plains indigenous, perhaps as many as fifty-thousand, within the zone of Chinese settlement, which exposed them to assimilation by the expanding emigrant population.[1] During the Zheng and early Qing periods, substantial numbers of plains indigenous rapidly identified themselves as Han, via marriage or parentage, in order to take advantage of favorable taxation policies. Others did not change their formal identification and thus retained indigenous status, even as they went through long-term processes of cultural transformation, adopting more and more of the socio-cultural practices of the Chinese with whom they lived in close proximity and frequently intermarried.[2]

The adoption by indigenous populations of imported norms and traditions was one part of Taiwan's Sinicization, which was paired with a counter-trajectory of localization. The installation of Qing administrative and security structures—prefectural and county magistrates, eventually a provincial governor, military garrisons—made Taiwan an increasingly regular piece of Qing territory.[3] The inscription of the Qing state was paired with discursive practices such as mapping, travel writing, and the description and classification of indigenous groups that, collectively, made Taiwan a more familiar place.[4] In contrast, Chinese who migrated to Taiwan usually did so because they were near the bottom of the socio-economic ladder in their home regions, and their ties to the Qing state were often tenuous at best. That disconnect manifested in frequent outbursts of civil unrest, over 150 between 1684 and 1895, many of them directed against the government institutions that tried to control Chinese settlement.[5] As some families remained in Taiwan for several generations, such as the Lins of Wufeng, they oriented themselves toward the state, studying for the civil service examinations, serving as leaders of rebellion-suppression campaigns, and establishing themselves as classic scholar-gentry families.[6] However, multi-generational habitation also promoted an increasing

1 John Robert Shepherd, *Statecraft and Political Economy on the Taiwan Frontier, 1600–1800* (Stanford, CA: Stanford University Press, 1993), 14.
2 Melissa J. Brown, *Is Taiwan Chinese?: The Impact of Culture, Power, and Migration on Changing Identities* (Berkeley: University of California Press, 2004), 66, 134. Brown distinguishes between "short-route" and "long-route" identity change.
3 Shepherd, *Statecraft and Political Economy*, 191–208.
4 Emma Teng, *Taiwan's Imagined Geography: Chinese Colonial Travel Writing and Pictures, 1683–1895* (Cambridge, MA: Harvard University Press, 2006), 3–6.
5 Chiukun Chen, "From Landlords to Local Strongmen: The Transformation of Local Elites in Mid-Ch'ing Taiwan, 1780–1862," in *Taiwan: A New History*, ed. Rubinstein, Murray A., Expanded Edition (Armonk, N.Y: M.E. Sharpe, 2007), 133–62, 136.
6 Johanna Margarete Menzel Meskill, *A Chinese Pioneer Family: The Lins of Wu-Feng, Taiwan, 1729–1895* (Princeton, N.J.: Princeton University Press, 1979).

focus on Taiwan and an identification with the specific locales in which they resided and built their economic foundations, clan organizations, and ancestral shrines.[7] That is, Chinese settlers became localized in Taiwan.

The final decades of Qing rule brought the first stages of modern globalization to Taiwan's shores. First came a limited integration into the global economy via the treaty ports established at Tamsui, Keelung, and Kaohsiung, where foreign traders came to collect tea, camphor, and sugar for distribution to markets across the world.[8] Two foreign incursions—a Japanese invasion of the southern tip of the island in 1874, and the French occupation of northern harbors in 1884–85—prompted the Qing to revise its management of Taiwan. Since the Japanese had acted because the Qing had long disclaimed jurisdiction over the indigenous groups and their lands in the east and southeast, the court responded by announcing a plan to eliminate the guard line and to "open the mountains and pacify the savages" (*kaishan fufan*).[9] The court later elevated Taiwan to the status of province and its first governor, Liu Mingchuan, was an advocate of self-strengthening policies who launched an ambitious initiative of infrastructure development in order to make Taiwan a model of modernization and a key node in China's foreign trade.[10] Liu's planned trans-island railway epitomized the limited extent to which these plans were fulfilled—by 1895, it ran only from Keelung to the provincial capital of Taipei—but even so, Taiwan's residents incorporated internally and externally focused perspectives into identities that stressed attachments to China, ancestral homeland, place of residence, and indigenous community. As yet, there were no Taiwanese.

2   The Colonial Infrastructure of Japanese Imperialism

The Japanese colonial regime shared many of the same objectives as its Qing predecessor: to establish and maintain control while expending as few

---

7   Chen, "From Landlords to Local Strongmen" 149–51; Chen Qinan, *Chuantong zhidu yu shehui yishi de jiegou: lishi yu renleixue de tansuo* (Traditional Systems and the Structure of Social Consciousness: The Deep Search of History and Anthropology) (Taipei shi: Yun chen wenhua shiye gufen youxian gongsi, 1998), 174–75.

8   Lin Man-houng, *Cha, tang, zhangnao ye yu wan Qing Taiwan* (The Tea, Sugar, and Camphor Industries and Late Qing Taiwan) (Taipei shi: Lianjing, 1997).

9   Teng, *Taiwan's Imagined Geography*, 207–36.

10 William M. Speidel, "The Administrative and Fiscal Reforms of Liu Ming-Ch'uan in Taiwan, 1884–1891: Foundation for Self-Strengthening," *The Journal of Asian Studies* 35, no. 3 (May 1976): 441–59.

resources as possible; to extract beneficial materials; to facilitate settlement by its native subjects; and to transform or civilize the existing residents. In contrast, however, it had the powerful administrative and security machinery of a modern nation-state at its disposal and, having just defeated the former regional hegemon, Japan's leaders approached their new acquisition with considerable imperialist confidence. Even though considerable opposition from the new imperial subjects challenged that confidence—the peoples of Taiwan did not easily abandon their traditions of anti-state violence—the new rulers implemented sweeping changes that re-engineered the island's administrative and physical topography.

Acting with a high degree of autonomy from the home government in Tokyo, the Government-General of Taiwan (GGT) created an administrative structure of breadth and depth that had no precedent in Taiwan. Its freedom of activity came from an 1896 act of the Japanese Imperial Diet known as Law 63, which gave Taiwan's Governor-General the authority to enact legislation via edict, along with broad judicial powers, and ensured that Japan's domestic laws would not automatically be extended to the colony.[11] The bureaucratic hierarchy went through a number of reforms between 1895 and 1920, and as it took shape it emanated out and down from the GGT to prefecture (*chō* or *shū*), subprefecture (*shichō*), county (*gun*), and city, town, or village (*shigaison*). By the end of this process, the administrative units were mostly the same as those in the home islands, although all officials were appointed by the GGT.[12] Beneath the formal bureaucracy, the GGT selected local elites to form neighborhood committees or town councils that served as intermediaries for the government.[13] The GGT also created consultative bodies at the municipal, prefecture, and colonial levels. These measures brought formal and informal agents of the state directly into the everyday lives of imperial subjects, at least those within the lowland zones.

The GGT also developed two policing institutions that gave it an additional mechanism of control over local society. In 1901, Governor-General Kodama

---

11   Huiyu Caroline Ts'ai, *Taiwan in Japan's Empire-Building: An Institutional Approach to Colonial Engineering* (New York: Routledge, 2009), 30–32. Law 31 replaced Law 63 in 1906, and was replaced in 1922 with Law 3, but all of them maintained the autonomy and administrative distinctives of the GGT.

12   Huang Zhaotang, *Taiwan zongdufu* (The Taiwan Government-General), trans. Huang Yingzhe, Xiuding yiban (Taipei shi: Qianwei chubanshe, 2004), chap. 5.

13   Evan N. Dawley, *Becoming Taiwanese: Ethnogenesis in a Colonial City, 1880s-1950s* (Cambridge, MA: Harvard University Asia Center, 2019), 52.

Gentarō and Civil Administrator Gotō Shinpei established the colonial police force, which existed within the civilian government as an autonomous body with authority to intervene in most aspects of governance. Spread throughout all layers of the GGT, and with officers recruited among both Japanese and islanders (*hontōjin*; this was the Japanese term for the peoples of Taiwan, primarily used for those with ties to China), the colonial police had tremendous potential for asserting control. However, because police officers were disproportionately concentrated in indigenous communities, they were a weaker presence in the lives of Chinese-descended islanders.[14] To augment the official police force, and to reach more deeply into these segments of the population, the GGT adapted an existing mutual responsibility system, the *hokō* or *baojia*, that placed a substantial burden for ensuring security and stability upon islander society.[15]

In order to fulfill its goals of making Taiwan a self-sufficient colony, the GGT developed infrastructure to maximize the efficiency of resource extraction, such as ambitious programs of road and railroad construction and harbor development. Railroads became the central feature of transportation infrastructure under Japanese rule, as the GGT moved quickly to complete a trans-island railway and then expand the network through a combination of locomotive and push-cart lines. In 1908, the GGT proudly opened a line running near the western coast from Keelung in the north to Kaohsiung in the south.[16] Railway construction continued until, by 1929, over one-thousand miles of track had been laid across the island.[17] Private companies accounted for some of this construction, such as the Keelung Light Rail Corporation (Kiirun keitetsu kabushiki kaisha), owned and financed by the mining magnates Kimura Kutarō, Yan Yunnian, and Yan Guonian, which built lines to bring coal to Keelung's harbor from the mines they ran in its hinterland.[18] Harbors were the other main area of focus, both for shipping Taiwan's valuable agricultural products—rice, sugar, camphor, tea, bananas—to Japan and other parts of the world, and for facilitating Japan's "Southern Advance"

---

14   Ts'ai, *Taiwan in Japan's Empire-Building*, 76–79 and 84–87.

15   Ts'ai, 98–105, 108–17.

16   Cai Longbao, *Tuidong shidai de julun: Ri zhi zhongqi de Taiwan guoyou tielu (1910–1936)* (Period of Promotion: Taiwan's National Railroads in the Middle Period of Japanese Control, 1910–1936) (Taipei shi: Taiwan guji, 2004).

17   Paul D. Barclay, "Japanese Empire in Taiwan," in *Oxford Research Encyclopedia of Asian History*, ed. David Ludden (New York: Oxford University Press, 2020), np.

18   Dawley, *Becoming Taiwanese*, 69–70.

during the 1930s and 1940s. The GGT poured huge sums of imperial funds into transforming the narrow, shoal-filled natural harbors of Keelung and Kaohsiung into deep-water ports capable of hosting 10,000-ton vessels and loading and unloading them with the most up-to-date equipment. Keelung, the early centerpiece of port construction, expanded exponentially: it welcomed 318 vessels carrying 148,496 tons of cargo in 1899, and 1,943 ships with 6,604,176 tons in 1931.[19]

Port construction was part of a broader program of urbanization that reflected both the practical need to entice Japanese settlers and the ideological need to justify Japanese colonization. The most high-profile manifestation of this project was the creation of the colonial capital, Taipei, as a unified entity out of the three distinct settlements that existed in 1895. The Taipei basin contained two merchant communities along the banks of the Danshui River, Wanhua/Mengjia and Dadaocheng/Twatutia, between which sat a walled administrative and military zone. Beginning with plans laid down by Gotō Shinpei in 1900, and subsequent iterations of urban design in 1905 and 1932, the GGT merged these three districts and extended the city south and eastward. Most of the Qing wall was destroyed—except for four gates—and replaced by wide boulevards and railway lines, and the planners knit the city together with broad and narrow streets that define the city's layout up to the present.[20] The dense neighborhoods of the older districts were largely preserved, albeit with substantial renovation, but because the city expanded into farmland, colonial architects were able to build anew. As Joe Allen describes it, "[T]he newer sections of town were populated by large modern, renaissance, and neoclassical buildings surrounded by open spaces. All of these just screamed 'colonialism.' "[21] Taipei was the most prominent example, but other cities like Keelung, Kaohsiung, and especially Taichung experienced even more dramatic urbanization because all of them had been mere villages when the Japanese arrived.[22] Urbanization also brought a notable demographic shift. The island remained primarily agrarian throughout the first half of the 20th century, but by 1920, 12.7 percent of Taiwan's population lived in its nine largest cities, a proportion that reached 17.3 percent in 1940.[23]

19   Dawley, 45–47.
20   Joseph Roe Allen, *Taipei: City of Displacements* (Seattle: University of Washington Press, 2012), 25–33, 75–80.
21   Allen, 74.
22   Dawley, *Becoming Taiwanese*, 48–50.
23   George W. Barclay, *Colonial Development and Population in Taiwan* (Princeton, N.J.: Princeton University Press, 1954), tables 2, 24.

3   Closing the Frontier

The Japanese colonial regime, and its adherents, developed an interest bordering on obsession with Taiwan's indigenous population. Even though the peoples identified as indigenous constituted only about two percent of the total, they occupied some of the most economically significant terrain and also afforded Japanese colonizers with the opportunity to prove their worth as civilizers. Through diplomatic, military, and administrative methods, the colonial regime and its agents erased the indigenous frontier and attempted to integrate the island within a framework of unified, continuous sovereignty.[24]

The GGT moved in stages to implement this plan, first replicating Qing policies to manage the frontier before altering the relationships within it. In northern Taiwan, the frontier economy had long revolved around the production of camphor, which Chinese settlers obtained through their interactions mostly with members of the Atayal group.[25] The GGT coveted the revenues from this valuable commodity, but initially did not have the capacity to facilitate direct access to camphor production, so it restored the indigenous guard line and promoted intermarriage between Japanese men and indigenous women to promote stability and commerce in the frontier. Although these unions were never legally recognized, nor did they always achieve their political and economic goals, they remained a part of Japanese frontier management into the 1920s.[26] Another key piece of the early policy was the practice of "wet diplomacy," whereby Japanese officials shared alcoholic beverages—sometimes from the same vessel—with leaders of the Atayal, Sediq, and other groups in order to secure diplomatic agreements.[27] However, these measures were only temporary, as the GGT supported Japanese capitalists in their takeover of camphor production and, in a more dramatic fashion, launched a series of military and construction campaigns in order to pacify the indigenes and push the guard line further into the interior. This was a lengthy and costly endeavor—the northern offensives lasted from 1907–14 and cost in the vicinity of 18 million yen—but at the end of it, the GGT had established a new boundary consisting

24   Paul D. Barclay, *Outcasts of Empire: Japan's Rule on Taiwan's "Savage Border," 1874–1945* (Oakland, CA: University of California Press, 2018), 17–19, 30–33.

25   Antonio C. Tavares, "The Japanese Colonial State and the Dissolution of the Late Imperial Frontier Economy in Taiwan, 1886–1909," *The Journal of Asian Studies* 64, no. 2 (May 2005): 361–85, 363–71.

26   Paul D. Barclay, "Cultural Brokerage and Interethnic Marriage in Colonial Taiwan: Japanese Subalterns and Their Aborigine Wives, 1895–1930," *The Journal of Asian Studies* 64, no. 2 (May 2005): 323–60, 340–51.

27   Barclay, *Outcasts of Empire*, 87–92.

of a road, guard posts, and deforested terrain demarcating the indigenous lands. The term guard line, as Paul Barclay notes, "soft-pedaled the physical magnitude of the scorched-earth installations."[28] Thereafter, an uneasy stasis prevailed, with some disruptions, for around fifteen years.

Japanese settlers and scholars devoted considerable attention to Taiwan's indigenes during these early decades. Beginning with the pioneering work of anthropologists Inō Kanori and Torii Ryūzō, Japanese scholars joined the ranks of imperialist academics as they catalogued and studied indigenous customs and used them to categorize the different groups in Taiwan. Inō worked mostly on the plains indigenous, developing a spectrum of civilization, or Sinicization, that charted the varying degrees of acculturation to Chinese culture. Torii, in contrast, did his fieldwork among the mountain indigenous, in order to explore theories of Malayo-Polynesian diffusion and the origins of the Japanese.[29] Torii's research agenda swiftly became the dominant Japanese approach to Taiwan's indigenes and paved the way for their inclusion in major exhibition venues, such as the Human Pavilion at the 1903 Industrial Exposition in Osaka, in the Formosa Hamlet at the 1910 Japan-British Exhibition in London, and at the Colonial Expositions in Tokyo and Osaka in 1912 and 1913, respectively.[30] Non-academic settlers also engaged in this exoticization and commercialization of the indigenous. For example, Japanese members of the Taiwan Branch of Japan's Patriotic Ladies Association (Aikoku fujinkai) ran trading posts in the guard line zone, where they took pictures of indigenous people and acquired indigenous handicrafts, which they then sold to customers in Taiwan and in the metropole, using the proceeds to sustain their activities. These operations included, somewhat contradictorily, lending moral and material support to the Japanese soldiers engaged in the suppression campaigns of the 1910s.[31]

The apparent effectiveness of these measures in suppressing indigenous opposition and incorporating them into the economic and administrative order of the colony hid the reality of continued indigenous discontentment, which exploded in the Wushe Incident of 1930. On October 27, a group of

---

28   Barclay, 103–111, quote on 106.

29   Paul D. Barclay, "An Historian among the Anthropologists: The Inō Kanori Revival and the Legacy of Japanese Colonial Ethnography in Taiwan," *Japanese Studies* 21, no. 2 (2001): 117–36, 117–18.

30   Kirsten L. Ziomek, *Lost Histories: Recovering the Lives of Japan's Colonial Peoples* (Cambridge, MA: Harvard University Asia Center, 2019), 46–49, 125–31, chap. 4.

31   Evan N. Dawley, "Women on the Move: Shifting Patterns in Migration and the Colonization of Taiwan," in *The Decade of the Great War: Japan and the Wider World in the 1910s*, ed. Toshihiro Minohara, Tze-Ki Hon, and Evan N. Dawley (Leiden: Brill, 2014), 281–300, 292–96.

some three hundred Sediqs, led by chieftain Mona Ludao and responding to a recent lapse in frontier diplomacy, attacked a Japanese settlement, killing 134. Colonial forces reacted with "genocidal fury," massacring over one-thousand indigenes during a months-long campaign, at the end of which they relocated all survivors from Mona's village.[32] Shocked to discover that the long-standing policy of using the guard line to fix indigenes within a separate administrative zone had failed to accomplish broader goals of civilization, the GGT began a more radical program of reorganizing indigenous society, advancing cultural transformation, and inculcating the indigenous peoples with loyalty to the Japanese Emperor. These actions dovetailed with the full-scale Japanization of the Kōminka movement, beginning in 1936. The incorporation of indigenes into the imperial order seemed evident in the recruitment of indigenous brigades during the Pacific War, and the popularity of the story of Sayon, a porter who purportedly sacrificed herself while helping a Japanese police officer leave Taiwan for the war in China.[33]

That success was largely ephemeral. It filled the discourses of late-colonial officials and writers, but in fact, Taiwan's indigenes were not passive recipients of colonial plans. As Kirsten Ziomek shows through the lives of people like Yayutz Bleyh—Atayal woman, widow of a Japanese pharmacist, translator, frequent traveler between colony and metropole with gravestones in both places—indigenes both created and navigated colonial Taiwan in pursuit of their own ambitions.[34] Their agency, combined with Japanese ambivalence regarding assimilation, meant that Taiwan retained what Paul Barclay refers to as "bifurcated sovereignty," with the indigenous zones never fully integrated with the rest of the island.[35] For these reasons, the indigenes themselves remained on the outside of the processes of Taiwanese identity construction that took place among the Chinese-descended islanders.

4   Creating New Subjects

The transformative agenda of Japanese colonialists depended upon the recreation of Qing subjects as subjects of the Japanese Emperor. That assimilationist goal was a part of Japanese colonialism from the outset, although GGT policies

---

32   Barclay, *Outcasts of Empire*, 1.
33   Leo T. S. Ching, *Becoming "Japanese": Colonial Taiwan and the Politics of Identity Formation* (Berkeley: University of California Press, 2001), 161–68.
34   Ziomek, *Lost Histories*, 196–223.
35   Barclay, *Outcasts of Empire*, 17–18.

oscillated between gradual and rapid timetables as they attempted to Japanize the islanders primarily through education and youth organizations.

The public education system was the centerpiece of this project, but its original structure almost guaranteed that true assimilation would be deferred into a long-distant future. Public education had to address two separate groups—the children of Japanese settlers and the children of islanders—therefore what emerged around the turn of the 20th century was a two-track system. Although schooling became mandatory for all children, Japanese went to Elementary Schools (*shōgakkō*) and islanders went to Common Schools (*kōgakkō*). In order to attract settlers from the home islands, the former track had to be at least on par with metropolitan schools, whereas the latter, in practice, had inferior facilities and, at least for a time, had to overcome obstacles of training and communication. Moreover, even after the Elementary Schools were opened to all students in the 1920s, entry requirements and Japanese settler resistance to granting the equality of islanders meant that very few of them gained admission. The colonial educational system saw impressive aggregate achievements: 5 percent of islanders were enrolled in 1906, but 15 percent by 1918, and over 70 percent in 1944; among girls, one-quarter were enrolled by 1935 and 60 percent in 1944.[36] A huge array of informal night schools, private schools, and other programs supplemented the formal institutions, and many shared the goal expressed in a 1941 teacher's manual: "It is not enough to give them the ability to speak Japanese. The goal is much more: it is to inculcate the Japanese way of thinking and of experiencing emotion and to cultivate the Japanese spirit."[37] However, not long before, colonial education had failed to reach even the first objective. Even in a city like Keelung, which felt the presence of the colonial state and Japanese settlers more heavily than most of Taiwan, in 1935 only about one-quarter of islanders could understand Japanese.[38]

Nevertheless, education had a dramatic impact upon the lives and identities of the islanders who received it. One result of the laxity of language policies, at least until the Kōminka-era prohibitions on Chinese instruction and publications, was that *baihuawen* (Mandarin), Romanized Taiwanese (Hokkien or Minnanhua), and Written Taiwanese movements flourished, establishing the basis for a plurality of linguistic identities.[39] Basic education in Taiwan also

36   E. Patricia Tsurumi, *Japanese Colonial Education in Taiwan, 1895–1945* (Cambridge, MA: Harvard University Press, 1977); the statistics come from 19, 45–46, 148, 219.

37   Tsurumi, 133.

38   Dawley, *Becoming Taiwanese*, 107–08.

39   Ann Heylen, *Japanese Models, Chinese Culture and the Dilemma of Taiwanese Language Reform* (Wiesbaden: Harrassowitz, 2012), 8–9.

opened doors for journeys to the metropole and elsewhere for more advanced degrees, producing in some a cosmopolitan consciousness that was not necessarily bound to a single nation-state.[40] One of the few forms of higher education available to islanders within Taiwan was medicine, and the process of training and practicing as doctors facilitated the early formation of a professionally based Taiwanese ethno-nationalism. Doctors such as Jiang Weishui became leaders of social and political movements that promoted Taiwan's independence from, or at least autonomy within, Japan.[41] Medical training and associated practices of hygiene and disease control also imparted a decidedly modern cast to the identities in formation in Taiwan, such that as islanders became Taiwanese, they defined that new consciousness as specifically modern, not exclusively rooted in the past.[42]

Alongside public education, the GGT utilized the institution of youth groups (*seinendan*) to assimilate and nationalize the islanders, but with complex and contradictory results. As Sayaka Chatani has demonstrated, youth groups appeared across Japan's national empire, and much of the world, during the early 20th century. Founded upon the "imagined universality of youth," these groups sought to organize and mobilize young citizens and subjects in the service of the state, but everywhere they had to contend with local needs and circumstances. In Taiwan, youth groups gained strength and popularity during the 1920s and early 1930s, particularly in rural areas where they dovetailed with moral suasion (*kyōka*) campaigns to formulate modern youth ideal-types, who would act to fulfill state objectives.[43] Following the launch of the Kōminka policies in 1936, and especially during the period of intense wartime mobilization, the youth groups evidently produced strong emotional bonds between rural Taiwanese and the Japanese empire, because it was through these groups that large numbers of young islanders submitted applications to the volunteer soldier program, beginning in 1942, and contributed their labor within and outside of Taiwan.[44] However, the GGT did not, in fact, achieve its

40   Komagome Takeshi, "Colonial Identity for an Elite Taiwanese, Lim Bo-seng: The Labyrinth of Cosmopolitanism," in Ping-hui Liao and David Der-wei Wang, eds., *Taiwan under Japanese Colonial Rule, 1895–1945: History, Culture, Memory* (New York: Columbia University Press, 2006), 141–59.

41   Ming-cheng Miriam Lo, *Doctors within Borders: Profession, Ethnicity, and Modernity in Colonial Taiwan* (Berkeley: University of California Press, 2002).

42   Michael Shiyung Liu, *Prescribing Colonization: The Role of Medical Practices and Policies in Japan-Ruled Taiwan, 1895–1945* (Ann Arbor, MI: Association for Asian Studies, 2009).

43   Sayaka Chatani, *Nation-Empire: Ideology and Rural Youth Mobilization in Japan and Its Colonies* (Ithaca: Cornell University Press, 2018), 13, 137–39, 145–48.

44   Chatani, 171–78.

goal of Japanization through youth mobilization. In Keelung, for example, a new youth group established in 1937 avowed a firmly nationalistic, patriotic agenda, but it was a part of an organization that local Taiwanese leaders had been using for their own purposes for over two decades, and the rural islanders came to see themselves as model rural youth rather than as model Japanese.[45] Much like the indigenes who pursued their own ambitions through colonial policies, Chatani argues that, "these supporters of Japanese militarism and agrarian nationalism in the countryside were subversive, career-seeking, and outward-looking modern beings."[46]

5   Taiwan's Socio-Economic Transformations

Education, youth mobilization, and the new mobility of indigenes were components of a much broader socio-economic transformation that occurred in rural and especially urban Taiwan, which provided the context within which islanders created and manifested Taiwanese identities. In this section, I will address these developments in three areas: the formation of new elites through social and economic engineering and personal initiative; the emergence of the "New Woman" in Taiwan; and conflict and contestation over local religious institutions and practices.

The defining features of Taiwan's economy during the era of Japanese rule were its incorporation into Japan's capitalistic economy and the creation of a native capitalist class.[47] In the first regard, a massive land survey, the arrival of Japanese capital in the hands of individuals and *zaibatsu*, and a reorientation of productivity to meet the demands of metropolitan consumers, facilitated Japanese economic domination. This ascendancy was most notable in the sugar sector, where Japanese capitalists held monopoly control over sugar manufacturing, which depended upon the exploitation of islander producers.[48] However, especially after World War I, islander landlords took advantage of Japanese demand for rice to control that sector of the economy and amass wealth in their own hands, a least until the end of the 1930s.[49] Similarly, even

---

45   Dawley, *Becoming Taiwanese*, 157–58; Chatani, *Nation-Empire*, 179.
46   Chatani, *Nation-Empire*, 16.
47   Thomas B. Gold, "Colonial Origins of Taiwanese Capitalism," in *Contending Approaches to the Political Economy of Taiwan*, ed. Edwin A. Winckler and Susan Greenhalgh (Armonk, N.Y.: M.E. Sharpe, 1988), 101–17.
48   Chih-ming Ka, *Japanese Colonialism in Taiwan: Land Tenure, Development, and Dependency, 1895–1945* (Boulder, CO: Westview Press, 1995), 62–82.
49   Ka, 133.

though Japanese dominated the shipping, mining, fisheries, and early industrial (mostly cement and chemical production) sectors, islanders played significant roles in all of these areas. For example, the Yan brothers parlayed their
family's late-Qing prominence in northern Taiwan into key mining licenses
from the GGT and expanding connections with Japanese settler business leaders, which they used to place themselves at the forefront of coal and gold mining in colonial Taiwan. Yunnian became known as the "Coal King of Taiwan,"
and Guonian expanded and extended the family businesses after his brother's
early death.[50]

Expanding wealth for some overlapped with the actions of the GGT to create a new generation of elites that partly displaced the old Qing-era gentry
and paved the way for late-colonial and post-war figures. Early in its rule, the
colonial regime selected, and thereafter relied upon, individuals to serve as
hokō leaders, neighborhood heads, temple managers, welfare commissioners,
and other types of intermediaries between itself and the population it sat
atop, but with which it had no meaningful connections. These figures were
almost exclusively male, had received some measure of classical Chinese
education—some had even sat for civil service examinations—and in many
cases came from already prominent local families, like Lin Xiantang, scion
of the aforementioned Lins of Wufeng. The GGT elevated and affirmed their
status by bestowing upon them the title of "gentlemen" (shenshi).[51] One representative of this new elite class was Keelung's Xu Zisang, who belonged to
a relatively minor lineage in the Qing port town, but a family with enough
money to send him to private academies. Within a decade of establishing
control of Taiwan, the GGT had tapped him as a neighborhood chief and temple manager, and thereafter he became the leader of Keelung's largest social
organization, a welfare commissioner, a member of the municipal consultative council, and a businessman.[52] Xu, the Yan brothers, and men like them
across Taiwan provided leadership—and crucial financing—for a dizzying
array of commercial, educational, and charitable activities, as well as political
and social movements.

A second key feature of colonial Taiwan's socio-economic transformation
was the expansion of roles and opportunities for female islanders. Much as
with educational and economic shifts, changes in the position of women and

---

50   Dawley, *Becoming Taiwanese*, 66–71.
51   Wu Wen-hsing, *Ri zhi shiqi Taiwan de shehui lingdao jieceng* (Taiwan's Social Elites during
      the Period of Japanese Rule) (Taipei shi: Wu nan, 2008), 5–7, 312–13.
52   Dawley, *Becoming Taiwanese*, 63–73.

girls in Taiwan had strong historic connections to recent and contemporaneous developments in Japan, which had witnessed a dramatic expansion in female education and employment since the 1880s, and where vibrant debates about the New Woman and Modern Girl occurred during the 1910s–1930s. As a result of these metropolitan developments, Japanese women settlers took it upon themselves to, as they saw it from their colonialist perch, elevate the status and lives of their colonized sisters. The Taiwan Branch of the Patriotic Ladies Association, an offshoot of an organization created in the wake of the First Sino-Japanese War to enlist Japanese women in the support of Japan's military, joined the broader campaign to stamp out foot binding and led the way in promoting girls' education and vocational training. The Training Centers that it established in Taipei around 1915, which taught both Japanese language and practical skills like sericulture and household management, merged in 1920 to form Taipei Girls' Vocational School, open to both islanders and Japanese.[53] Although women constituted a minority of the labor force throughout the Japanese era, they held a prominent position in some sectors, such as factory work, food-processing, and tea-production.[54]

Furthermore, circulating discourses and representations of the New Woman and Modern Girl meant that, especially in urban settings, female islanders became both subjects of and participants in the production of modernism. As Jina Kim demonstrates with her research on women's magazines in Taiwan and Korea, the new images of femininity presented allowed islander women readers to engage in "racial masquerade," shifting between Chinese, Japanese, Taiwanese, and even Western roles as they put on and removed particular styles of dress. Furthermore, the New Woman and Modern Girl were both discursive icons, presented for either emulation or critique, and actual figures of lived experience that reflected the modernity of Taiwanese women. As Kim puts it, "it was through consumption of these images that real women moved toward naming themselves and thus forging their own subjectivity."[55]

The regular practice of popular religion became an arena of intense contestation, in which Japanese colonizers sought to install their familiar institutions and replace those of the islanders, whereas the islanders built their communities and identities around their temples and festivals. Japanese settlers, with direct and indirect support from the GGT, moved quickly to establish Shintō

---

53   Dawley, "Women on the Move," 296–98.

54   Barclay, "Japanese Empire in Taiwan," np.

55   Jina Kim, *Urban Modernities in Colonial Korea and Taiwan* (Leiden: Brill, 2019), 145–53, 163–64.

shrines and Buddhist temples in their new hometowns and cities, not infrequently displacing existing temples with their own imports until such reconsecration was forbidden in 1908. The GGT altered the leadership structure of islanders' temples by requiring each one to have a temple manager (*kanrijin* or *guanliren*) and representative (*daihyōsha* or *daibiaozhe*), who it hoped would facilitate state observation and control. Even with these early intrusions into islanders' sacred spaces, colonial officials and settlers made few efforts to reform them for several decades, preferring to observe and study local traditions. Inō Kanori paired his studies of indigenous customs with research on islander religions, and a scholar-bureaucrat named Marui Keijirō led a major survey of religious institutions and practices in the late 1910s, a project that was supplemented by new research in the 1930s. However, aside from a very brief period of restriction between 1895–97, Taiwanese temples and festivals flourished into the mid-1930s. In major cities like Keelung, local elites renovated temples and expanded their festivals in honor of important deities like Mazu, or annual events like the summer Ghost Festival. In times of prosperity and scarcity, religious activities absorbed substantial amounts of islanders' energies and resources, becoming even more central foci of everyday life than they had been before 1895.

When Japanese settlers and the GGT took more aggressive steps to overwrite Taiwan's religions (*Taiwan shūkyō*) during the 1930s, they met with firm, if understated, resistance. Japanese efforts reached a peak in the late 1930s when, as part of the Kōminka policies, the GGT launched a Temple Restructuring movement (*Jibyō seiri undō*), the core objective of which was to amalgamate and then shut down Taiwanese temples, and replace them with Shintō shrines. This plan began amidst the first peak of wartime mobilization and, with the full weight of the colonial state behind it, it met its goals in some locations. In Okayama (Gangshan), near Kaohsiung, the county shrine assumed control of all local temples in 1939 and built more Shintō shrines. In Taitung, 93 percent of Taiwanese temples were closed, and in Tainan, the city government commandeered temple resources in 1940. But these apparent successes were far from the full story. In Taipei, a mere 7 percent of temples were "restructured" and not a single temple was formally closed in either Tamsui or Keelung. In the last city, Taiwanese leaders met during the summer and fall of 1940 and elected to merge their main temples under unified leadership rather than close them. These acts of measured opposition sustained key institutions until the GGT decided to ease the Temple Restructuring campaign in 1941. A year later, a leading Japanese scholar of Taiwanese religion, Masuda Fukutarō, visited Keelung, where he found a festival in honor of Mazu underway and lamented the fact that the monks at a major Buddhist temple, founded and run by islanders but ostensibly part of a Japanese Zen sect, did not yet display proper training.[56] Temple Restructuring, and the attempted spiritual transformation of Taiwan, shared a key feature in common with colonialist socio-economic engineering and liberation of women: in all cases, islanders redirected and utilized these projects in their construction of new identities.

6   Manifesting Taiwanese Identities

The real effects of the transformational projects of Japanese colonialism frequently diverged from the intended objectives, for the Chinese-descended islanders formed and expressed their identities through a range of social and political activities. They did not create a single Taiwanese consciousness, rather they constructed both ethnic and national varieties that geographically and demographically transcended the particularistic ties to ancestral home, clan, and present location that had defined their identities in 1895.

Group identities depend upon the formation of a community that, through its interactions with other communities, coalesces to define itself as a reasonably united entity. The GGT facilitated this process by classifying almost all non-Japanese residents as islanders and then establishing educational and security institutions specific to the majority who originated in southeastern China. These islanders formed their own organizations for charitable and reformist purposes, one type of which appeared in several locations under the name of Customs Assimilation Associations (Tongfeng hui), before merging with the hokō system in a network of local and regional groups that became especially strong in northern Taiwan. Run by members of the new islander elite class, often with official oversight, these groups counted only other islanders among their members as they worked to provide assistance, extra-curricular education, and medical services, and to reform customs such as footbinding, the queue hairstyle, marital and funerary practices, and religious rituals like the burning of ghost money.[57] The community-definition work of these organizations was augmented by the gradual development of an island-wide social welfare system that combined privately established and publicly mandated institutions in a remarkably dense web that, although broadly unified, largely

---

56   Dawley, *Becoming Taiwanese*, 161–204.
57   Dawley, 144–58. See also Wang Shih-ch'ing, "Huangminhua yundong qian de Taiwan shehui shenghuo gaishan yundong: yi Haishan qu wei li, 1914–1937" (Taiwan Society's Everyday Life Reform Movement before the Kōminka: The Case of Haishan District, 1914–1937), *Si yu yan* 29, no. 4 (1991.12): 5–63.

divided the provision of assistance into islander and Japanese segments. Most of the private organizations worked only with one demographic group, such as the well-known Keelung Fraternity Group (Bo'ai tuan) that Yan Yunnian founded in 1920, with his business associates Gu Xianrong and Lin Taizheng, as a sort of settlement house for poor islanders. Even the ostensibly universal system of publicly supported, semi-professional local welfare commissioners (*hōmen iin*) mirrored these divisions because the elite islanders who joined could only assist other islanders.[58] In conjunction with the contestation over sacred spaces, social organizations and social welfare defined a border around the people who became Taiwanese.

Within that border, social and political movements and cultural reform programs promoted identity formation, especially during the 1920s and 1930s. Wakabayashi Masahiro has defined four main types of activity, all of which shared a fundamentally anti-Japanese perspective: the new culture, petition, labor, and farmer's movements. The first two were sparked by the Taiwan Culture Association (Taiwan wenhua xiehui) and Taiwan People's Party (Taiwan minzhong dang), and the others had their own political apparatus.[59] The Taiwan Culture Association, formed under the leadership of Lin Xiantang and Jiang Weishui, launched a series of Culture Lectures across the island that sparked discussions regarding the practices and customs that needed to be preserved, altered, or jettisoned within a broad agenda of modernization.[60] It also led the drive for political participation through annual petitions to Japan's Imperial Diet for the creation of an elected Taiwan Assembly that would govern the island through popular sovereignty and break the monopoly of the GGT. Although the petition movement disbanded in 1934 without achieving its stated objective, it nevertheless deepened the divide between islanders and Japanese by promoting a sense of Taiwanese autonomy.[61] Local politics also became an important arena for the development and expression of Taiwanese consciousness, because it was in local contexts that islanders and Japanese confronted each other and their respective, occasionally overlapping, interests. Popular advocacy for elected legislative councils reached a peak in 1931

58   Dawley, *Becoming Taiwanese*, 216–25.
59   Wakabayashi Masahiro, *Taiwan kang Ri yundong shi yanjiu* (Research on the History of Taiwan's Anti-Japanese Movement), trans. Taiwan shi Riwen shiliao dianji yandu hui (Taipei shi: Bochong zhe, 2007), 8, 171–72.
60   Lo, *Doctors within Borders*, 64–68; Dawley, *Becoming Taiwanese*, 104–05.
61   Chou Wan-yao, *Riju shidai de Taiwan yihui she zhi qingyuan yundong* (The Taiwan Assembly Petition Movement during the Era of Japanese Occupation) (Taipei shi: Zili baoxi wenhua chubanbu, 1989), 6–9, 182–84.

when mock elections for local, prefectural, and colonial assemblies took place across Taiwan. The results left little doubt as to the formation of Taiwanese consciousness: at the prefecture level, Taiwanese won all seats, and Japanese only garnered a few seats at the municipal level, where settlers lived in higher concentrations.[62]

Taiwanese also expressed their identities through literature. Amidst the stylistic and canonical debates between the New and Old Literature camps, there was agreement on the importance of using Chinese and Taiwanese language literature to resist Japanization.[63] Some writers relied on literature as an escape from the difficulties of colonial rule, and explored modernist and proletarian identities in their writing, while others drew heavily on ethnological research in order to preserve what they saw as the dying traditional cultures of Taiwan.[64] The paradigmatic example was Wu Zhuoliu's *Orphan of Asia*, written in secret during the last years of the war, which Leo Ching reads as a record of consciousness in formation, as Wu's efforts to grapple with the cultural change around him. For Ching, the story of Hu Taiming and his movement through classical and modern education in Taiwan, higher education in Japan, and experiences teaching in Taiwan and China, reveal the "irreducible colonial-national-local triangulation between Japan, China, and Taiwan" that produced Taiwanese consciousness.[65] This literary production shows, more than anything else, that islanders embraced a range of identities, including a highly complex and difficult sense of being Taiwanese. Taking the fictionalized experience of Hu Taiming as a guide, at the end of Japanese rule, Taiwanese consciousness was a rootless identity, verging on madness.[66]

However, the fifty years of Japanese rule should be viewed as an era of creation, not just destruction or oppression. There is certainly evidence for Reo Matsuzaki's analysis of Japanese colonization of Taiwan as a successful example of "statebuilding by imposition."[67] By 1945, the peoples of Taiwan had evidently abandoned mass violence as a form of dispute resolution or grievance

---

62   Dawley, *Becoming Taiwanese*, 108–09.

63   Huang Mei-er, "Confrontation and Collaboration: Traditional Taiwanese Writers' Canonical Reflection and Cultural Thinking on the New-Old Literatures Debate During the Japanese Colonial Period," in Liao and Wang, *Taiwan under Japanese*, 187–209.

64   Peng Hsiao-yen, "Colonialism and the Predicament of Identity: Liu Na'ou and Yang Kui as Men of the World," and Tarumi Chie, "An Author Listening to Voices from the Netherworld: Lu Heruo and the *Kuso* Realism Debate," in Liao and Wang, 210–13, 262–76.

65   Ching, *Becoming "Japanese,"* chap. 5, quote on 176.

66   Zhuoliu Wu, *Orphan of Asia* (New York: Columbia University Press, 2006), 199–247.

67   Reo Matsuzaki, *Statebuilding by Imposition Resistance and Control in Colonial Taiwan and the Philippines* (Ithaca, N.Y.: Cornell University Press, 2019), 3.

redress, in favor of the opportunities provided by the modern state. However, as Andrew Morris suggests, Japan's success was largely imagined, at least in the sense of recreating Taiwan as Japanese.[68] Education and socio-economic transformation opened doors for new generations of elites to emerge and gain some measure of autonomy from the colonial state that depended upon them to carry out its programs. Social organizations and social welfare programs, and the new youth groups, gave definition and support to an emerging trans-island community, although one that, because of the ongoing bifurcation between indigenes and those of Chinese ancestry, did not include everyone. Nevertheless, within the latter group, political and social movements articulated identities that either promoted nationalism and independence from Japan and China, or foregrounded the linguistic, religious, and other socio-cultural dimensions of ethnicity. Being Taiwanese in 1945 meant that one had been through a creative process that had diverged from the construction of modern Chinese national identity without being subsumed into imperial Japanese nationalism.

7   Legacies of the Japanese Era

The significance of these transformations became evident almost immediately following the transfer of sovereignty over Taiwan to the Republic of China. Divergent historical trajectories meant that Taiwan and the Taiwanese did not fit the national imaginings of the Chinese state and settlers. The Nationalist Chinese vision of Taiwan, by the end of the war, was a contradictory one: it was Chinese and held resources and industries essential to the reconstruction of post-war China; it had been fundamentally tainted by five decades of Japanese enslavement; and it had been largely locked out of historical time and so remained a backward place in need of Chinese modernization and tutelage. Little to none of this meshed with the Taiwanese views of themselves, but they nonetheless accepted, even welcomed, incorporation into China when it arrived and promptly asserted themselves and their autonomous interests within their new nation. However, the disconnect between Taiwanese and Chinese emerged through disputes over the pace and direction of reconstruction, over the allotment—and extraction—of resources, over local and island-wide governance, over language, religion, and a host of other issues. The most

---

68   Andrew D. Morris, "Introduction: Living as Left Behind in Postcolonial Taiwan," in
      Japanese Taiwan: Colonial Rule and Its Contested Legacy, ed. Andrew D. Morris (London:
      Bloomsbury Academic, 2015), 5.

explosive clash occurred in February and March of 1947, but that was just one manifestation of a deep divide that most of the policies of the new government did little to bridge.

Taiwan's post-1945 history only makes sense with an understanding of what took place during the preceding five decades. The Taiwan Independence Movement, *dangwai* politics, the Taiwanization of the Nationalist Party, and democratization all emerged from the identity construction and political engagement of the Japanese era. The prolonged marginalization of indigenous peoples, as well as the very slow turn to transformational justice, have deeper roots, but the academic and administrative classification by Japanese scholars and officials continues to shape indigenous communities and identities, as does the bifurcated sovereignty of that period. The pronounced religiosity of contemporary Taiwan has at least part of its basis in the fact that temples and festivals were building blocks for Taiwanese identities, and links may also exist between Taiwan's contemporary welfare system and the earlier network of social work institutions. Even the preference among early 21st century Taiwanese for the status quo in cross-straits relations—*de facto* independence without *de jure* statehood—reflects the earlier drive for an autonomous Taiwan Assembly. Although Japanese colonizers did not change Taiwan and its residents in all of the ways they had planned, the developments of that period have asserted a powerful influence ever since.

References

Allen, Joseph Roe. *Taipei: City of Displacements*. Seattle: University of Washington Press, 2012.

Barclay, George W. *Colonial Development and Population in Taiwan*. Princeton, N.J.: Princeton University Press, 1954.

Barclay, Paul D. "An Historian among the Anthropologists: The Inō Kanori Revival and the Legacy of Japanese Colonial Ethnography in Taiwan." *Japanese Studies* 21, no. 2 (2001): 117–36.

Barclay, Paul D. "Cultural Brokerage and Interethnic Marriage in Colonial Taiwan: Japanese Subalterns and Their Aborigine Wives, 1895–1930." *The Journal of Asian Studies* 64, no. 2 (May 2005): 323–60.

Barclay, Paul D. "Japanese Empire in Taiwan." In *Oxford Research Encyclopedia of Asian History*, edited by David Ludden. New York: Oxford University Press, 2020; https://oxfordre.com/asianhistory.

Barclay, Paul D. *Outcasts of Empire: Japan's Rule on Taiwan's "Savage Border," 1874–1945*. Oakland, CA: University of California Press, 2018.

Brown, Melissa J. *Is Taiwan Chinese?: The Impact of Culture, Power, and Migration on Changing Identities.* Berkeley Series in Interdisciplinary Studies of China 2. Berkeley: University of California Press, 2004.

Cai, Longbao. *Tuidong shidai de julun: Ri zhi zhongqi de Taiwan guoyou tielu (1910–1936)* (Period of Promotion: Taiwan's National Railroads in the Middle Period of Japanese Control, 1910–1936). Chuban. Taiwan Shufang. Taibei shi: Taiwan guji, 2004.

Chatani, Sayaka. *Nation-Empire: Ideology and Rural Youth Mobilization in Japan and Its Colonies.* Ithaca: Cornell University Press, 2018.

Chen, Chiukun. "From Landlords to Local Strongmen: The Transformation of Local Elites in Mid-Ch'ing Taiwan, 1780–1862." In *Taiwan: A New History*, edited by Rubinstein, Murray A., Expanded Edition., 133–62. Armonk, N.Y: M.E. Sharpe, 2007.

Chen, Qinan. *Chuantong zhidu yu shehui yishi de jiegou: lishi yu renleixue de tansuo* (Traditional Systems and the Structure of Social Consciousness: The Deep Search of History and Anthropology). Chuban. Yun Chen Daxue Congshu 1. Taibei shi: Yun chen wenhua shiye gufen youxian gongsi, 1998.

Ching, Leo T. S. *Becoming "Japanese": Colonial Taiwan and the Politics of Identity Formation.* Berkeley: University of California Press, 2001.

Chou, Wan-yao. *Riju shidai de Taiwan yihui she zhi qingyuan yundong* (The Taiwan Assembly Petition Movement during the Era of Japanese Occupation). Chuban. Taiwan bentu xilie 2: 18. Taibei shi: Zili baoxi wenhua chubanbu, 1989.

Dawley, Evan N. *Becoming Taiwanese: Ethnogenesis in a Colonial City, 1880s-1950s.* Harvard East Asian Monographs 420. Cambridge, MA: Harvard University Asia Center, 2019.

Dawley, Evan N. "Women on the Move: Shifting Patterns in Migration and the Colonization of Taiwan." In *The Decade of the Great War: Japan and the Wider World in the 1910s*, edited by Toshihiro Minohara, Tze-Ki Hon, and Evan N. Dawley, 281–300. Leiden: Brill, 2014.

Gold, Thomas B. "Colonial Origins of Taiwanese Capitalism." In *Contending Approaches to the Political Economy of Taiwan*, edited by Edwin A. Winckler and Susan Greenhalgh, 101–17. Studies of the East Asian Institute, Columbia University. Armonk, N.Y.: M.E. Sharpe, 1988.

Heylen, Ann. *Japanese Models, Chinese Culture and the Dilemma of Taiwanese Language Reform.* 1. Aufl. Studia Formosiana 7. Wiesbaden: Harrassowitz, 2012.

Huang, Zhaotang. *Taiwan zongdufu* (The Taiwan Government-General). Translated by Huang Yingzhe. Xiuding yiban. Taiwan Wenshi Congshu 113. Taibei shi: Qianwei chubanshe, 2004.

Ka, Chih-ming. *Japanese Colonialism in Taiwan: Land Tenure, Development, and Dependency, 1895–1945.* Transitions: Asia and Asian America. Boulder, CO: Westview Press, 1995.

Kim, Jina. *Urban Modernities in Colonial Korea and Taiwan.* Leiden: Brill, 2019.

Liao, Ping-hui, and David Der-wei Wang, eds. *Taiwan under Japanese Colonial Rule, 1895–1945: History, Culture, Memory.* New York: Columbia University Press, 2006.

Lin, Man-houng. *Cha, tang, zhangnao ye yu wan Qing Taiwan* (The Tea, Sugar, and Camphor Industries and Late Qing Taiwan). Chuban. Taiwan Yanjiu Congkan. Taibei shi: Lianjing, 1997.

Liu, Michael Shiyung. *Prescribing Colonization: The Role of Medical Practices and Policies in Japan-Ruled Taiwan, 1895–1945.* Asia Past & Present: New Research from AAS 3. Ann Arbor, MI: Association for Asian Studies, 2009.

Lo, Ming-cheng Miriam. *Doctors within Borders: Profession, Ethnicity, and Modernity in Colonial Taiwan.* Colonialisms 1. Berkeley: University of California Press, 2002.

Matsuzaki, Reo. *Statebuilding by Imposition Resistance and Control in Colonial Taiwan and the Philippines.* Ithaca, N.Y.: Cornell University Press, 2019.

Meskill, Johanna Margarete Menzel. *A Chinese Pioneer Family: The Lins of Wu-Feng, Taiwan, 1729–1895.* Princeton, N.J.: Princeton University Press, 1979.

Morris, Andrew D. "Introduction: Living as Left Behind in Postcolonial Taiwan." In *Japanese Taiwan: Colonial Rule and Its Contested Legacy*, edited by Andrew D. Morris, 3–23. Studies in Modern and Contemporary Japan. London: Bloomsbury Academic, 2015.

Shepherd, John Robert. *Statecraft and Political Economy on the Taiwan Frontier, 1600–1800.* Stanford, CA: Stanford University Press, 1993.

Speidel, William M. "The Administrative and Fiscal Reforms of Liu Ming-Ch'uan in Taiwan, 1884–1891: Foundation for Self-Strengthening." *The Journal of Asian Studies* 35, no. 3 (May 1976): 441–59.

Tavares, Antonio C. "The Japanese Colonial State and the Dissolution of the Late Imperial Frontier Economy in Taiwan, 1886–1909." *The Journal of Asian Studies* 64, no. 2 (May 2005): 361–85.

Teng, Emma. *Taiwan's Imagined Geography: Chinese Colonial Travel Writing and Pictures, 1683–1895.* Harvard East Asian Monographs 230. Cambridge, MA: Harvard University Press, 2006.

Ts'ai, Huiyu Caroline. *Taiwan in Japan's Empire-Building: An Institutional Approach to Colonial Engineering.* Academia Sinica on East Asia. New York: Routledge, 2009.

Tsurumi, E. Patricia. *Japanese Colonial Education in Taiwan, 1895–1945.* Harvard East Asian Monographs 88. Cambridge, MA: Harvard University Press, 1977.

Wang, Shih-ch'ing. "Huangminhua yundong qian de Taiwan shehui shenghuo gaishan yundong: yi Haishan qu wei li, 1914–1937" (Taiwan Society's Everyday Life Reform Movement before the Kōminka: The Case of Haishan District, 1914–1937). *Si yu yan* 29, 4 (1991.12): 5–63.

Wakabayashi, Masahiro. *Taiwan kang Ri yundong shi yanjiu* (Research on the History of Taiwan's Anti-Japanese Movement). Translated by Taiwan shi Riwen shiliao dianji yandu hui. Chuban. Taibei shi: Bochong zhe, 2007.

Wu, Wen-hsing. *Ri zhi shiqi Taiwan de shehui lingdao jieceng* (Taiwan's Social Elites during the Period of Japanese Rule). Chuban. Taibei shi: Wu nan, 2008.

Wu, Zhuoliu. *Orphan of Asia.* New York: Columbia University Press, 2006.

Ziomek, Kirsten L. *Lost Histories: Recovering the Lives of Japan's Colonial Peoples.* Harvard East Asian Monographs 418. Cambridge, MA: Harvard University Asia Center, 2019.

CHAPTER 4

ROC-ROK International Fate

Decolonization, Democratization, and Pragmatism

Moises de Souza and Fabricio A. Fonseca

1   Introduction

Dramatic geopolitical developments such as the Chinese Civil War, World War II (WWII), and the Korean War, along with the status inside of the United Nations (UN) created the grounds for the diplomatic position of Taiwan (Republic of China, ROC)[1] and South Korea (Republic of Korea, ROK)[2] in 20th century global politics that still persists unto the present. Years later, economic development and democratization would also be important factors in the elaboration of these countries' foreign policies, as well as the maintenance or expansion of their international space, and their responses to the challenges posed by their powerful neighbors who claim those territories as part of their own, namely the Democratic People's Republic of Korea (DPRK) and the People's Republic of China (PRC)[3].

This chapter briefly discusses some elements that played essential roles, first from 1949 until 1971 when both Koreans and Taiwanese were fighting for their place inside the UN, and later from 1972 to the present, when the Sino-American rapprochement changed the balance of power in the region. The first part is organized around the idea that the way that Taipei, Seoul, and Beijing reacted to the decolonization process after WWII was one of the drivers behind the fate of Koreans and the Nationalist Chinese inside the UN.

Similarly, the PRC, via a radical change in its way of conducting its foreign affairs, skillfully captured the trends represented by the decolonization and non-aligned movements, to not only change its international image but also to finally assume its place in the UN as a member of the Security Council. The flexibility demonstrated by Koreans and the Communist Chinese would prove critically important for the achievement of their diplomatic goals

---

1   In this chapter, Taiwan and ROC have been used interchangeably.
2   In this chapter, South Korea and ROK have been used interchangeably.
3   In this chapter, China and PRC have been used interchangeably.

© MOISES DE SOUZA AND FABRICIO A. FONSECA, 2021 | DOI:10.1163/9789004461314_005

while the rigidity of the Kuomintang worked in exactly the opposite fashion.[4] Nonetheless, pragmatism finally prevailed among the policy makers in Taipei once it was clear the PRC also embraced the One China Principle and made it an inseparable element of its own foreign policy.

The second part of this chapter presents the transformations in South Korea and Taiwan's foreign relations after the UN episodes, paying special attention to the elements of democratization, international cooperation, and their relations with the United States (US), and to a lesser extent, with Japan. The pragmatic approaches followed by these governments, characterized by a clear separation between politics and economics, have ensured the stability of the region and contributed to the rise of the Indo-Pacific as the most dynamic engine of economic growth in the world. Paradoxically, being the most critical points to the maintenance of regional security, the pragmatism and ambivalence displayed when addressing the situation in the Korean Peninsula and the Taiwan Strait, not only by the ROC and the ROK, but also by the other major powers, have contributed to the delay in their final resolution.

2 The ROC-ROK Evolving Position at UN: Decolonization as a Game Changer

Both the ROC and ROK confronted many challenges regarding their presence in the UN during the Cold War years. However, two fundamental aspects set them apart. First, is the fact that the ROC was already a UN member holding a permanent seat at the Security Council. Taipei's struggle was to keep itself as the legitimate representative of China at UN due the ascendancy of the PRC as an important geopolitical player. On the other hand, South Korea was seeking admission to the UN as a new state-member. The second aspect that set them apart was Seoul's awareness about the developments in global politics during the 1960s in contrast to Taipei's inability to adjust itself to facing the changing international scenario. The first movements initiated to integrate South Korea,

---

4 The PRC flexibility here was essentially visible in the way the Communist regime saw the UN. Beijing never lost the opportunity to denounce it as an appendix of the US State Department which, according to China, had utilized it as a way to penetrate into the Third World countries economically and culturally. Mao was also uneasy playing the game of the big powers inside the UN, which, from his perspective, used most of the states simply as pawns and invariably disrespected their sovereignty. As the chapter will demonstrate, gradually, the PRC would become less vocal and more practical towards the agency, without however, yielding their adamant principle of One-China. For more, see Samuel S. Kim, "The People's Republic of China in the UN: A Preliminary Analysis," World Politics 26, no. 3 (April 1974), 299–330.

with the active support of ROC, as a member of the UN, are understood as a piece in the complex puzzle that East Asia had become immediately after World War II, with the Chinese Civil War and the Korean War as its more dramatic facets.

Under the banner of the anti-communist movement leadership, the ROC and ROK both locked into their own territorial stalemates with their Communist counterparts, transforming the UN as a whole, especially the Security Council and the General Assembly,[5] in another front for their respective domestic dramas. Under these circumstances, with an international order that at that time seemed immutable in many ways, it is possible to understand the sequence of the ROK's failures in attempting to obtain membership in 1949. From that moment, all attempts to include ROK in the UN and to replace (or keep) ROC by the PRC, would provide the same results: constant resistance from the Soviet Union and its allies against ROK membership and ROC permanence, with the American allies working in opposite fashion.[6] Notice that despite the crucial role played by the Security Council in the process of admission – or rejection – of new members, the applications can transit in different ways until facing the perspective of veto by any permanent-member. In a normal procedure, a UN membership must start with the country submitting an application to the Secretary-General and formally stating that it accepts the obligations under

---

5 Despite the lack of Security Council decision-making power, the role of the General Assembly to discuss, debate, and make recommendations about international questions has transformed it along with the Security Council where the ideological clashes and the level of controversy around specific topics becomes visibly identified. The examples abound as the case of Nikita Khrushchev's shoe-banging incident in 1960 and Yasser Arafat's olive branch or gun speech in 1974 among others. Specifically, during the 1950s the General Assembly also gained some prominence with resolution 377 A (V), known also as the "Uniting for Peace," a strategy elaborated by the Americans to circumvent future Soviet vetoes against Security Council determinations of further actions in the Korea Peninsula. Thus, when discussing the Korean and Chinese questions, both the General Assembly and Security Council were widely utilized by all sides to defend their positions. See: UN General Assembly, uniting for peace, November 3, 1950, A/RES/377. https://www.refworld.org/docid/3b00f08d78.html, accessed August 23, 2019.

6 In January 1950, Moscow had its proposal of non-acceptance of the ROC representative credentials rejected by the Security Council. In response, the Soviet representative Jacob Malik walked out in protest. Although not a veto per se (given it was understood as a procedural question), the "empty chair" policy conducted by Moscow, boycotting most of the Security Council meetings, worked in the same fashion by indicating the level of resistance against Taipei representation at the UN by the Soviet regime. Finally, from 1951 to 1960, the Soviet Union used the General Assembly to bring Chinese representation to discussion, but it was always rejected. See: Evan Luard, "China and the UN," *International Affairs* (Royal Institute of International Affairs 1944-), 47, no. 4 (Oct. 1971), 729–730.

the UN Charter. After analysis, the applications are sent for consideration to the Security Council, where it must receive the support of nine of the fifteen members, and no vetoes from any of the permanent ones. After that, the applicant still must gather a two-thirds majority vote in the General Assembly to finally be admitted as a new member. However, this is an outside-in process utilized by a non-member to apply for membership directly.

In the cases of both the ROC and ROK, most of their applications were made by state-members through UN internal commissions. As indicated by Jonsson, a good example happened in 1949, when Australia presented, at the 25th meeting of the UN General Assembly's Commission on Special Political Affairs, a proposal regarding UN membership for nine countries, including South Korea. The Australian proposal had as its main goal to recommend the Security Council to reexamine the membership application issue for these countries. As the first filter, the Australian proposal was first adopted by the General Assembly before being vetoed by the Soviets, therefore avoiding any further discussion at the Security Council.[7] The same happened in 1954, when the General Assembly decided:

> ... not to consider, at its ninth regular session during the current year, any proposals to exclude the representatives of the Government of the Republic of China or to seat representatives of the Central Government of the People's Republic of China.[8]

As the case illustrates, the proposal to alter the Chinese status quo inside the UN was not the subject of specific analysis by the Security Council but, exclusively, a matter discussed by the General Assembly. This is also understood by the fact that the seat of China had existed since the beginning of the organization. Therefore, the so-called "China issue" was not observed as the admission of a new member, but as a decision regarding which regime should occupy the seat of an already admitted member in opposition to the Korean case.

Besides the relations between the two major powers, we also need to pay attention to the importance of the process of decolonization. Regarding the quest of ROC-ROK to assure their position in the UN, the anti-colonial movement impacted it in three ways: 1) The fight for independence was literally

---

7 Jonsson Gabriel, *South Korea in The United Nations: Global Governance, Inter-Korean Relations and Peace Building* (London: World Scientific, 2017),32.

8 The UN General Assembly, (IX) Question of the representation of China in the General Assembly. 473rd plenary meeting, September 21, 1954. Available: https://undocs.org/en/A/RES/903(IX), accessed: June 22, 2019.

against the European powers making the incipient nations (principally in Africa) in many ways more pro-East and more sympathetic to the leftists anti-imperialist rhetoric; 2) the hesitance of the US to side with the anti-colonial movement due to its commitment with the European powers to contain the Soviet Union under bipolar rationale; and, 3) the skillful diplomatic efforts by the PRC to support nationalist movements, anti-colonial wars, and become a vocal partner of the so-called non-aligned movement. All three of these factors would prove decisively influential to the Chinese and Koreans interests at the General Assembly.[9]

In this regard, the ROK and ROC opted for different tactics. After the first veto in April 1949, South Korea tried five more application attempts unsuccessfully[10]: 1949 (October), 1951, 1954, and 1955 (twice).[11] Despite the failures, the ROC-ROK relations were, as usual, enjoying a highly positive moment, seeing themselves as "brothers in arms" against the communists. As an example, in 1954 the government of Syngman Rhee helped in the repatriation of more than 14,000 Chinese prisoners of war to Taipei who had refused to return to the mainland.[12] In response, in 1955, even after the exclusion of South Korea from the groups of nations accepted as new UN members, Chiang Kai-shek instructed his diplomats to coordinate efforts for a new attempt. Thus, on December 10, the ROC representation issued an official recommendation for South Korean membership that, in contrast from their first attempt, was not even considered for a vote by the General Assembly. The ROC would demonstrate its support to South Korean membership one last time in 1957, signing a

---

9   The discussion of the Kuomintang (KMT) government in Taiwan as colonial rule, despite important, is not considered as such in this study. The presence of the Kuomintang on Taiwanese soil was a result of diplomatic negotiations among the ROC, the United Kingdom (UK) and the US (with Moscow's consent) as registered by the 1943 Cairo Conference and later incorporated into UN framework. From this perspective, the KMT was "restoring" a territory stolen by a – de-facto and internationally recognized – colonial power, Japan. The debate about the KMT as an alien power in Formosa would be raised only later by the local indigenous independent movements receiving little or no international support.

10   The vetoes by the USSR against South Korean membership was also part of a consistent policy to reject the admission of any new member by Moscow during the early years of the UN. As result, until 2015 the Soviet Union (later Russia) had been the Security Council member that had cast most of the vetoes, a total of 141. See: "The Veto." Security Council Report. October 19, 2015. Available: https://www.securitycouncilreport.org/un-security-council-working-methods/the-veto.php, accessed: August 21, 2019.

11   Jonsson Gabriel, *South* Korea in *The United Nations: Global Governance, Inter-Korean Relations And Peace Building* (London: World Scientific, 2017), 31.

12   See: "When 'Brother Nations' Meet Together." Taiwan Today, March 1, 1966. Available: https://taiwantoday.tw/news.php?unit=4&post=6892, accessed: March 1, 2019.

joint draft resolution along with the US and other members, that also did not manage to be approved by the Security Council.[13]

The last two failed membership applications were followed by the striking realization by the South Korean diplomats at the UN that the world order that had emerged after WWII was not working in favor of their interests. Symbolically, in this regard, a report by a UN *ad hoc* committee in the year of 1953, recommended a set of guidelines for the General Assembly to follow when considering recognition of a former colonial state and during their membership application process: 1) The state shall demonstrate the ability to carry on international responsibilities through treaties; 2) full administrative and economic autonomy; and 3) absolute freedom to form a government of their preference.[14]

With these guidelines finally set after years of delays and negotiations, the anti-colonial movement gained momentum inside the UN.[15] As a result, by 1965, with 117 members, the General Assembly was composed of a majority of recently independent former colonies.[16] Therefore, the Korean question along with the Chinese question was no longer being discussed in a European-led world scenario. Regarding the role of the US, China's performance in the Korean conflict against a mighty coalition led by Washington was a game-changer in terms of perception."[17] For many former colonies in Africa, China's

---

13   Gabriel, South Korea, 32.

14   Domenico Mazzeo, "The United *Nations* and the Problem of Decolonization: The Special Committee of Twenty-Four," (PhD diss., Department of Political Science of the Faculty of Social Sciences of the University of Ottawa, 1969).

15   It is important to highlight though, that the decolonization process did not happen in a linear temporal line. It had different moments obeying different drivers according to the historical circumstances. Mazzeo, proposes three main phases of this development: from 1919 to 1945 is the awakening of the Middle East, from 1946 to 1955 is the victory of Asian nationalism, from 1956 to 1963 the majority of the African countries accede to independence (1969, 12).

16   Michael Collins, "Decolonization," in *The Encyclopedia of Empire*, ed. John M. Mackenzie (Oxford: Wiley-Blackwell, 2016), 2.

17   The challenges faced by the PRC to engage in a war in the Korean Peninsula were indeed tremendous. First, due to the demobilization of 1.4 million People's Liberation Army (PLA) soldiers in May 1950 in consequence of its lack of financial resources; second, the PRC military leaders had not followed closely the developments in the Korean Peninsula, the PRC ambassador to Pyongyang was only chosen in late August 1950. Finally, when the conflict started the PLA had only one division along the Yalu River, mainly for crop production purposes, while the others were scattered in different parts of the territory. Having been able to sustain combat with a world coalition by the American forces, preventing them from crossing the Chinese border, is seen by many as a great military prowess. See: Hao Yufan and Zhai Zhihai, "China's Decision to Enter the Korean War: History Revisited." *The China Quarterly*, no. 121 (March 1990), 99–100.

ability to achieve a military stalemate in Korea was nothing short of a stunning demonstration of resilience, bravery, and commitment to the cause of "anti-imperialism" a term that was rapidly becoming synonymous with "anti-Americanism." At the same time, Beijing – in contraposition to Moscow – began to be perceived as an exemplar of the same brand of socialist ideology that was emerging in the newly decolonized African nations.[18] Hence, the US did not have to find its place of whether or not to support anti-colonial movements, due to the strategic imperatives of the Cold War. For many in the White House – during different administrations from Roosevelt to Kennedy – sympathy for the concept of self-determination rights for all people around the world was conditioned to the American geopolitical interests, and the latter always had prominence over the former. In general, *"the US adopted a very conservative view of the anti-colonial movement seeing the independence of the colonies as inimical to Western European recovery and the Anti-Soviet alliance, but, also, believed, that it "would create weak nations unable to resist penetration and subversion by Moscow."* In sum, by giving priority to Europe over the incipient independent nations, the US ended up being seen as a guarantor of the continuity of the European colonial possessions between 1948 and the beginning of the 1970s.[19]

It was with this background and in response to this new reality that South Korea and its diplomatic allies decided to radically change its approach and diplomatic objectives. Thus, in 1968 Seoul stopped submitting the Korean question to the General Assembly every year as it had been doing since 1949. As Jonsson points out, "the purpose of the new South Korean policy was to prevent the unfavorable and unproductive debates on the Korean question in the UN that was the major arena for the inter-Korean rivalry."[20]

---

18   James I. Matray, "Beijing and the Paper Tiger: The Impact of the Korean War on Sino-American Relations," *International Journal of Korean Studies* 15, no. 1 (Spring 2011), 170.

19   Ebere Nwaubani, "The United States and the Liquidation of European Colonial Rule in Tropical Africa, 1941–1963," *Cahiers d'Etudes africaines* 43, no. 171 (2003), 505.

20   Needless to say, that Communist North Korea worked in frontal opposition to the South Korean approach. Under the leadership of the Soviets, Pyongyang instructed its supporters to keep submitting draft resolutions calling for the withdrawal of all foreign troops from South Korea and the dissolution of the UN Commission for the Unification and Rehabilitation of Korea (UNCURK), what in practice was the recognition of the regime in Pyongyang as the sole legitimate government of Korean Peninsula. South Korea, instead of submitting for UN membership per se, required its allies to present counter submissions asking for intensification of the role of the UNCURK, free elections in North Korea and reiterated the UN position on the ROK as the legitimate government of Korea. See: Gabriel, South Korea, 34–35.

These unproductive debates are better explained by looking back at the inception of the UN. Since 1947, the organization worked under the premise of establishing a unified, independent and democratic Korea under a representative form of government, and full restoration of international peace and security. With the American influence at its apex, the Western bloc at the UN was able to provide the majority of votes necessary to keep the ROK with a representative attending the sessions of the General Assembly. The status of observer had ever since provided a comparative advantage to Seoul compared to Pyongyang in having its positions heard.[21] The tides changed for the ROK in 1960, when during the 15th session of the General Assembly, the first wave of African and Asian states was accepted as new members, altering the balance of power between the West and the Communist bloc at the floor of the General Assembly.

It is important to highlight that, together with the new strategies the ROK adopted at the GA, they followed up with an aggressive bilateral diplomacy initiative aimed largely at this bloc of new members. From 1961 to 1971, the ROK established relations with more than 60 countries around the world. Of these, 29 were Afro-Asian, and 19 were Latin American nations. By 1971, as Sang-Seek Park argues, there were 41 new African states and the ROK had official relations with 23 of them. Taking into account that until 1960 Seoul did not have any diplomatic relations in Africa, this demonstrates the magnitude of how radical its approach towards this new world scenario really was. A similar approach would be implemented by the North Koreans, and by 1972 they had established relations with 36 new countries, of which 16 were African.[22]

After the shift in 1968, Seoul would, in 1973, set a new turning point in the question of Korean UN membership. Having observed that the great powers and other members had finally agreed on the dual admission of West and East Germany to the UN that year, South Korean representatives announced the ending of their opposition to separate UN admission for the two Koreas, something that until that moment had been absolutely inconceivable for both the South and North regimes. Hence, South Korea would show that, in the long term in international relations, the need to have a plan B and a more pragmatic approach is always a powerful tool. A tool that for many reasons Taipei at that time completely lacked.

---

21   Chong-Ki Choi, "The Korean Question in The United Nations" (Paper presented at Sixth General Conference of the International Peace Research Association, Turku, Finland, August 15, 1975), 398.

22   Sang-Seek Park, "Africa and Two Koreas: A Study of African Non-Alignment," *African Studies Review* 21, no. 1 (April 1978), 76–77.

At the moment that South Korea stopped submitting its regular membership application, the Chinese question had become, since 1951, a topic *in the moratorium*, meaning that the question was not to be discussed until favorable conditions were reached. In this regard, the postponement worked in favor of the ROC and American allies in opposition to the Soviet bloc that advocated the immediate expulsion of the ROC representative and the acceptance of the PRC as a UN member. This way, the question regarding the legitimate representative of China in the UN, which consequently included a seat at the Security Council, was – directly or indirectly – to be voted on continuously every year until 1960 without the need of one of the members submitting a draft resolution. However, by 1960 it had become unavoidable for Washington to postpone the Chinese question, as they faced the reality that the PRC had established itself as the effective power in the mainland, and its presence in the community of nations was increasingly accepted.[23]

Again, the changes in the profile of the General Assembly, with the continuous arrival of new members that had impacted South Korea diplomatic strategies, would soon start to peel away the support of the ROC's UN allies. As a consequence of the international outrage caused by the North Korean attack in 1950, from 1951 to 1955, Taipei experienced continuous growth of support for its permanence as the representative of China at the UN.[24] Taipei had

---

23   Washington's proposal to put the Chinese question in moratorium was part of its strategy to keep the PRC distant of any form of international recognition. Here, it is important to keep in mind that the level of distrust between the two sides was at its climax. Not only in consequence of the wounds of the Korean War and the presence of the seventh-fleet in the area, but also due to the two Taiwan Strait crises in 1954–1958. According to Matray, the US had decided to keep Beijing under constant diplomatic siege during the entire period by getting approval at the UN for a resolution calling PRC an aggressor, freezing financial assets, imposing a trade embargo, exclusion of all UN-related bodies, among other measures. See: Matray, Beijing and the Paper Tiger, 160.

24   The Soviet stayed out of the UN from January to August 1950. A study describes the Soviet return as "... marked the beginning of a new policy of active participation in international and regional organizations." Indeed, in "Data and Analyses of Voting in the UN General Assembly" Erik Voeten registered the Soviet consistent presence at voting sessions during the period of the Korean War (1950–1953) and after. On the other hand, Dallin points out, that the Soviet presence at the UN during this period "was more token than real" given the lack of disengagement of Moscow and its satellites from the debates and commissions works. See: Raymond E. Zickel and Eugene K. Keefe, *Soviet Union: A Country Study*, (Washington, D.C.: Federal Research Division, Library of Congress, 1991), 445; Erik Voeten et al. "UN General Assembly Voting Data" & "UN General Assembly Voting Data," Harvard Dataverse, V21,; and Alexander Dallin, *The Soviet View of the UN*, (Cambridge: Center for International Studies, Massachusetts Institute of Technology, 1959), 33.

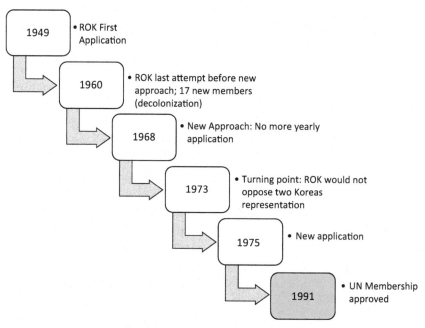

FIGURE 4.1   ROK UN membership timeline (1949–1991)
            SOURCE: AUTHOR'S COMPILATION BASED ON KIM, 1974: 302

56 percent of the votes in 1951 and would see this number increase to 62 percent in 1952, reaching its peak with 73 percent of the votes in 1953. But this started to change as the number of countries began to grow. From 1954 to 1972, the ROC would see the erosion of its diplomatic status decline steadily to an average of 47 percent through the whole of the 1960s. By 1970, before the famous trip of Richard Nixon to Beijing in 1972, Taipei had, for the first time since the establishment of the UN, already lost the majority in the General Assembly by gathering only 39 percent of votes. Later, in 1971, it reached its lowest level at 27 percent, already making Taipei's position inside of the UN and as a member of the Security Council simply unsustainable, resulting in its withdrawal in October of the same year.

Along with the ideological preferences of the recently independent countries, other strategic factors also had an important role in explaining the downward trend of the ROC's diplomatic support at the UN. The changing attitudes of the great powers, especially France and the United Kingdom, towards the Chiang Kai-shek regime in Taiwan were combined with the consolidation of the Communist regime in the mainland, the latter's split with Moscow, and its eventual acquisition of nuclear weapons. Similarly, as pointed out by Samuel S. Kim, the drastic change conducted by the communist regime in Beijing in the way that they conducted their foreign affairs after the climax of the Cultural Revolution had passed, played a very important role as well.[25]

Since 1949, the year of the establishment of the People's Republic of China, sixteen countries immediately recognized it as the "real" China. At that time, the ROC had diplomatic relations with 37 countries, although only seven decided to move their embassies to Taipei. With the advent of the Korean War in 1950 and the realities of the Cold War, along with pressures from Washington, the ROC was able to maintain and even add more diplomatic allies to its side. From 1960 to 1963, 13 African nations established relations with Taipei, while the Mao regime only received five new diplomatic allies.[26] However, after the period of international isolation marked by a perceived promotion of support to revolutionary groups in other parts of the world, mainly in Southeast Asia, the People's Republic of China (PRC) assumed a more amicable and less defensive attitude towards the UN, principally with the anti-colonial groups,[27] leading to a complete inversion of the conditions as discussed above.[28]

It is important to highlight that the Kuomintang regime had a clear picture of the importance of the new African nations and about the impact that the decolonization could have at the UN. The problem, however, was Taipei's inability to compete with China in terms of resources and diplomatic appeal. With an emergent economy highly dependent on US aid, Chiang Kai-shek largely relied upon cultural exchanges and joint educational programs focused on agricultural development as his main tools to persuade the former colonies

25 Samuel S. Kim, "The People's Republic of China in the United Nations: A Preliminary Analysis," *World Politics* 26, no. 3 (April 1974), 299–330. http://journals.cambridge.org/abstract_S0043887100012909, accessed March 20, 2019.

26 Timothy S Rich, "Renting Allies and Selling Sovereignty: Taiwan's Struggle for Diplomatic Recognition," in *The Changing Dynamics of the Relations Among China, Taiwan and the United States*, ed. Cal Clark (Newcastle: Cambridge Scholars Publishing, 2011), 181.

27 The accurate sense of opportunity demonstrated by the PRC to explore the overtures of the new international reality proved surgically efficient to reposition the country internationally. The words of A.D. Hassan, High Commissioner for the Republic of Tanzania in India, and active voice for the anti-colonial movements and the non-aligned group, offers a good summary of how both groups saw the PRC at that moment: "China is an ally of the oppressed, dominated, colonized and segregated people in the world. China is an ally of non-aligned countries in our fight against colonialism, neo-colonialism, and imperialism. This fact has been recognized and still being recognized by the non-aligned movement." See: A.D. Hassan. "China and the non-aligned." International Centre Quarterly, No. 13, N. 3. 1976, 66.

28 Kim, "The People's Republic of China in the United Nations," 303.

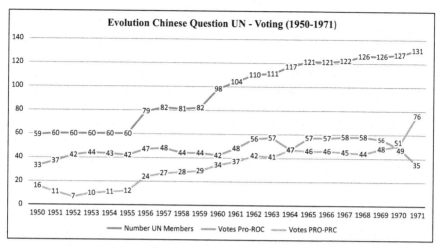

FIGURE 4.2   Evolution of the Chinese question at UN – voting
SOURCE: AUTHOR'S COMPILATION BASED ON JONSSON, 2017 AND UN ARCHIVES

to maintain their diplomatic support. In the long term, these tools showed themselves to be insufficient to turn the international tides to be less favorable to Beijing. As Lin contends, Zhou Enlai's achievements in terms of diminishing the fears of Communist China had taken away Taipei's most powerful tool in its relations with new African states, states that had long had a fear of communist interference that prevented them from having an amicable relationship with Beijing.[29] Zhou not only removed these anxieties but also made the PRC an ally of the non-aligned group.

Finally, with the PRC announcing in 1964 that it had successfully developed its own nuclear bomb and conducted its first atomic tests, followed by the country's pacification with the end of the Cultural Revolution in 1967, the international profile of the communist regime in Beijing had reached a point that was impossible to ignore. And even less to keep it outside of the UN. Without a new facet in its diplomatic strategy, as exhibited by the South Koreans later in 1973,[30] to cope with the new international reality, the ROC saw its days as a UN

29   Bih-jaw Lin, "The Republic of China and Africa: A Case of Positive Adaptation," *in Foreign Policy of the Republic of China on Taiwan: An Unorthodox Approach*, ed. Yu San Wang (New York: Praeger, 1990), 145–160.

30   As mentioned earlier, the 1973 decision to end its opposition to the dual-recognition Seoul removed an important barrier against its membership that would happen in 1991 when both Koreas were admitted as UN members. Flexibility that Taipei took too long to exhibit.

member, and its powerful position in the Security Council, dwindle day after day. When Chiang Kai-shek finally gave permission to discuss the possibility of a dual representation (two Chinas) in 1971, as a way to escape from the deadlock established since the 1950s, it was already too late.[31]

With its official expulsion from the UN on October 27, 1971,[32] the ROC would join both Koreas in the group of nations without official international representation in the majority of diplomatic decision-making bodies formed after WWII. This new condition did not put Taipei in exactly the same condition as Seoul or Pyongyang, however. At the beginning of the 1970s, Seoul and Pyongyang had reached equal geopolitical importance and diplomatic weight making them each unable to exercise their will or gain the upper hand over the other. Although South Korea underwent impressive economic development between the 1970s and 1990s, it could not translate this economic power into additional geopolitical weight on the Korean Peninsula question. In other words, there were no conditions for a "One-Korea policy" or even a "One-Korea representation policy." With lessons learned from the sequence of failures of its application for UN membership, Seoul switched to the tactic of blocking the

---

31   J. Bruce Jacobs makes the question of Chiang Kai-shek's regime adherence to One-China very clear. He argues that despite the fact the idea be mostly associated as a PRC demand, the KMT equally did not signal any possibility of flexibility and also worked actively to its maintenance, even after its expulsion from the UN in 1971. A new approach would only happen with the arrival of Lee Teng-hui to the presidency in 1988. For that, Jacobs adds: "Taiwan maintained a rigid "One-China policy" in which the ROC or Taiwan, was the only China. By the time of the flexibility of 1988, more than fifteen years had passed since China had "re-entered" the world with the Kissinger and Nixon visits, the entry of the PRC into the UN, and the establishment of diplomatic relations with most countries. Thus, Lee Teng-hui's pragmatism came much too late to be internationally effective for the newly emerging nation of Taiwan. Today's democratic Taiwan continues to suffer from the consequences of the stubborn obduracy of the prior rigidly dogmatic authoritarian Kuomintang (KMT, Nationalist Party) regime." See: J. Bruce Jacobs, 'One China, diplomatic isolation and a separate Taiwan'. In *China's Rise, Taiwan's Dilemmas and International Peace*; edited by Edward Friedman (London and New York: Routledge, 2006), 85–109; Also see "Taiwan and the UN – Withdrawal in 1971 was an historic turning point." Taipei Times, September 12, 2001. Available: http://www.taipeitimes.com/News/local/archives/2001/09/12/102595, accessed August 24, 2019.

32   The New York Times, in its October 27, 1971 edition, described the reaction at the UN: "After the tension and drama of last night, today was spent in efforts at reconciliation and in political introspection and analysis." It also noted, "Secretary General Thant appealed to all members to 'endorse the tremendous step forward' represented by Peking's admission and to set aside suspicion and bitterness." See: "UN Awaits Peking Delegates; Taipei Clings to Affiliate Ties; Roger Calls Outer a Mistake." October 27, 1971. Available: https://learning.blogs.nytimes.com/on-this-day/october-25/, accessed August 24, 2019.

acceptance of the North as an alternative. With the mutual blocking strategy implemented by Seoul, the Korean question at the UN would continue for two decades as an unsolved issue until both Koreas finally gained membership in 1991.[33]

However, with diplomatic support for Taipei's adherence to the idea of One-China representation eroding quickly, Chiang Kai-shek lost the opportunity to add a new element that could give time for the new UN to consider choices besides Taiwan's complete expulsion in 1971.[34] The US Ambassador George H.W. Bush would later say the lack of enough time to consolidate the support for the American proposal resolution of dual recognition as one of the factors behind the adoption of the resolution 2758.[35] With the PRC enjoying a reinvigorated international profile after years of isolation and hostility towards the western powers, the majority of the UN members did not hesitate a second to switch sides.

3   The Role of Democratization and International Cooperation

South Korea and Taiwan embarked on a process of political liberalization due to both domestic and external factors and have been considered as two stable 'Third Wave' democracies in Asia.[36] According to the modernization theory, the economic success of those countries in the previous decades allowed them to increase the size of their middle-class, which eventually became instrumental

---

33   On August 8, 1991, Security Council Resolution 702 recommended to the General Assembly the admission of both Koreas. It was later confirmed by the General Assembly resolution 46/1, September 17, 1991.

34   Taipei's adherence to the One-China policy had until the 1970s international diplomatic support that provided basis for its insistence. Later, the PRC developed the leverage to sustain the same demand, first due to its geopolitical importance as a result of the Sino-American rapprochement, and later also with the weight of its economic growth. Seoul and Pyongyang never had at their disposal enough of either geopolitical or economic resources to emulate the Chinese case, thus making it impossible for any side of the Korean Peninsula to impose a unilateral UN membership.

35   "We lost the China vote. The People's Republic of China was admitted to the UN – which we supported – but Taiwan was expelled … In the end, it became more of an anti-American vote than anything else … Some anti-American delegates literally danced in the aisles. … I felt it was a dark moment for the UN and international diplomacy." See: Pamela Falk, "George H.W. Bush Stood out As Tough Negotiator on the World Stage," cbsnews. com, last modified December 2, 2018, https://www.cbsnews.com/news/george-hw-bush-stood-out-as-tough-negotiator-on-world-stage/, accessed: August 24, 2019.

36   J. Bruce Jacobs, "Taiwan and South Korea: Comparing East Asia's Two 'Third-Wave' Democracies," *Issues & Studies* 43, no. 4 (2007), 227–260.

in the demand for more participation in the political process of their societies.[37] Nonetheless, in a time when modernization theory has seemed to be
challenged by the current developments in places like China and Russia, it is
also necessary to consider other important elements that help us explain the
democratization process in places like the ROK and ROC.[38]

Being close allies to the US during the Cold War, Taipei and Seoul reached an
informal understanding with Washington, which according to the hegemonic
stability theory, the latter would open its markets and promote loans and pro-
ductive investments pouring into these countries, and in exchange, they would
commit themselves to contain the advance of Communism in the region.[39]
Lacking an instrument similar to the Marshall Plan, the US signed bilateral
cooperation and defense treaties with the ROK and the ROC, in 1953 and 1954
respectively, and devoted large amounts of money not only for the acquisition of defensive weapons and equipment, but also for the promotion of infant
industries and economic growth.[40]

Considering the need for these governments to avoid growing dependence
on US aid, cooperation efforts eventually included the development of important export industries that would allow them to maintain constant access to
foreign currency. Different from what had happened with the ROC government
during the final years of the Chinese Civil War in the mainland, with constant
allegations of mismanagement and corruption, the cooperation funds that
were devoted to Taiwan between the mid-1950s and 1960s were the ones showing the best performance among the nations in East Asia receiving American
funds, including countries like the Philippines and Thailand.[41]

---

37   Seymour M. Lipset, "Some Social Requisites of Democracy: Economic Development and
      Political Legitimacy," *American Political Science Review* 53, no. 1 (1959), 69–105.
38   Adam Przeworski and Fernando Limongi, "Modernization: Theories and Facts," *World
      Politics* 49, no. 2 (1997), 164–165.
39   Charles P. Kindleberger, *Power and Money: The Economics of International Politics and the
      Politics of International Economics* (New York: Basic Books, 1970).
40   Hsiao-Ting Lin, *Accidental State: Chiang Kai-Shek, The United States, and the Making of
      Taiwan* (Cambridge, MA: Harvard University Press, 2016).
41   According to USAID data, during the first two decades after WWII, most of the foreign aid
      provided by the US government to Asia was concentrated in Thailand, the Philippines,
      Turkey, South Korea, and Taiwan. Together with Thailand, Taiwan was the place where
      each dollar received from the US reported the highest achievements, as observed in the
      high GDP and GDP per capita growth rates. After 1965, when Washington stopped provid-
      ing civilian aid to Taiwan, the ROC government, concerned by the potential negative mac-
      roeconomic effects of the lack of foreign currency sources, adopted an export-led growth
      strategy, replicating the success observed in Japan. Neil H. Jacoby, *US Aid to Taiwan: A
      Study of Foreign Aid, Self-help, and Development* (New York: F.A. Praeger, 1966), 150–162;

The rise of US-supported developmental states in South Korea and Taiwan had the goal, among many others, to consolidate capitalism and offer a viable option to the communist alternatives as being developed in North Korea and mainland China. Therefore, domestic political considerations came on second place to foreign-policy makers in Washington. The economic miracles in the ROC and ROK were carried out by authoritarian regimes, with a relatively autonomous bureaucracy, isolated from the interests of the business class and the workers. In South Korea, a succession of military dictatorships, initiated with strongman Park Chung-hee's rule after his coup in 1971, and the imposition of martial law and the creation of a new constitution one year later, were instrumental in the implementation of the successful developmental policies in place until the 1990s. In Taiwan, it was a hegemonic party rule with Chiang Kai-shek at the top, that also allowed the organization of periodical elections at the local level but continued martial-law and put a tight grip on opposition leaders in a period that was known as 'White Terror'.[42]

However, when Jimmy Carter sanctioned the inclusion of the international promotion of human rights, particularly among the allied countries, in the US foreign policy agenda, pressure for regimes like those of the ROK and ROC to liberalize their political systems began to grow. The vision of the USSR as an 'empire of evil' by the Reagan Administration, also contributed to the continuation of the US worldwide advancement of democracy. According to this logic, Washington would not have the moral ground to condemn authoritarianism in Communist nations while supporting military dictatorships and authoritarian regimes in allied countries in East Asia and Latin America. As a result, the incidents involving heavy state repression of social protests calling for democratization in Zhongli (1977) and Kaohsiung (1979) in Taiwan, and Gwangju (1980) in South Korea, received international attention and drew heavy criticism from important organizations in the US and Europe.[43] These

Yuezhao Li, "Guoji shehui dui Taiwan de yuanzhu" (The International Community's Aid to Taiwan)," in *Guoji fazhan hezuo de gainian yu shiwu* (*Overview of International Cooperation and Development*) (Taipei: International Cooperation and Development Fund (ICDF), 2007).

42   Chien-chao Hung, *A New History of Taiwan: Asia's First Republic in the New Millennium* (Taipei: The Central News Agency, 2011), 367–370.

43   Hung-Mao Tien, *The Great Transition: Political and Social Change in the Republic of China* (Taipei: SMC Publishing, 1989), 95–98; Bruce J. Jacobs, *The Kaohsiung Incident in Taiwan and Memoirs of a Foreign Big Beard* (Leiden: Brill, 2016).

events were also influential in the ensuing political liberalization in the ROC and the ROK.[44]

One year after the popular movements known as the EDSA Revolution overthrew Ferdinand Marcos out of power in the Philippines and started the third wave of democratization, in 1987, Seoul announced political reforms, including the first direct presidential elections in its history. Taipei also carried out important changes, allowing the formation of new opposition political parties and lifting martial law. Democratization was part of a larger trend of transformations, framed in a changing international system, marked by the end of bipolarity and the rapid embrace of globalization. Opening their political systems also meant the relaxation of state-led economic policies, diminishing the role of the developmental state. In South Korea, this meant a continuous effort by the state to limit the increasing role of *chaebols'* interests in the policy-making process, albeit with mixed results.[45] In Taiwan, it signified a bigger challenge, by conciliating the domestic security concerns with the interests of the so-called *Taishang* (Taiwanese businesspeople) in continuing their investments in mainland China.[46]

The way these countries were ruled during the Cold War also affected the way democracy evolved. Having been ruled by strong military dictators, South Korea did not experience the creation of strong and deep-rooted political parties, hence affecting political negotiation and the way the Legislative branch interacted with the Executive after democratization.[47] This situation has made possible the impeachment and removal of President Park Geun-hye, and her ensuing arrest on charges of influence-peddling and abuse of power, as well as the incarceration of former president Lee Myung-bak, accused of corruption, embezzlement and bribery.

The ROC, on the other hand, being dominated by the KMT until democratization, evolved into an effective two-party system after the creation of the PP in

---

44   Bruce J. Jacobs, "Two Key Events in the Democratisation of Taiwan and South Korea: The Kaohsiung Incident and the Kwangju Uprising," *International Review of Korean Studies* 8, no. 1 (2011), 28–56.

45   Mark A. Abdollahian, et al, "Economic Crisis and the Future of Oligarchy," in *Institutional Reform and Democratic Consolidation in Korea*, ed. Larry Diamond and Doh Chull Shin (Stanford, CA: Hoover Institution Press, 2000), 191–231.

46   Shelley Rigger, *Why Taiwan Matters: Small Island, Global Powerhouse* (Lanham: Rowman & Littlefield, 2013).

47   Hoon Jaung, "Electoral Politics and Political Parties," in *Institutional Reform and Democratic Consolidation in Korea*, ed. Larry Diamond and Doh Chull Shin (Stanford: Hoover Institution Press, 2000), 43–71; Kie-Duck Park, "Political Parties and Democratic Consolidation in Korea," in *Asian New Democracies: The Philippines, South Korea and Taiwan Compared*, ed. Hsin-Huang Michael Hsiao (Taipei: TFD-CAPAS, 2008), 127–156.

1986, and the eventual *Taiwanization*[48] of the Kuomintang.[49] The existence of other minor parties has forced the two largest parties to join forces with them, forming two large camps, known as Pan-blue and Pan-green, and defined by their different approaches to ethnicity and the future of the island regarding its position towards the mainland. In this sense, the element of identity has become an important cleavage in ROC politics.[50] The KMT control of the Legislative Yuan during the government of Chen Shui-bian from the DPP was also determinant to its return to power under the leadership of Ma Ying-jeou in 2008, and to the detention of Chen on charges of corruption that same year. The alternation of the presidency between the two largest parties completed with the victory of Tsai Ing-wen in 2016, has also consolidated the democratic transformation of Taiwan.

Therefore, the transition to democracy in both the ROC and the ROK has put them more in line with the interests of other major democratic countries, in what can be identified by the Constructivist theory as socialization of the states, and their shared commitments to maintain and defend democratic practices.[51] The governments of both countries have encouraged the use of

---

48 The *Taiwanization* of the KMT is the name given to the process pursued by the ROC hegemonic party to give more prominence to ethnically Taiwanese cadres and politicians, appointing them to key positions in the administration under the tenure of Chiang Ching-kuo (1978–1988). The most relevant case was that of Lee Teng-hui, nominated and elected by the National Assembly to the position of Vice president during the rule of Chiang Ching-kuo. Originally, the process was intended to gain more support for the ruling party among the majority Hoklo population on the island. After the split of the Kuomintang in the 2000 elections, and the triumph of DPP candidate Chen Shui-bian, Lee was expelled from the party and the process was notably slowed down. As a result, the KMT had to find new ways to remain competitive. One of them was the idea of "New Taiwanese," embraced by Ma Ying-jeou, who was originally born in Hong Kong from Hunanese parents, but promoted the idea of "Taiwaneseness" of KMT politicians, which had now a new generation of politicians born and raised on the island, who in spite of having mainlander descent, now claim to be as Taiwanese as the other ethnic groups that conform the population of the ROC. Nonetheless, the close ties with the PRC that the Ma administration pursued has been seen as one of the reasons for the KMT failure in the 2016 presidential elections, with many young people showing their concerns about the future of the island, as seen during the social protests known as the Sunflower Movement in 2014. See: Malte P. Kaeding, "Taiwanized "New Taiwanese": The Effect of Taiwanization on the 2008 Presidential Election Campaign of Ma Ying-jeou," *Asia-Pacific Social Science Review* 9, no. 2 (2009); Bruce J. Jacobs, *Democratizing Taiwan* (Leiden: Brill, 2012), 5–18.
49 Tien, *The Great Transition*, 253–254.
50 Thomas B. Gold, "Taiwan's Quest for Identity in the Shadow of China," in *The Shadow of China: Political Developments in Taiwan since 1949*, ed. Steve Tsang (Hong Kong: Hong Kong University Press, 1993), 169–192.
51 Alexander Wendt, *Social Theory of International Politics* (Cambridge: Cambridge University Press, 1999).

contemporary methods of public diplomacy with other democratic countries, and the other power branches, particularly the legislative one, have also
gained experience in extending their contacts with their counterparts in other
parts of the world.[52] In the case of the ROC, there has been a visible effort
to consolidate a support network including European Parliamentarians and
Representatives and Senators of the US, who often are invited to visit Taiwan,
and to host unofficial visiting delegations from Taiwan in their countries.[53]

Democratization and economic development also affected the way Taiwan
and South Korea practiced their international cooperation. In the same way
they paid close attention to the developmental policies implemented by Japan
after the end of WWII, Seoul and Taipei also emulated the mechanisms of
cooperation developed by Tokyo. If, as mentioned above, international cooperation during the Cold War was aimed at the establishment of relations with
recently independent countries looking for their support on their positions in
the UN, the process of democratization brought more pressure to make cooperation more institutionalized, effective, and transparent. After Tokyo established the Japan International Cooperation Agency (JICA) in 1974, and fifteen
years later, in 1989, Japan became the largest provider of official development
assistance in the world,[54] decision makers in Seoul and Taipei also decided to
follow a similar path.[55]

Therefore, in order to coordinate the efforts of economic aid and technical assistance to least developed countries, the ROC government set up the
International Economic Cooperation Development Fund (IECDF) in 1989,
under the supervision of the Ministry of Economic Affairs. In 1996, this fund
was merged with an organ dedicated to technical assistance and was granted
larger autonomy, then forming the International Cooperation Development

---

52   Gary D. Rawnsley, *Taiwan's Informal Diplomacy and Propaganda* (Hampshire, UK:
      Palgrave, 2000).

53   Yuchunv Lan, "The European Parliament and the China-Taiwan Issue: An Empirical
      Approach," *European Foreign Affairs Review* 9 (2004), 115–140.

54   The official development assistance (ODA) offered by countries like Japan, and later
      emulated by governments like those from the ROC and ROK, have been the subject of
      study, noting how it has acquired elements of hard and soft power, sometimes imply-
      ing different types of strategic demands, both economic and political, from the donor
      countries. See: Alberto Alesina and David Dollar, "Who Gives Foreign Aid to Whom and
      Why?" *Journal of Economic Growth* 5, no. 1 (2000), 33–63. For a comparison between Japan,
      South Korea, and Taiwan, some of their motivations and amounts, see Joel Atkinson,
      "Comparing Taiwan's foreign aid to Japan, South Korea and DAC," *Journal of the Asia
      Pacific Economy* 22, no. 2 (2017), 253–272.

55   Robert M. Orr, *The Emergence of Japan's Foreign Aid Power* (New York: Columbia University
      Press, 1990).

Fund (ICDF), which has been an advanced mechanism of cooperation not only with diplomatic allies but also with other less developed regions in the world.[56] Similarly, the ROK government established the Economic Development Cooperation Fund (ECDF) in 1987, which later evolved into the more autonomous Korea International Cooperation Agency (KOICA), in 1991. Using a more extensive network of diplomatic channels, the ROK has established offices in several emerging and developing countries around the globe.[57]

These agencies have served their governments to advance an idea of success stories, with their countries having been recipients of aid during the 1950s and 1960s, and then transforming themselves into important economic powerhouses and therefore aid donors. Hence, in their own views, theirs is an effort at giving back, sharing their experience and becoming an inspiration to others. Similarly, the governments in both countries have intended to project an image of being responsible players in the system. After years of consideration and a few months of negotiation, South Korea was finally admitted into the Organization for Economic Cooperation and Development (OECD) in 1996, hence performing multiple reforms to be more in tune with the goals of the institution, specifically democracy and market economy. Limited by the "One China" policies observed by the different members of the organization, the ROC has been unable to join the OECD. Nonetheless, since the late 1980s, the government in Taiwan has followed closely the reports and recommendations issued by the organization, and in many cases, it has unilaterally implemented reforms in areas like governance, transparency, economic freedom, rule of law, among others, the same way it is expected for the member countries.[58]

Taiwan's ICDF and South Korea's KOICA also represent an important show of difference with their self-proclaimed Communist neighbors. Despite the increased volume of official development assistance and technical cooperation with other nations in the past two decades, the institutionalization of the PRC international cooperation remains underdeveloped. Chinese international cooperation continues being a non-transparent and non-centralized process, without a single agency in charge, therefore involving many different

---

56   International Cooperation and Development Fund (ICDF), *Guoji fazhan hezuo de gainian yu shiwu* (*Overview of International Cooperation and Development*) (Taipei: ICDF, 2007).

57   Eun Mee Kim and Jinhwan Oh, "Determinants of Foreign Aid: The Case of South Korea," *Journal of East Asian Studies* 12, no. 2 (2012), 299–330.

58   Zhao Linian, *Woguo jiaqiang canyu OECD guoji hezuo huodong zhi kenengxing* (*Analysis on the possibilities of our country to increasingly participate in the OECD international cooperation activities*). *Working Paper no. 21005*, (Taipei: Ministry of Economy, ROC, 1992).

official agents and levels, usually with opposing views.[59] The PRC is also among the few countries in the world that are both donor and recipient of aid. The DPRK, on the other hand, despite having carried out some efforts to provide technical assistance to recently independent countries in the past, is now among the countries more in need of receiving official development assistance (ODA). The minimal international cooperation practiced by North Korea in the past was also highly influenced by its desire to export the ideology of *Juche* as a viable alternative for less-developed nations.[60] As a result, the international cooperation agencies developed by the ROK and the ROC as a result of democratization, advance their cause as promoters of shared values like democracy and social justice, and for the case of Taiwan, it has helped the island to maintain and increase its international space.

4   Security Challenges and Increasing Pragmatism

Since the 1970s, South Korea paid close attention to the political developments in Germany. As discussed above, when both Bonn and East Berlin were admitted as members to the UN in 1973, Seoul also changed its strategy and showed its willingness to be admitted to the organization together with Pyongyang. When both countries finally joined the UN in 1991, after the Cold War ended, Germany was also under the process of reunification, with the capitalist West taking the lead and absorbing the East. These events boosted the confidence of South Korea, now under the rule of democratically elected president Roh Tae-woo, who also imitated the successful German policy known as *Östpolitik*, and embarked on a new trend later branded as *Nordpolitik*.[61] Using its economic miracle as a promotion tool and the successful organization of the 1988 Olympic games, Seoul approached effectively Beijing and Moscow, seeking to eventually achieve similar results as those obtained by the Federal Republic of Germany in the past.

Once admitted to the UN, and attracted by the scale of economic reforms in the PRC, South Korea decided to switch diplomatic recognition, abandoning

---

59   Carol Lancaster, "The Chinese Aid System," Center for Global Development, last modified June 2007, https://www.cgdev.org/files/13953_file_Chinese_aid.pdf, accessed August 23, 2019.

60   Alzo David-West, "Between Confucianism and Marxism-Leninism: Juche and the Case of Chong Tasan," *Korean Studies* 35 (2011), 104–110.

61   Victor Cha, *The Impossible State: North Korea, Past and Future* (London: The Bodley Head, 2012), 323–328.

its traditional political alliance with Taiwan, and being the last country in Asia to formalize diplomatic relations with Beijing.[62] The PRC, nonetheless, has played a vital role in the continued existence of the DPRK, as its largest trading partner and provider of aid. After the Cold War, the pragmatism of Seoul contrasted with the increasing hermetic response from Pyongyang. After years of promoting the policy of *Juche* or 'self-reliance' as a response to the Sino-Soviet split, the government in North Korea went into further isolation from the outside world and heavy militarization, making huge sacrifices to develop a nuclear program as the only way to ensure regime survival.[63]

For the past 25 years, the acquisition of nuclear weapons by Pyongyang has remained the greatest security concern of Seoul, and one of the largest threats to the development of East Asia. Successive democratically elected governments in South Korea have transitioned from the *Nordpolitik*, to the more pragmatic Sunshine Policy, which contemplated direct contacts with North Korea and gradual steps of cooperation in different areas, and to the mediation of other regional powers in the framework known as Six-Party Talks.[64] None of those policies were successful in convincing Pyongyang to abandon its nuclear ambitions. After the 'strategic patience' shown by the Obama administration towards North Korean missile tests, the governments of Lee Myung-bak and Park Geun-hye decreased cooperation with the North and tried to find mechanisms to put more pressure on Kim Jong-un to stop North Korea's nuclear program.[65]

The formal security alliance with the US has been an important factor in the evolution of the ROK's policy towards the DPRK. The lack of a peace treaty negotiated after the armistice of the Korean War has made the Korean Peninsula to remain a hot topic in East Asia, even three decades after the end of the Cold War. The deployment of a Terminal High Altitude Area Defense (THAAD) system in South Korea, in 2016, with the cooperation of the US Department of Defense, raised the level of regional tensions. Not only did the North Korean government increase the number of missile tests throughout 2017, but the

62   Wenshou Chen and C.X George Wei, "Separating Economics from Politics: Contemporary Taiwan-South Korea relations" in China-*Taiwan Relations in a Global Context: Taiwan's Foreign Policy and Relations*, ed. C.X George Wei (New York: Routledge, 2012), 115–139.

63   Soyoung Kwon, "State building in North Korea: from a 'self-reliant' to a 'military-first' state," *Asian Affairs* 34, no. 3 (2003), 286–296.

64   Chung-in Moon, *The Sunshine Policy: In Defense of Engagement as a Path to Peace in Korea* (Seoul: Yonsei University Press, 2012).

65   Yangmo Ku, "Inter-Korean relations and reunification," in *Politics in North and South Korea: Political Development, Economy, and Foreign Relations*, ed. Yangmo Ku, Inyeop Lee, and Jongseok Woo (New York: Routledge, 2018), 192–214.

Chinese government also reacted angrily. Fearful of the possible negative implications to its own security, Beijing encouraged calls on social media to boycott Korean brands, companies and even K-pop stars in China, harming considerably South Korea's business interests in that country, but also the level of bilateral trust.[66] These developments led to a change, with the arrival of Moon Jae-in to the Blue House and Donald Trump to the White House.

Moon has promoted a revival of the Sunshine Policy, encouraging more cooperation with the DPRK and bilateral summits with his counterpart in the North, Kim Jong-un. Similarly, a more personalist approach has characterized the style of Trump, who also has met Kim personally, and in spite of the lack of a formal commitment to denuclearization, the joint US-ROK military exercises were halted, while Pyongyang also temporarily refrained from testing new missiles. In spite of the changes regarding the threat posed by the North Korean nuclear program, Seoul has maintained its security alliance with Washington, and South Korea still hosts some of the largest US military bases in East Asia. The armed forces of the US are still an important element in the security of the ROK, and its sustained economic growth has also depended on the protection offered by the former.[67] Therefore, it is difficult to think about a change in the nature of the bilateral commitments in the coming years.

On the other hand, the relationship between the US and the ROC has adopted a more ambivalent quality. Since the ROC government refused to abandon its commitment to the "One China" ideal after its walkout from the UN, fearful of a backlash from the nationalist military who migrated to Taiwan with the hope of eventually retaking the mainland and reuniting with their families and loved ones, the rest of the countries in the world had to carry different versions of "One China" policies. This situation limited their interactions with Taiwan.[68] After the 1972 Shanghai Communique agreed by Nixon and Zhou Enlai, where the US government abstained from recognizing the PRC's sovereignty over Taiwan but acknowledged that both sides considered themselves as part of one China, among the first states to develop a pragmatic approach was Japan. In this case, different from the continuously tense relations between Tokyo

---

66   *The Economist* (London). "A geopolitical row with China damages South Korean business further," October 19, 2017. https://www.economist.com/business/2017/10/19/a-geopolitical-row-with-china-damages-south-korean-business-further, accessed August 23, 2019.

67   Mark E. *Manyin*, et al, "US-South Korea Relations," in *South Korea: International Relations, Trade and Politics*, ed. Alan K. Becker (New York: Nova Science Publishers, 2011), 1–26.

68   Tien, 240–41.

and Seoul,[69] manifested by the negative views still held among many Koreans regarding the Japanese colonial domination and its behavior during WWII, the people of Taiwan tend to have a very positive impression of Japan, its government and its people.[70]

This was demonstrated when, in 1972, after establishing official diplomatic ties with the People's Republic of China and abrogating the 1952 Sino-Japanese Peace Treaty that formally ended the war between Japan and the ROC, the government of Japan established the Interchange Association to serve as a de facto embassy in Taiwan. Since Japan was the second-largest source of cooperation and aid to the ROC during the first years of the Cold War, Tokyo paid special attention to the political and economic developments on the island, and maintained intense commercial, cultural and academic links even after the recognition of Beijing as the legitimate government of China.[71]

The Japanese ambivalent attitude has also been reflected by the support that some right-wing factions have offered to Taiwanese movements and politicians in favor of independence at different periods of time. This situation has tended to create tensions between Japan and the PRC, and also with the movements favoring reunification with the mainland in Taiwan.[72] Nonetheless, Tokyo has continued to show its support to the island by renaming its representative office as Japan-Taiwan Exchange Association in 2017. This bold move, including for the first time the name Taiwan, instead of the more traditional and conservative name of Taipei, has been seen as deepening its ambivalence regarding the situation of cross-strait developments.

After Japan, many other countries have established informal relations with the ROC and have opened representative offices in Taipei, while allowing the creation of similar offices in their capital cities. The end of the Cold War and democratization allowed Taipei to fully embrace pragmatism and warm ties with the government in Beijing. Starting with people-to-people exchanges, both sides of the Taiwan Strait developed a series of policies to improve economic, cultural, social and academic exchanges, hence clearing the way for Taiwan to do the same with third countries.[73] During the administration of Lee

---

69   Victor Cha, *Alignment Despite Antagonism: The United States-Korea-Japan Security Triangle* (Stanford, CA: Stanford University Press, 1999), 9–35.

70   Chen and Wei, "Separating economics from politics," 115–39.

71   Jing Sun, "Japan-Taiwan Relations: Unofficial in Name Only," *Asian Survey* 47, no. 5 (2007), 790–810.

72   Thomas S. Wilkins, "Taiwan-Japan Relations in an Era of Uncertainty," *Asia Policy* 13 (2012), 113–132.

73   For further studies on Taiwan's foreign policymaking process, see Jie Chen, *Foreign Policy of the New Taiwan: Pragmatic Diplomacy in Southeast Asia* (Cheltenham, UK: Edward Elgar,

Teng-hui, the creation of semi-official bodies in Taiwan and China for the con-
duction of Cross-Strait affairs in the early 1990s, also permitted both sides to
reach an unofficial understanding on the use of the term "One China," although
with different interpretations. This was later known as the "1992 Consensus."[74]
Nonetheless, in practice, the observance of the "One China" policy by other
governments and international organizations has limited the international
space of the ROC. With only 15 countries maintaining official diplomatic relations with Taiwan at the beginning of 2020, in past decades the country has
found it difficult to access other institutions or be readmitted to the UN.[75]

Unlike the ROK, that has been able to expand its international economic
presence through the signature of FTAS and PTAS, as well as other cooperation agreements, the ROC faces constant isolation and self-imposed barriers by
countries who fear a backlash from an increasingly powerful PRC, in case they
decide to forge closer ties with Taiwan. Even so, the Taiwanese authorities and
businesspeople have been able to find pragmatic answers to these obstacles,
as represented by the diplomatic truce with the mainland, in effect during the
years of President Ma Ying-jeou,[76] or by the New Southbound Policy implemented by his successor, President Tsai Ing-wen.[77]

The ambivalent example set by Japan in its relations with Taiwan was
closely watched by the US. Hence, when the Carter administration decided to
take the step to establish formal diplomatic ties with the PRC, it also created
the American Institute at Taiwan to serve as its de facto embassy on the island.
Abrogating the 1954 bilateral defense treaty, which meant the removal of all
troops and active military personnel from the island, Washington came under

---

2002); Dennis V. Hickey, *Foreign Policy Making in Taiwan: From Principle to Pragmatism*
(New York: Routledge, 2007).

74   The Straits Exchange Foundation (SEF) operates in Taiwan, and the Association for
Relations Across the Taiwan Straits (ARATS) was set up in mainland China. Both bod-
ies were created in 1990–1991 and represented an effort to conduct Cross-Strait high-
level talks. Ying-jeou Ma, "Policy Towards the Chinese Mainland: Taipei's View," in *In
The Shadow of China: Political Developments in Taiwan since 1949*, ed. Steve Tsang (Hong
Kong: Hong Kong University Press, 1993), 193–211.

75   In case they managed to join international organizations, due to pressure from the PRC,
it has been under a different name, usually "Chinese Taipei," in order to avoid the idea of
the existence of two Chinas, or one China and one Taiwan.

76   T.Y. Wang, et al, "Structural realism and liberal pluralism. An assessment of Ma Ying-
Jeou's Cross-Strait policy," in *New Thinking about the Taiwan Issue: Theoretical insights
into its origins, dynamics, and prospects*, ed. Jean-Marc F. Blanchard and Dennis V. Hickey
(New York: Routledge, 2012), 137–171.

77   Bonnie Glaser, et al, *The New Southbound Policy: Deepening's Taiwan Regional Integration*
(Washington, DC: CSIS – Rowman & Littlefield, 2018).

heavy pressure by the so-called China Lobby and the US Congress moved fast
to pass the Taiwan Relations Act (TRA). The TRA and the 1982 Six Assurances
offered by the US to Taiwan, and derived from another bilateral communique
agreed with the PRC, became the base of the informal relations between the
US and the ROC.[78] In all of the communiques, Washington has expressed its
opposition to the use of force and any unilateral changes in the cross-strait status quo, which not only means a rejection of any forced unification by the PRC
but also to any radical move at proclaiming independence by the government
of the island. Nonetheless, the US has also committed itself to continue its
arms sales to Taiwan, although it agreed to reduce its volume and intensity.[79]

The US government has also shown evidence of its continued commitment
at different times, such as in 1996, when it sent the Pacific Seventh Fleet to
the Taiwan Strait after Chinese forces launched missiles into the water as a
way to influence the first direct presidential elections in the ROC. And recently,
especially after the election of Donald Trump and the rise of tensions between
Washington and Beijing, US legislators from both parties have endorsed
and passed new acts promoting further interaction between American and
Taiwanese officials, and have pledged to contribute toward the construction of
a domestic submarine fleet for Taiwan.[80] These moves have also contributed
to the increasing hostility from the PRC government towards the administration of President Tsai Ing-Wen, and the continuous calls by Chinese leaders to
President Xi Jinping, to set a deadline for the reunification of Taiwan with the
mainland.

This situation shows the way the US is perceived by the governments of the
ROC and the ROK as the most important ally in terms of their national security. For the case of Taiwan, Japan is also seen as a strategic player. Meanwhile
South Korea sometimes reluctantly cooperate with Japan, encouraged mainly
by the US.[81] Nonetheless, with the increasing role that the PRC is playing in
the region, both Taipei and Seoul need to develop different strategies when
dealing with Beijing and its close ally Pyongyang. For the case of South Korea,
the PRC can be the key to find a sustainable solution to its problems with the
DPRK, and eventually dream of successful Korean reunification. For the case

78   Rigger, *Why Taiwan Matters*, 174–84.
79   Henry Kissinger, *On China* (London: Penguin, 2011), 381–86.
80   Richard Bush, "Why a new office building in Taiwan is heightening US-China tensions,"
      Brookings: Order from Chaos (May 29, 2018), online, https://www.brookings.edu/blog/
      order-from-chaos/2018/05/29/why-a-new-office-building-in-taiwan-is-heightening-u-s-
      china-tensions/, accessed August 23, 2019.
81   Cha, *Alignment Despite Antagonism*, 3.

of Taiwan, the options are more limited, and even considering a more pragmatic approach towards mainland China in the future, it does not affect the
fact that the majority of the people in the island still prefer to maintain the
status quo and to leave the choice between independence or unification to
future generations.[82]

5   Conclusion

After geopolitical events created the structural conditions of the current situation in the Korean Peninsula and the Taiwan Strait, their process to access or
remain in the UN contributed to their perpetuation. In that sense, if a state's
geography is fated as they say, the position of those states inside of the international system is inevitably a question of interpretation by other members of
the system. There were interpretations that gave North and South Koreans a
different destiny than the one granted to the ROC. It was not the PRC that initially isolated the ROC in world affairs, but the latter's original embrace of the
One China principle and its ensuing interpretation by UN members that made
its diplomatic exile a reality. What makes Taipei's misfortune different from the
Korean one? The answer is tragically simple: Koreans are a member of the UN,
and Taiwan is not, and that makes a difference.

The UN's interpretation about the role that the ROC is supposed to play in
world politics rendered it dismissible when compared to the importance of the
PRC on the world stage, and the majority of the members have accepted this
perspective. In their attempt to gain (or retain) a seat at the organization, Seoul
did not have a powerful piece to move on this new board, so it decided to stop
playing, and eventually to stop the game itself. On the other hand, Taipei also
did not have good pieces to play and yet did not yield, with results being the
ones we have observed.

The democratization of both Taiwan and South Korea was an important
game-changer. Both countries could present a renewed image to the world,
after years of also being perceived as important successful cases of industrialization and economic development. The end of the Cold War, achieved in part
through the Sino-American rapprochement, served the ROK to accomplish its
goal to join the UN and to maintain diplomatic ties with the major powers in
the system, including the PRC. On the other hand, Taiwan initially intensified

---

82   Election Study Center (ESC). "Taiwan Independence vs. Unification with the Mainland
        (1992/06~2018/12)," *ESC-National Chengchi University*, (January 28, 2019), online, https://
        esc.nccu.edu.tw/course/news.php?Sn=167, accessed August 23, 2019.

the competition for allies, but also took a more pragmatic approach with the major powers, maintaining informal relations and increasing economic ties. Nonetheless, once the balance of power between both sides of the Taiwan Strait changed dramatically during the past two decades, being significantly unfavorable to Taipei, it is difficult to think about a future abandonment of the "One China" principle by the PRC. This means that the government on the island must dedicate its limited resources to maintaining and eventually increasing its international space, and to avoid any unfavorable unification with the mainland in the near future. Conversely, now that the nuclear program in North Korea starts looking like a reality more than a future project, the peaceful unification of the peninsula also seems like a yet distant goal.

The analysis of the evolution of the foreign policies of both the ROC and the ROK is indeed a complex task. Nonetheless, the introduction of the different elements, as exemplified first in their relations to the UN, and later democratization, economic growth and their interactions with strategic players like the US and Japan, contribute to the understanding of the similarities and differences in the responses to external challenges faced by these two countries throughout contemporary history. The peaceful resolution of the situations in the Korean Peninsula and the Taiwan Strait, and the maintenance of peace in the Indo-Pacific region, will require the constant attention and communication between the different actors presented in this chapter. So far, the abandonment of ideological positions and the embrace of pragmatism can be seen as effective steps in that direction.

References

Abdollahian, Mark A., et al. "Economic Crisis and the Future of Oligarchy." In *Institutional Reform and Democratic Consolidation in Korea*, edited by Larry Diamond and Doh Chull Shin, 191–231. Stanford, CA: Hoover Institution Press, 2000.

Alesina, Alberto, and David Dollar. "Who Gives Foreign Aid to Whom and Why?" *Journal of Economic Growth* 5, no. 1 (2000): 33–63.

Atkinson, Joel. "Comparing Taiwan's foreign aid to Japan, South Korea, and DAC." *Journal of the Asia Pacific Economy* 22, no. 2 (2017): 253–272.

Briggs, Herbert W. "Chinese Representation in the UN." *International Organization* 6, no. 2 (1952): 192–209.

Bush, Richard. "Why a new office building in Taiwan is heightening US-China tensions." *Brookings: Order from Chaos* (May 29, 2018), https://www.brookings.edu/blog/order-from-chaos/2018/05/29/why-a-new-office-building-in-taiwan-is-heightening-u-s-china-tensions/, accessed August 23, 2019.

Cha, Victor. *Alignment Despite Antagonism: The United States-Korea-Japan Security Triangle.* Stanford, CA: Stanford University Press, 1999.

Cha, Victor. *The Impossible State: North Korea, Past and Future.* London: The Bodley Head, 2012.

Chen, Jie. *Foreign Policy of the New Taiwan: Pragmatic Diplomacy in Southeast Asia.* Cheltenham, UK: Edward Elgar, 2002.

Chen, Wenshou, and C.X. George Wei. "'Separating economics from politics': Contemporary Taiwan-South Korea relations." In *China-Taiwan Relations in a Global Context: Taiwan's Foreign Policy and Relations*, edited by C.X. George Wei, 115–139. New York: Routledge, 2012.

Choi, Chong-Ki. "The Korean Question in the UN." Paper presented at *Sixth General Conference of the International Peace Research Association*, Turku, Finland, August 15, 1975.

Collins, Michael. "Decolonization." In *The Encyclopedia of Empire*, edited by John M. Mackenzie, 1–14. Oxford: Wiley-Blackwell, 2016.

Dallin, Alexander. *The Soviet View of the UN.* Cambridge: Center for International Studies, Massachusetts Institute of Technology, 1959.

David-West, Alzo. "Between Confucianism and Marxism-Leninism: Juche and the Case of Chong Tasan." *Korean Studies* 35 (2011): 93–123.

"Decolonization of Asia and Africa, 1945–1960." Office of the Historian. https://history. state.gov/milestones/1945–1952/asia-and-africa, accessed March 20, 2019.

Election Study Center (ESC). "Taiwan Independence vs. Unification with the Mainland (1992/06~2018/12)." ESC-National Chengchi University, January 28, 2019. https://esc. nccu.edu.tw/course/news.php?Sn=167, accessed August 23, 2019.

Falk, Pamela. "George H.W. Bush Stood out as Tough Negotiator on the World Stage." cbsnews.com. Last modified December 2, 2018. https://www.cbsnews.com/news/ george-hw-bush-stood-out-as-tough-negotiator-on-world-stage/, accessed August 24, 2019.

Fallaci, Oriana. *Interview with History.* Boston: Houghton Mifflin, 1976.

Glaser, Bonnie, et al. *The New Southbound Policy: Deepening's Taiwan Regional Integration.* Washington, DC: Center for Strategic and International Studies – Rowman & Littlefield, 2018.

Gold, Thomas B. "Taiwan's Quest for Identity in the Shadow of China." In *The Shadow of China: Political Developments in Taiwan since 1949*, edited by Steve Tsang, 169–192. Hong Kong: Hong Kong University Press, 1993.

Hassan, A.D. "China and the non-aligned." *International Centre Quarterly* 13, no. 3 (1976): 66.

Hickey, Dennis V. *Foreign Policy Making in Taiwan: From Principle to Pragmatism.* New York: Routledge, 2007.

Hilger, A. "Communism, Decolonization and the Third World." In *The Cambridge History of Communism*, edited by N. Naimark, S. Pons, and S. Quinn-Judge, 317–340. Cambridge: Cambridge University, 2017.

Hill, Christopher. *The Changing Politics of Foreign Policy*. London: Macmillan, 2003.

Hung, Chien-chao. *A New History of Taiwan: Asia's First Republic in the New Millennium*. Taipei: The Central News Agency, 2011.

Huntington, Samuel P. *The Third Wave: Democratization in the Late Twentieth Century*. Norman, OK: University of Oklahoma Press, 1991.

International Cooperation and Development Fund (ICDF, editor). *Guoji fazhan hezuo de gainian yu shiwu* (Overview of International Cooperation and Development). Taipei: ICDF, 2007.

Jacobs, J. Bruce. *Democratizing Taiwan*. Leiden: Brill, 2012.

Jacobs, J. Bruce. "Taiwan and South Korea: Comparing East Asia's Two 'Third-Wave' Democracies." *Issues & Studies* 43, no. 4 (2007): 227–260.

Jacobs, J. Bruce. *The Kaohsiung Incident in Taiwan and Memoirs of a Foreign Big Beard*. Leiden: Brill, 2016.

Jacobs, J. Bruce. "Two key events in the democratisation of Taiwan and South Korea: The Kaohsiung incident and the Kwangju uprising." *International Review of Korean Studies* 8, no. 1 (2011): 28–56.

Jacoby, Neil H. *US Aid to Taiwan: A Study of Foreign Aid, Self-Help, and Development*. New York: F.A. Praeger, 1966.

Jaung, Hoon. "Electoral Politics and Political Parties." In *Institutional Reform and Democratic Consolidation in Korea*, edited by Larry Diamond and Doh Chull Shin, 43–71. Stanford, CA: Hoover Institution Press, 2000.

Jonsson, Gabriel. *South Korea in The UN: Global Governance, Inter-Korean Relations and Peace Building*. London: World Scientific, 2017.

Kaeding, Malte Philipp. "Taiwanized 'New Taiwanese': The Effect of Taiwanization on the 2008 Presidential Election Campaign of Ma Ying-jeou." *Asia-Pacific Social Science Review* 9, no. 2 (2009): 19–34.

Kim, Eun Mee, and Jinhwan Oh. "Determinants of Foreign Aid: The Case of South Korea." *Journal of East Asian Studies* 12, no. 2 (2012): 251–274.

Kim, Samuel S. "The People's Republic of China in the UN: A Preliminary Analysis." *World Politics* 26, no. 3 (April 1974): 299–330.

Kissinger, Henry. *On China*. London: Penguin, 2011.

Kindleberger, Charles. *Money and Power: The Economics of International Politics and the Politics of International Economics*. New York: Basic Books, 1970.

Krishnan, R.R. "North Korea and The Non-Aligned Movement." *International Studies* 20, no. 1–2 (1981): 299–313.

Ku, Yangmo. "Inter-Korean relations and reunification." In *Politics in North and South Korea: Political Development, Economy, and Foreign Relations*, edited by Yangmo Ku, Inyeop Lee, and Jongseok Woo, 192–214. New York: Routledge, 2018.

Kwon, Soyoung. "State Building in North Korea: From a 'Self-Reliant' to a 'Military-First' State." *Asian Affairs* 34, no.3 (2003): 286–196.

Lan, Yuchun. "The European Parliament and the China-Taiwan Issue: An Empirical Approach." *European Foreign Affairs Review* 9 (2004): 115–140.

Lancaster, Carol. "The Chinese Aid System," *Center for Global Development*, June, 2007, https://www.cgdev.org/files/13953_file_Chinese_aid.pdf, accessed August 23, 2019.

Li, Yuezhao. "Guoji shehui dui Taiwan de yuanzhu" (The International Community's Aid to Taiwan), In *Guoji fazhan hezuo de gainian yu shiwu* (Overview of International Cooperation and Development), edited by International Cooperation and Development Fund, 213–242. Taipei: ICDF, 2007.

Lin, Bih-jaw. "The Republic of China and Africa: A Case of Positive Adaptation." In *Foreign Policy of the Republic of China on Taiwan: An Unorthodox Approach*, edited by Yu San Wang, 145–160. New York: Praeger, 1990.

Lin, Hsiao-ting. *Accidental State: Chiang Kai-Shek, The United States, and the Making of Taiwan.* Cambridge, MA: Harvard University Press, 2016.

Lipset, Seymour M. "Some Social Requisites of Democracy: Economic Development and Political Legitimacy." *American Political Science Review* 53, no. 1 (1959): 69–105.

Luard, Evan. "China and the UN." *Royal Institute of International Affairs 1944- 47*, no. 4 (1971): 729–744.

Ma, Ying-jeou. "Policy Towards the Chinese Mainland: Taipei's View." *In In The Shadow of China: Political Developments in Taiwan since 1949*, edited by Steve Tsang, 193–211. Hong Kong: Hong Kong University Press, 1993.

Manyin, Mark E., et al. "US-South Korea Relations." In *South Korea: International Relations, Trade and Politics*, edited by Alan K. Becker, 1–26. New York: Nova Science Publishers, 2011.

Matray, James I. "Beijing and the Paper Tiger: The Impact of the Korean War on Sino-American Relations." *International Journal of Korean Studies* 15, no. 1 (Spring 2011), 155–186.

Mazzeo, Domenico. "The UN and the Problem of Decolonization: The Special Committee of Twenty-Four." Ph.D. diss., Department of Political Science of the Faculty of Social Sciences of the University of Ottawa, 1969.

Ministry of Foreign Affairs, Republic of China (Taiwan). "When 'Brother Nations' Meet Together." *Taiwan Today*. Last modified March 1, 1966. https://taiwantoday.tw/news.php?unit=4&post=6892, accessed March 1, 2019.

Mitter, Rana. "Nationalism, decolonization, geopolitics and the Asian post-war." In *The Cambridge History of the Second World War*, edited by Michael Geyer and Adam Tooze, 599–622. Cambridge, UK: Cambridge University Press, 2015.

Moon, C.I. *The Sunshine Policy: In Defense of Engagement as a Path to Peace in Korea.* Seoul: Yonsei University Press, 2012.

Myrice, Erin. "The Impact of the Second World War on the Decolonization of Africa." Paper presented at *17th Annual African Studies Research*. Bowling Green, OH: Bowling Green State University, 2015.

Namboodiri, P.K.S. "China and Nonaligned." *Strategic Analysis* 3, no. 6 (1979): 221–224.

Nwaubani, Ebere. "The United States and the Liquidation of European Colonial Rule in Tropical Africa, 1941–1963." *Cahiers d'Etudes Africaines* 43, no. 171 (2003): 505–551.

Orr, Robert M. *The Emergence of Japan's Foreign Aid Power.* New York: Columbia University Press, 1990.

Przeworski, Adam, and Fernando Limongi. "Modernization: Theories and Facts," *World Politics* 49, no. 2 (1997): 155–183.

Park, Kie-Duck, "Political Parties and Democratic Consolidation in Korea." In *Asian New Democracies: The Philippines, South Korea and Taiwan Compared,* edited by Hsin-Huang Michael Hsiao, 127–156. Taipei: TFD-CAPAS, 2008.

Park, Sang-Seek. "Africa and Two Koreas: A Study of African Non-Alignment." *African Studies Review* 21, no. 1 (1978): 71–88.

Rawnsley, Gary D. *Taiwan's Informal Diplomacy and Propaganda.* Hampshire, UK: Palgrave, 2000.

Rich, Timothy S. "Renting Allies and Selling Sovereignty: Taiwan's Struggle for Diplomatic Recognition." In *The Changing Dynamics of the Relations Among China, Taiwan and the United States,* edited by Cal Clark, 175–190. Newcastle: Cambridge Scholars Publishing, 2011.

Rigger, Shelley. *Why Taiwan Matters: Small Island, Global Powerhouse.* Lanham, MD: Rowman & Littlefield Publishers, 2011.

Su, Chi. "The International Relations of the Republic of China during the 1980s." In *Taiwan in Transition: Political Development and Economic Prosperity,* edited by Bernard T.K. Joei, 101–116. Taipei: Tamkang University, 1988.

Sun, Jing. "Japan-Taiwan Relations: Unofficial in Name Only." *Asian Survey* 47, no. 5 (2007), 790–810.

Taipei Times (Taipei). "Taiwan and the UN – Withdrawal in 1971 was a historic turning point." September 12, 2001. http://www.taipeitimes.com/News/local/archives/2001/09/12/102595, accessed August 24, 2019.

The Economist (London). "A geopolitical row with China damages South Korean business further," October 19, 2017. https://www.economist.com/business/2017/10/19/a-geopolitical-row-with-china-damages-south-korean-business-further, accessed August 23, 2019.

Tien, Hung-mao. *The Great Transition: Political and Social Change in the Republic of China.* Taipei: SMC Publishing, 1989.

UN Dag Hammarskjöld Library. "Resolutions and Decisions adopted by the General Assembly during its 15th session: GAOR, 15th session, Supplement No. 16 + 16A." Last modified February 26, 2019. https://research.un.org/en/docs/ga/quick/regular/15, accessed August 23, 2019.

UN General Assembly. *10th Session, Admission of New Members to the UN. 555th Plenary.14 December 1955.* New York: UNGA, 1955.

Wang, T.Y. et al. "Structural realism and liberal pluralism. An assessment of Ma Ying-Jeou's Cross-Strait policy." In *New Thinking about the Taiwan Issue: Theoretical insights into its origins, dynamics, and prospects*, edited by Jean-Marc F. Blanchard and Dennis V. Hickey, 137–171. New York: Routledge, 2012.

Wei, George C.X. and Chen Wenshou. "Recent Taiwan-Japan Relations. Interactions, trends and perspectives." In *China-Taiwan Relations in a Global Context: Taiwan's Foreign Policy and Relations*, edited by C.X. George Wei, 92–114. New York: Routledge, 2012.

Wendt, Alexander. *Social Theory of International Politics*. Cambridge, UK: Cambridge University Press, 1999.

Wilkins, Thomas S. "Taiwan-Japan Relations in an Era of Uncertainty." *Asia Policy* 13 (2012): 113–132.

Yu, George T. "China's Role in Africa." *The Annals of the American Academy of Political and Social Science*, no. 432 (1977): 96–109.

Yufan, Hao, and Zhai Zhihai. "China's Decision to Enter the Korean War: History Revisted." *The China Quarterly* 121 (1990), 94–115.

Zhao, Linian. *Woguo jiaqiang canyu OECD guoji hezuo huodong zhi kenengxing* (Analysis on the possibilities of our country to increasingly participate in the OECD international cooperation activities). Working Paper no. 21005, Taipei: Ministry of Economy-ROC.

Zickel, Raymond E., and Eugene K. Keefe. *Soviet Union: a Country Study*. Washington, D.C.: Federal Research Division, Library of Congress, 1991.

CHAPTER 5

Tzu-Chi and the 'Moonies'

New Religious Movements in Taiwan and South Korea

Niki J.P. Alsford and Nataša Visočnik

Is religion a product of society, merely a human intervention and projection? Is it an impulse? A response perhaps to specific external variables? What happens when two culturally different societies follow similar economic, political, and socio-cultural paths? This latter question forms the basis of this edited volume that explores the similar pathways taken by South Korea (hereinafter Korea) and Taiwan. In the two case studies presented in this chapter, it is argued that new religious movements, or NRMs, are part of the very fabric of modernization theory. In the absence of state-led welfare, it often falls to grassroots-level organizations to provide assistance—religion playing a key role here. In societies marked by an economic imbalance between the rich and the poor (a product of an emerging middle-income group), it is at the grassroots level that more organizations, charities, and foundations tend to form.

In the 1950s and 1960s, in both Korea and Taiwan, the emerging middle-class—which would prove instrumental in the later democratic movements in both locations—would see the establishment of two religiously motivated organizations, the chief aim of one of which is charity. However, both have been accused of engaging in cult-like practices. The Tzu-Chi Foundation founded in Taiwan and the Unification Church (UC) in South Korea have a number of similarities that warrant further investigation.

It may be argued that producing a like-with-like reduces a study to what Marcel Detienne disdainfully called '*comparer l'incomparable*'.[1] Yet, the differences can easily be discerned—Tzu-Chi was founded on the principles of Buddhism, while UC is an interpretation of Christianity. The height of the success of Tzu-Chi was principally found after democratization.[2] In contrast, the highlight of the UC was during the period of dictatorship. What is more, the Buddhism practiced by Tzu-Chi is not esoteric, whereas UC arguably is, since it

---

1   Marcel Detienne, *Comparer l'incomparable. Oserexpérimenter et construire* (Paris: Editions du Seuil, 2009).

2   Richard Marsden, *Democracy's Dharma: Religious Renaissance and Political Development in Taiwan* (Berkeley: University of California Press, 2007), 17.

© NIKI J.P. ALSFORD AND NATAŠA VISOČNIK, 2021 | DOI:10.1163/9789004461314_006

keeps parts of its doctrine secret from non-members: a practice known as the 'heavenly deception'. Thus, a principal motivation for the comparison lies in the consideration that both were established during a period of high economic growth in the countries on which this edited volume is centered. Both hold their teachings to the concept of 'fallen humanity'. For Tzu-Chi, all humans are considered in essence equal, but it is the human heart that has fallen. For UC, it teaches that humanity has fallen and can only be restored through a messiah (a new Adam). UC argues that Jesus was a messiah, but his execution was premature in that he fathered no children. As a result, this was passed onto Sun Myung Moon (the founder of UC). Both have been accused of being a cult (discussed in more detail below) for the manner in which they have practiced their beliefs. It is true that other organizations could have been proposed as a comparative for the study of religion in Korea and Taiwan, and it is important to note that alternatives could have easily been made elsewhere. Good examples could perhaps have been made on the role of the Presbyterian Church in Taiwan and Korea, or a focus placed on the role of *Juche* in North Korea. An even more rigorous comparison could perhaps have been made in exploring the role of Conservative Christianity and the American military presence in both locations. A factor, thus, for this comparison lies foremost at the central importance they place on welfare, charity, and international relief efforts.

In Korea and Taiwan, as in other parts of Asia, the two most recognized features of religion are diversity and inclusiveness as people could belong to more than one religion at the same time. This also means that they can seek various advantages from different religions and philosophies—"education from Confucianism, offspring from Buddhism, and protection from dangers and evil forces through the mediation of a shaman.[3]"

Since religion is deeply rooted in many communities in the countries under discussion, it therefore makes sense that faith-based non-governmental organizations (NGOs) would be established and begin work in those communities. The problems that are frequently identified revolve around the practice of religious conversion: this is especially true in South Korea and Taiwan, where Buddhism is widely practiced. However, the practices and social performance of Tzu-Chi and the UC are in the minority. This is not to say that religious NGOs play no role as social service providers. On the contrary, evidence shows that a faith-based approach has the ability to develop deeper relationships with

---

3 While the role of the shaman in Korea is mostly hereditary and performed by women, the case in Taiwan is different, the shamans are mostly men. Peter Clarke, *New Religions in Global Perspective* (London and New York: Routledge, 2006), 292.

communities in the developing world.[4] This ability to foster deep connections should not be overlooked. Faith-based NGO s have the ability to fight for the marginalized. Yet, certain faith-based NGO s—and this is especially true of Christian evangelism—are often conflated with colonialism. Their primary goals being economic and political exploitation and conversion by manipulation. Both the UC and Tzu-Chi offset this to some degree as being non-Western faith-based groups. Nevertheless, the faithful of both organizations have shaped and moulded the socio-political landscape of New Religious Movements (NRM s) in their respective nations. In the context of humanitarianism, religion has been a double-edged sword. Aid can be seen as an entrée to spreading doctrine with specific aid being withheld until specific practices have been stopped. An example of this was the suggested guidelines (no alcohol or meat consumption, no smoking, and no chewing betel nut) that Tzu-Chi imposed on the indigenous communities in the relocation project that followed Typhoon Morokot in Taiwan.[5]

The link between notions of welfare and religious practice is well-documented. Religious groups play a key role in determining how well a country's welfare system has developed.[6] Their reach includes education, medical care, and other social services. In an East Asian context, unlike the dominant European welfare models, they lack uniformity. This is instead frequently centered on informal provision at the community level rooted in strong cultural-religious values.

It is within this provision of welfare that often an individual decides to follow a *Path* and set out a new *Way* to develop spiritualism. In the context of this research, both organizations are peripheral and have been born and socialised from a society's dominant religious culture. As a result, both Tzu-Chi and the UC can trace their roots to part of a wider religion, while remaining distinct from pre-existing denominations. These NRM s either push for embracing individualism and the idea of individual responsibility (as in the case of Tzu-Chi) or they seek a tightly-knit collective ideal (the UC). Since they are built upon a religious base, they frequently face a hostile reception from other religious organizations and secular institutions. The extent of this criticism is generally over the lack of agency given to its members. In other words, they are perceived

4 Wendy Tyndale, "Idealism and Practicality: The Role of Religion in Development," in *Development* 46, no. 4 (2003).

5 Chiaoning Su, "An Alternative Chronicle of Natural Disaster: Social Justice Journalism in Taiwan," *International Journal of Communication* 13 (2019): 3330.

6 Birgit Rommelspacher, "Religion and Welfare," *European Journal of Social Work* 20, no. 6 (2017).

as having been indoctrinated and are members not by their own choosing but rather through a process of coercion.

The phrase 'exercising excessive control over members'[7] is often found in the standard dictionary definition of the word 'cult'. The sinister connotation and the lack of a standard usage makes the claim of cult difficult to define.[8] This lack of a common denominator make an analysis of UC and Tzu-Chi as being cult-like a mooted line of inquiry. Yet the criteria used by Campbell addresses three markers: (1) deviance; (2) individualism; and (3) mysticism.[9] It is here that this chapter can address the similarities between UC and Tzu-Chi in the context of accusations made against them. Before doing so, it is impor-tant to note that when referring to 'cult' in a theological rather than a soci-ological sense, typically the term is applied to all religious movements with which a writer disagrees. This is typical of Christian writers who apply the term 'sect' or 'cult' synonymously to separate the 'my church' from 'your church' con-cept.[10] A key factor for a number of concerns would be the issue of 'influence'. Moreover, not all would demonstrate intolerance of other faith systems. In the case of Tzu-Chi, as a cultural institution in Taiwan, there have been attempts on the part of Tzu-Chi to mould Taiwanese society in its own moral image, while maintaining a degree of tolerance for other faith systems, particularly the Abrahamic religions. Membership, however, is counted on the regularity of donation. The accusations, thus, come largely from the claim of having four million members in Taiwan, and, therefore, an ability to exert significant social and political influence. The allegations of being cult-like generally refer to the recruitment of volunteers and doctors in their hospitals not on merit, but rather on how they display appreciation for the group's founder, Cheng Yen, and on the size of their donations.[11] It is in the enactment of their mysticism and the individualized prostration to the founder, coupled with coerced donations that centers the accusations of it being cult-like or having cult-like practices. The charisma of the group's leadership and the ability to attract converts on a significant scale is important. Yet when this clashes and disrupts traditional socio-cultural concepts of family ties and values, this leads to accusations of

---

7   Oxford English Dictionary 2013.

8   Colin Campbell, "Clarifying the Cult," *The British Journal of Sociology* 28, no. 3 (1977), 377.

9   Campbell, "Clarifying," 379.

10   Geoffrey Nelson, *Cults, New Religions and Religious Creativity* (London: Routledge, 1987), 116.

11   Pau Pernghwa Kung, "A Curious Case in Tzu Chi Foundation's Recent Scandal," *Part News (2015)*, https://partnews.mit.edu/2015/03/17/a-curious-case-in-tzu-chi-foundations-recent-scandal/, accessed May 17, 2019.

indoctrination and brainwashing. This is especially true in the cult labeling of the UC. The allegations made against the UC are far more numerous than those against Tzu-Chi. Stories of being 'brainwashed' blossomed in the 1970s as people (mainly in the United States (US)) spoke out on the 'cult problem' and 'cult techniques of recruitment' employed by the UC.[12]

Societal responses to NRM s are revealing. They highlight the difficulties of state regulation of religious practice and religious NGO s. This is particularly true in cases when the NRM s threaten perceived values and institutional structures, as was the case of the UC in the 1970s. Resistance was perhaps inevitable given the fear that change initiated by these movements would threaten existing power structures. Most notable is the role of the media. To give an example, in 1981, the UC sued the *Daily Mail* for libel against their accusation that they ended marriages and brainwashed converts. The case was dismissed by the court, and this resulted in a decline in UC activities within the UK.[13]

In a book that assesses the landscape of the studies of Korea and Taiwan, this chapter brings a comparison of two NRM s in the study of links between religion and welfare. In so doing, it argues that both Tzu-Chi and the UC were founded during a period of rapid economic growth and in the welfare needs of the accompanying growing gap between those that have and those that have not.

1   Buddhist Compassion Relief Tzu Chi Foundation

Dharma Master Cheng Yen was the religious innovator of the Buddhist Compassion Relief Tzu Chi Foundation. Since its founding in 1966, the foundation's mission has been to make a humanistic contribution to the improvement of social and community services, while providing medical care and education, both within Taiwan and abroad. Its role, therefore, is similar to that of Christian Aid in Taiwan's post-war period.[14] It was founded on 'the two-cent savings' model, which encouraged homemakers (predominately women) to put aside a bit from their daily grocery money. In many ways, this means that the active participants, who call themselves *huiyuan,* are part of an

---

12   David G. Bromley, and Anson D. Shupe Jr., *'Moonies' in America: Cult, Church and Crusade* (London: Sage, 1979), 211.

13   Geoffrey Nelson, *Cults, New Religions and Religious Creativity* (London: Routledge, 1987), 117.

14   Niki J.P. Alsford, "We Believe in Life Before Death: The Christian Aid Movement in Taiwan, 1970–78," *Journal of Historical Archaeology & Anthropological Sciences* 3(2) (2018a).

organization that, in its initial form, was similar to the mutual-aid associations that provided support to local communities. These were common elite-driven social organizations that arose in a number of developing countries, and their formation was in part prompted by insufficient state-led public support programs.[15] It is from this phenomenon that the religious movement now has volunteers in 50 countries, with 502 offices globally.

The core belief of those running the foundation is that suffering is not caused by material deprivation, but rather by spiritual poverty. During a period of high economic growth in the 1970s and 1980s, relative poverty (defined as the number of households receiving 50 percent less income than the average household) increased, whereas absolute poverty did not. This can be described as 'relative deprivation' since the people living in this category are not living in abject poverty, but rather than enjoying the exact same standard of living, they lack specific provisions.[16] This could be a television, clean clothes, or access to specific kinds of education. This state of deprivation could be permanent. Specific families that are trapped in a low-income category would stand no chance of social mobility. The emphasis for Tzu-Chi was not to look at material gain, but rather spiritual enlightenment. The term 'help the poor and educate the rich' was thus a guiding principle. By focusing on aid, Tzu-Chi employs what is referred to as the 'Four Major Missions': Charity, Medicine, Education, and Humanity. If we add to that the ongoing efforts in bone marrow donation, environmental protection, volunteerism, and international relief, these eight campaigns are collectively known as 'Tzu Chi's Eight Footprints'.

The emphasis on the rejection of economic materialism and its replacement with a collectivist lifestyle reinforces the mystical notions. A core belief of Tzu-Chi is that it is only possible for the rich to find happiness and meaning in life when they give to the poor. There is, therefore, a subsequent understanding that this would then translate downwards to the poor being motivated to help those even less fortunate than them. This downward giving is not always financial (though donations to the foundation are compulsory for uniformed volunteers). Often this is done by non-uniformed volunteers (*weiyuan* commissioners) who collect donations and distribute resources in hospitals and other day-care hospices. Volunteers would often wear vests to indicate their role, and they may be accompanied by the blue-and-white clad uniformed volunteers, the *weiyuan*.

---

15   Niki J.P. Alsford, *Transitions to Modernity: The Spirit of 1895 and the Cession of Formosa to Japan* (London: Routledge, 2018b).

16   Gordon J. Melton, "Unification Church," *Encyclopaedia Britannica* (2017), https://www.britannica.com/topic/Unification-Church, accessed December 28, 2019.

The medical mission side of Tzu-Chi was founded in 1972 by Cheng Yen. Opened as the Tzu-Chi Free Clinic for the Poor, it took on a role similar to the Presbyterian Church medical missions of the late 19th century.[17] In 1986, the Hualien Tzu-Chi General Hospital opened, and this was later followed by hospitals in Yuli, Guanshan, Dalin, Taipei, and Taichung. To foster the development of future medical professionals who share the moral collective ideals of the foundation, Cheng Yen established the Tzu Chi Nursing College in 1989. This college had a particular focus on addressing the lack of employment opportunities for indigenous women in eastern Taiwan. In July 2000, Tzu-Chi formally completed its education mission by establishing a series of programs that offered a complete curriculum, from preschool to university. The objective of Tzu-Chi schools is to enhance collective moral value based on the principles of the foundation.

These values, according to Tzu-Chi, are based on its mission of 'Humanistic Culture' that is designed to purify the human mind and pacify society.[18] Its mission is to create 'a new history for mankind' (Tzu-Chi Organisation, Mission of Humanistic Culture). This culture is predicated on compassion. Often in the spirit of *daai* (Great Love), the principal culture for Tzu-Chi is self-cultivation.[19] The charisma of leadership, however, means that principally all literature on the methods of self-cultivation and on the interpretations and practices of religious teachings is written by its founder, Cheng Yen. This means that uniformity exists in what are defined as the moral values of the movement.[20] Much like the UC, it is this charismatic leadership that has aided in the group's transnational mobilization efforts. Tzu-Chi is able to provide goods and services that states and private companies have been unable, or unwilling, to provide.

On the night of April 29, 1991, one of the deadliest tropical cyclones recorded struck the Chittagong district of south-eastern Bangladesh, with wind speeds reaching 155 mph. The storm killed 138,866 people and left as many as 10 million homeless. The global emergency response to this marked Tzu-Chi's first international relief effort. Beyond the donation of food and clothing, Tzu-Chi aided in the rebuilding of houses and schools, connecting these to a water

---

17   Niki J.P. Alsford, *Chronicling Formosa: Setting the Foundations for the Presbyterian Mission, 1865–1876* (Taipei: Shung Ye Museum, 2015).

18   Richard Marsden, *Democracy's Dharma: Religious Renaissance and Political Development in Taiwan* (Berkeley: University of California Press, 2007), 22.

19   Arnold Lindros Lau, and Jayeel Serrano Cornelio, "Tzu Chi and the Philanthropy of Filipino Volunteers," *Asian Journal of Social Science* 43: 376.

20   Marsden, *Democracy's Dharma*, 16.

supply, and setting up medical clinics. Given its origins as a local charity in Taiwan,[21] Tzu Chi is considered a broad-based humanitarian organization. In 2003, it became the first non-government organized charity group in Taiwan to attain association status within the United Nations Department of Information. According to Lee and Han,[22] there has been a recognizable shift in the way that two of Tzu-Chi's periodicals (*ciji yuekan*, Tzu-Chi Monthly; and *jingdian yuekan* Rhymes Monthly) refer to environmental awareness. There have been a series of shifts in the frequency with which references to environmental protection, recycling, and climate change appear.

'Environmental protection', as a concept, appears first and follows a lecture given by Cheng Yen in 1990. This appears as a result of communal implication, as she stated that Tzu-Chi should concentrate not just on 'teaching the wealthy' and 'assisting the poor', but also on promoting the 'task of environmental protection'.[23] This then shifted to the role of 'recycling', and again this had links to the writings of Cheng Yen, who wrote that the goal of environmental protection is living in comfortable and clean neighborhoods by helping to save resources through the act of frugality and the process of recycling. Today, the average Taiwanese person produces 850 grams of waste per day. This is down from 1.2 kilograms just 15 years ago. Recycling rates now exceed 50 percent, and many of Taiwan's incinerators run below capacity.[24] The most recent reference in the periodical, according to Han and Lee[25] is 'climate change'. The first reference to this followed Hurricane Katrina in 2005. Cheng Yen urged members to reduce unnecessary consumption in order to lower their carbon footprints. The discourse on environmentalism and climate change within Tzu-Chi clearly follows other global movements. They not only provide a call to action but are also directly involved in environmental practices. In many ways, Tzu-Chi is considered an organization rather than a religious movement. Having looked at Tzu-Chi in the case of Taiwan, this chapter will next look at Sun Myung Moon and the Unification Church.

---

21   Yu-Shuang Yao, *Taiwan's Tzu Chi as Engaged Buddhism* (Leiden: Global Oriental, 2012), 1.
22   Chengpang Lee, and Han Ling, "Recycling Bodhisattva: The Tzu-Chi Movement's Response to Global Climate Change," *Social Compass* 62, no. 3 (2015).
23   Lee and Han, "Recycling Bodhisattva," 3019.
24   Marcello Rossi, "How Taiwan Has Achieved One of the Highest Recycling Rates in the World," *Smithsonian Magazine*, https://www.smithsonianmag.com/innovation/how-taiwan-has-achieved-one-highest-recycling-rates-world-180971150/, accessed June 16, 2019.
25   Lee and Han, "Recycling Bodhisattva."

2   Unification Church and Social Welfare

The Unification Church is one of the new religious movements that has generated a great deal of controversy since its establishment, however, it has been also enormously active in all kinds of social, educational, political, and other types of activities, with the stated goal of making a harmonious society. This part of the article presents an analysis of the life and work of its controversial founder, Sun Myung Moon, focusing on the range of UC-affiliated organizations, especially those involved in social welfare, and presenting their purposes and activities. Reverend Moon was well-known as a religious figure; he was also motivated to establish many groups that are not strictly religious in their purposes. Moon was not directly involved with managing the day-to-day activities of the numerous organizations that he indirectly oversaw, yet all of them can attribute the inspiration behind their work to his leadership and teachings.

Although two of the main features of Korean religiosity are diversity and inclusiveness, when Christianity arrived on their shores, it significantly changed the religious outlook. It also reduced the level of multiple religious belonging, as Clark[26] points out. Christianity has become an influential religion in South Korea, with the number of believers in the various denominations of Catholicism and Protestantism increasing, including the new religious movements. Whenever the discussion turns to new religious movements in Korea, the focus is immediately on the Holy Spirit Association for the Unification of World Christianity (HAS-UWC, 1954–1994): a name that was later changed to the Family Federation for World Peace and Unification (FFWPU, 1994–). This organization is, of course, known widely as the Unification Church (UC), or the Moonies, after the name of founder Sun Myung Moon. As such, it is based on one man's charisma.[27] While this is the most widely known and discussed Korean movement in the West, the country has several hundred other NRMs,[28]

---

26   Clarke, *New Religions*, 292.

27   An exact number of members is extremely difficult to obtain. The UC does not publish official statistics for outsiders, explaining that the media may use these statistics against the organization. Membership is estimated at 1–2 million worldwide, with the largest number in Korea, and a US membership of approximately 10 to 30 thousand. (Unification Church History website).

28   Another such NRM is the World Mission Society Church of God (WMSCG) which is very similar to the UC in that it involves relief programs and volunteering. This group has also been very successful in achieving its goals, having been conferred the UK-based Queen's

all of which have millenarianism features as a core component of their
message.[29]

Unification Church (UC) (T'ongil-gyo) was founded in Korea in May 1954
by the Reverend Sun Myung Moon,[30] who was born into a Presbyterian family
in 1920 in what North Korea is today. The UC is also strongly millenarian in
orientation, believing that in these last days, the Lord of the Second Advent
will appear to complete the mission left unfinished by Christ, and establish the
Kingdom of Heaven on Earth.[31] Moon claims that, after praying near Mount
Myodu, Jesus Christ appeared to him and asked him to take on a special mission on Earth having to do with Heaven's work. At the beginning of the Korean
War (1950–1953) he escaped to the South Korean port city of Pusan and began
writing and teaching the Divine Principle. In 1960, he married his second wife,
Dr Hak Ja Han Moon, and together they founded an array of religious, academic, educational, arts, and peace organizations working in more than 190
nations[32]. In 1994, Moon declared that the era of the HSA-UWC had ended, and
he inaugurated a new organization: The Family Federation for World Peace
and Unification (FFWPU). This new group would include HSA-UWC members
as well as members of other religious organizations working toward common

---

Award for Voluntary Service in 2016 (WMSCG). WMSCG was established by Ahn Sang-
hong in 1964 and claims to have '1.7 million members and established 2,200 local churches
in 150 countries in just half a century' (WMSCG 'Home page'). It is also based on the charisma of one man, who even proclaimed himself to be a second Jesus, while also believing
in God the Mother, who is his wife herself and living in South Korea. The WMSCG recruits
people on the street, later proselytizing to them about their church and their importance
in the world. (WMSCG; interview with a member).

29   Clarke, *New Religions*, 293.
30   Sun Myung Moon studied engineering, first in Korea and later in Japan, where he became
      involved in the Korean independence movement and was arrested for his political activi-
      ties. Moon returned to Korea in 1945 and concentrated on developing the Divine Principle,
      the UC's most authoritative sacred text (Barker 1984). Moon's ideas were rejected as
      heretical by Christian groups in the South, so he moved to North Korea to preach his
      message of the imminent arrival of the Lord of the Second Advent, and the establishment
      of the Kingdom of God on earth—an activity that was construed by the authorities in
      the North as espionage on behalf of the South. He was imprisoned and tortured more
      than once, and even spent time as prisoner No. 596 in the notoriously repressive labour
      and concentration camp at Hungnam for inciting 'social chaos'. Hungnam was liberated
      by UN troops at the start of the Korean War in 1950, and Moon fled to Pusan, where he
      continued preaching. In 1952, he completed the draft of the Divine Principle at Pusan and
      founded the Unification Church. Soon afterward, he was imprisoned again, this time for
      alleged illicit sexual practices, a charge that was later dropped. The UC was given legal
      status by the South Korean Government in 1963. (Clarke 2006, 296–97).
31   Clarke, *New Religions*, 296.
32   Rev. Sun Myung Moon website.

goals, especially on issues of morality and reconciliation between people of different religions, nations, and races.[33]

Unlike most of the other minor religious groups in Korea, Unificationism was unique in having spread beyond the peninsula's shores: first to Japan and the US in 1959; in 1972 to the United Kingdom and Europe; and by 1975 a UC presence had been established in 120 nations.[34] The Unification vision of the creation, fall, and restoration of humanity is not unique, however. Robbins[35] presents Reverend Moon's movement as an attempt at a totalitarian response to the cultural fragmentation of society. There are many controversies surrounding the UC, sometimes derided as the 'dark side of the Moon',[36] the most well-known of which is undoubtedly their mass weddings where hundreds or even thousands of couples are married. Moreover, the UC's teachings are viewed unfavourably by most mainstream Christian churches, and those who join are allegedly subjected to 'heavenly deception'[37] and various brainwashing techniques, and thus the UC is denoted as a cult. The public controversy over the group's methods raises questions as to whether this movement should even be treated as a religion.[38]

The 1990s appeared far more favourable to the movement than the 1970s and 1980s when accusations of brainwashing, heavenly deception, and tax evasion were leveled at the UC by anti-cult groups in various parts of the world,

---

33   see Melton, "Unification Church"; Family Federation for World Peace and Unification, http://familyfedihq.org/about/, accessed January 20, 2019.

34   Georg D. Chryssides, *The Advent of Sun Myung Moon: The Origins, Beliefs and Practices of the Unification Church*, (Basingstoke: Macmillan, 1991), 21.

35   Thomas Robbins, Dick Anthony, Madeline Doucas and Thomas Curtis, "The Last Civil Religion: Reverend Moon and the Unification Church," *Sociological Analysis* 37, no. 2 (Summer 1976): 111.

36   Rachael Bletchly, "Dark Side of the Moon: How Megalomaniac Moonie Leader Built a Billion-dollar Business Empire Through Sinister Cult," *Mirror*, (September 4, 2012), https://www.mirror.co.uk/news/Cworld-news/inside-the-sinister-moonie-cult-how-1301689, accessed January 15, 2019.

37   Eileen Barker, "Living the Divine Principle. Inside the Reverend Sun Myung Moon's Unification Church in Britain," *Archives de sciences sociales des religions* 23, no 45.1 (Jan.–Mar., 1978): 75, http://www.jstor.org/stable/30124308.

38   As Chryssides (1991, 3) points out, some new religious movements like the UC are fronts for political organizations or business operations, and for that reason they are depriving the new religions of the right to a specific religious identity. This can also raise the methodological question of how to study this new religious movement, whether the normal canons of religious scholarship can be applied, while the sociological approaches to understanding the Unification Church cannot provide a single answer to the question of what is the sociological problem of the UC (Beckford 1978, 98; see also Parsons 1989, 209–10).

and Reverend Moon was jailed in the US on charges of tax evasion.[39] Held together by the reverend's charismatic authority, the Unification Church and Movement have so far avoided serious fragmentation. There are, however, signs of routinization and a loss of motivation among some long-term and second-generation members. Some of the former regret having dedicated so much time and energy to the neglect of their families and friends. They no longer have a sense of commitment and remain involved as much for practical reasons as out of conviction.[40] Today, seven years after Reverend Moon's death in 2012, his work is being continued by his widow, Dr Hak Ja Han Moon (who is known as the True Mother), and some of their children, and many of the organization's operations are still flourishing all around the world.

There are many social, educational, political, media and other types of organizations that have been founded in the name of the UC. The Unification Church has also developed into an international crusade, known as the Unification Movement (UM), that is spread through education at a few universities in the US and South Korea, a Theological seminary, and even the Bolshoi Ballet Academy in Washington, DC.[41] Likewise, the Professors World Peace Academy (PWPA; see website) is an educational organization that supports the academic community's role in the pursuit of world peace. It can be considered social action in the sense that it strives to unite science and values and seeks to apply scientific knowledge to the betterment of the human community.[42] The group's involvement in the media is apparent in its establishment of many newspapers worldwide,[43] and there is also a political wing of the UM, like CAUSA[44] whose principal function has been to undermine communism by publishing some treatises.[45]

As a Korean War refugee himself, Reverend Moon understood first-hand the importance of humanitarian relief in situations of war, disaster, and poverty. Following his vision of living for others, Moon has founded several worldwide humanitarian organizations. A unique feature of these relief organizations are programs of personalized service: service internships and volunteer programs

---

39   Clarke, *New Religions*, 299.
40   Clarke, *New Religions*, 299.
41   Clarke, *New Religions*, 298.
42   Richard Quebedeaux, ed. *Lifestyle: Conversations with the Members of Unification Church* (New York: Unification Theological Seminary, 1982), 83.
43   Like the *Washington Times*, as well as the Korean daily *Segye Ilbon*, the *Sekai Nippon* in Tokyo, and the Latin American daily *Tiempos Del Mundo*, published in Buenos Aires, Argentina.
44   Confederation of Associations for the Unity of the Societies of America.
45   Clarke, *New Religions*, 298.

that provide opportunities for thousands of individuals to go and personally serve in places of need.[46] While social welfare[47] is defined as a means to provide organized public or private social services for the assistance of disadvantaged individuals, church-based social welfare is founded upon the Christian philosophy as proposed by theologians. Su Kang[48] introduces the term 'Church social welfare' and defines welfare as 'An enjoyable condition consisting of good health, abundant life, and easy environment'. Kang adds that people involved in social welfare not only help other people but also experience personal satisfaction—an assertion that can be confirmed by some members of the UC as well. As such, the Family Federation's Social Welfare ideology of UC is based on interdependence, mutual prosperity, and universally shared values. That kind of society is a community, 'where God is in the centre and all the members of the society live together, prosper together, and live a life of ethics. A perfect society is God's purpose of creation and that is a society of welfare'.[49] The aim and purpose of Family Federation's social welfare are to realize a welfare state that is 'a Heaven on Earth'. They are trying to solve the problem of poverty for members by creating jobs, helping immigrant women and multicultural families with economic and educational support for children and adults, running counseling programs, offering professional training, and providing health, economic, and family therapy to maintain and restore the family.[50]

---

46 Rev. Sun Myung Moon: His Works, http://www.reverendsunmyungmoon.org/works_humanitarian.html, accessed January 26, 2018. See also Hwang Po Kun 황보군, "Segyepyeong hwatong-il gajeong-yeonhab bogjij eongchaeg-e gwanhan yeongu—gyeong-gi bugbugyoguleul sungsim-eulo세계평화통일가정연합 복지정책에 관한 연구—경기북부교구를 숭심으로 (A Study on the Welfare Policy of the Family Federation for World Peace and Unification. Centered on North Kyeonggi Region)," PhD Thesis, (Gyeonggi: Seonhak UP Graduate School, 2017).

47 Generally, social welfare is a generic term for various social services such as social policy, social security, public health, medical treatment, housing, employment, and education, all of which provide protection, promotion, guidance, treatment, and rehabilitation for those who are unable to do so on their own, and it also guarantees health and happiness for all citizens. In other words, social welfare helps people to satisfy the basic human need for food, housing, and clothing, including profit, health, knowledge, leisure, and cultural desires. Social welfare is also legislation, programs, and services that are arranged to help a person to maintain a healthy relationship with family and companions at work (Kang 2010, 18–19).

48 In Su Kang, "Church Growth through Social Welfare in South Korean Churches: Its Situation and Reformation Plan," PhD Thesis (Lynchburg, Virginia: Liberty Baptist Theological Seminary, 2010), 16–17.

49 Hwang, "Segyepyeong," 22.

50 Hwang, "Segyepyeong," 22.

Furthermore, the best known and most widespread organization promoting world peace and solving conflicts through interreligious initiatives—and whose aim is to strengthen the family as the basic unit for the wellbeing of society beside FFWPU (or UC) itself—is the Universal Peace Federation (UPF), otherwise known as the International Interreligious Federation for World Peace (IIFWP)[51], whose goal is to achieve an ideal world of peace—proposed by Sun Myung Moon through his messages on eliminating borders and building a peace bridge.[52] This organization also has a global reach in its provision of humanitarian aid. In response to natural disasters, UPF provides donations and volunteers to help with immediate relief and longer-term clean-up. After the tsunami in Japan, UPF-affiliated youths cleaned debris from homes. When Thailand was struck by floods, volunteers brought food and water to stranded survivors, as well as cleaning an Islamic school. Other projects aided people in Haiti, Pakistan, Russia, and India,[53] which is another example of how many charitable efforts were initiated by the churches and by Sun Myung Moon's influence on the emerging social work profession.

Today, some church-related organizations have secularized, dropping their former church affiliation. Others have maintained these ties, often wondering how to balance demands from both secular and religious sectors.[54] Most of these organizations are independently incorporated and non-profit organizations. Some are completely staffed by Unification people; others are a mixture; others still are non-Unification but are substantially funded or otherwise aided by the Unification Church. Another big and widely known organization is The International Relief Friendship Fund (IRFF), which has been active in sending aid to underdeveloped countries. It is an independent public foundation funded by members and non-members alike. IRFF now has operations in 27 countries. It works with various organizations through which it can provide

---

51 Founded in 1999, IIFWP is an NGO that has Special Consultative Status with the Economic and Social Council of the United Nations. One of its most important aims is the establishment of an interreligious council of the leaders of the world's religions and political leaders to advise and support the United Nations in its efforts for world peace. (UPF website).

52 An Yonhee 안연희, "Munseonmyeong seonsaeng-ui isangsahoelongwa segyegongdongche bijeon: 'guggyeongcheolpye'wa 'pyeonghwaui gil'eul jungsim eulo문선명 선생의 이상사회론과 세계공동체 비전: '국경철폐'와 '평화의 길'을 중심 으로 (Rev. Sun Myung Moon's Thought of Ideal World and Vision of World Community)." 평화와 종교 3 (2017): 155–85.

53 Rev. Sun Myung Moon; Universal Peace Federation, A global Network of Peacebuilders, http://www.upf.org/, accessed January 18, 2019.

54 Ellen F. Netting, "Church-related Agencies and Social Welfare," *Social Service Review*, (September 1984): 404–5.

social services overseas to help people struck by disaster, poverty, famine, and war. The IRFF aims to improve humankind's physical health; the pharmaceutical and machine tool companies owned by Reverend Moon aid in creating a prosperous society.[55] To address these problems, IRFF has established programs of rural development, educational and technical training, urban and community service, and emergency disaster relief.[56] As they explain on the website, regarding short-term relief assistance, IRFF provides shipments of supplies to alleviate the hardship of people left helpless by disasters. Mobile medical teams were formed to provide emergency service to troubled areas. Their mission statement is 'IRFF provides immediate humanitarian relief to individuals and families devastated by poverty, illness, natural disasters, and conflict while also providing opportunities for long-term sustainable development through educational and economic opportunities'.[57]

There are a few other groups providing services that were established in the US, like Project Volunteer, which is the social services entity of the California Unification Church. They have distributed tons of food to people in need and are involved in recycling, vocational training, and many other community projects. They are innovative; they deal with networking resources for the benefit of local community needs.[58] A similar group is called New Society Social Programs, which is a project-based in Harlem, New York. It is run by Unification people from Harlem and elsewhere who feel that God wants them to help in that particular situation. Their services have been very successful and include distribution; they are widely recognized.[59]

The Reverend Moon had an interest in medical service as well, specifically in the implications of his divine principle for holistic health and the relationship between acupuncture, chiropractic, shiatsu, and other traditional medicines and thus established the group World Medical Health Foundation, which holds conferences and seminars and has plans to open clinics in the near future. An institution called Isshin Hospital Medical Teams, founded in 1978 in Japan, sends out medical teams to crisis areas in Asia, Africa, and Latin America.[60] Bringing together people from long-time enemy nations,

55   Chryssides, *The Advent of Sun Myung Moon*, 174.
56   George D. Chryssides, and Margaret Z. Wilkins, eds., *A Reader in New Religious Movements: Readings in the Study of New Religious* (London and New York: Continuum, 2006), 278.
57   International Relief Friendship Foundation, https://www.irff.org/, accessed January 20, 2019.
58   Quebedeaux, *Lifestyle*, 82; see also Chryssides and Wilkins, *A Reader*, 278.
59   Quebedeaux, *Lifestyle*, 82.
60   Quebedeaux, *Lifestyle*, 83.

such teams help overcome national prejudices to serve the greater good, thus embodying Moon's vision of service projects that help others and also heal divisions of nationality, race, and religion.

The following two organizations provide care for the elderly, children, and women. Aewon Voluntary Service Foundation (AVSF), which was founded in 1994 in Korea, works primarily in Korea and runs programs for the elderly, needy children, orphanages, and the disabled. It is an active member of the Korea Council of Volunteer Organizations. Founded in 1992 to promote the value of women, the Women's Federation for World Peace Service Projects (WFWP) runs humanitarian aid and service projects, the most famous and important of which began in 1993 when WFWP sent teams of 10 Japanese service volunteers to serve for three years in 60 of the world's neediest nations.[61] Another group involved in providing services to children is the Religious Youth Service (RYS). Founded in 1986 to respond to post-modern disillusionment and promote the twin ideals of interreligious harmony and public service, RYS is a unique service organization where youth leaders of various faiths work on-site together to serve a needy community, like reforestation and the building of schools and clinics.[62]

The establishment of these social organizations that provide services to people in need is seen as a restoration of themselves and humanity from divine principle, which requires tangible actions; it should show how solutions should be approached and executed in the real world of particular political situations and social complexities. The research into the many relief organizations that spread out of the UC shows the enormous influence and inspiration of Reverend Moon and, according to UC members, the Principle.[63] There are people inspired by Him who are seeking answers in prayer and in their personal lives, within the racial and cultural admixtures that their communities represent. As Stark points out, people are drawn into these organizations by searching for a way to practically achieve the goal of restoration and personal satisfaction, which give them the energy to commit with volunteering and as results can be personally awarded.[64] But they can also be paying a high price for their membership. However, when commitment levels are high, groups can

---

61   WMSCG, http://watv. org/, accessed July 21, 2019.
62   Chryssides, *The Advent of Sun Myung Moon*, 168; see also RYS Brochure (2013), http://www.upf.org/transfer/2013-upf-pr-kit/rys-brochure-1024-11a-vw.pdf, accessed January 18, 2019.
63   Quebedeaux, *Lifestyle*, 75, 83.
64   Rodney Stark, "Why Religious Movements Succeed or Fail: A Revised General Model," *Cults and New Religious Movements. A Reader,* edited by Lorne L. Dawson (Malden, MA, et al.: Blackwell Publishing, 2003), 263.

undertake all manner of collective actions and these are not limited only to the psychic realm.

3   Conclusion

It is said that one purpose of these non-sectarian organizations is to pursue social respectability, as Moon and his followers believe that their authoritarian reconstitution of the civil religion will optimally communalize the whole of society. The UC has been able to envision and substantially begin a network of non-profit organizations. They are run by persons who, while not primarily interested in personal fulfilment, are trying to be unselfish and are serving at a high level of freedom and authenticity. Service has to do with reaching out to the genuineness of humanity and human nature. It exists to address the human condition. These service projects founded by Moon were designed to meet emergency needs in times of natural disaster, disease, poverty, and war, and they have brought hope and relief to millions of people across national, racial, and religious boundaries, and as such, they also assert people's need to create order in the world. However, a civil religion which may maintain their plausibility only by actively attempting to control secular institutions and which provides rationales for sacrificing individual interests in favor of the common good may appear superfluous[65] and—with its rhetoric of achieving world unification—also utopian, as Hendricks points out.[66]

Tzu-Chi is the largest and most influential Buddhist organization in Taiwan. Its impact extends far beyond this boundary and is a clear influencer in many other countries. The multiple angles from which one can look at Tzu-Chi makes the organization hard to define. The charisma of its leader and the emphasis on conforming to moral values has meant that Tzu-Chi can be considered a cult. Its base as a form of Buddhism—but not coherent to any school—has given it the label of a New Religious Movement. The exclusive emphasis on Cheng Yen's teaching and interpretation has given the organization the title of being a charismatic movement. What is more, the uniformed volunteers—those who have financially donated—has given rise to a belief that Tzu-Chi is simply a middle-class movement.

---

65   Robbins et al., "The Last," 123.
66   Tyler O. Hendricks, 2004–2005, "Unification Politics in Theory and Practice," *Journal of Unification Studies* 6, https://journals.uts.edu/volume-vi-2004-2005/57-unification -politics-in-theory-and-practice.

Given the position of Tzu-Chi and its comparison with the UC, it is argued here that Tzu-Chi's efforts in international humanitarian relief makes it less comparable with the UC and perhaps more comparable with the Red Cross or Christian Aid. Comparisons can be made in terms of the charisma of these groups' respective leader-founders, and their incoherence as to specific schools within their respective faiths. No other church follows the principles of the UC, just as no other Buddhist organization follows Tzu-Chi. The similarities in the economic development of both South Korea and Taiwan make a case that a comparison could be made of the middle-class element of donation and membership between the two.

References

Alsford, Niki J.P. *Chronicling Formosa: Setting the Foundations for the Presbyterian Mission, 1865–1876*. Taipei: Shung Ye Museum, 2015.

Alsford, Niki J.P. "We Believe in Life Before Death: The Christian Aid Movement in Taiwan, 1970–78." *Journal of Historical Archaeology & Anthropological Sciences* 3, no. 2 (2018a): 219–27.

Alsford, Niki J.P. *Transitions to Modernity: The Spirit of 1895 and the Cession of Formosa to Japan*. London: Routledge, 2018b.

An, Yonhee 안연희. "Munseonmyeong seonsaeng-ui isangsahoelongwa segyegong-dongche bijeon: 'guggyeongcheolpye'wa 'pyeonghwaui gil'eul jungsim eul 문선명 선생의 이상사회론과 세계공동체 비전: '국경철폐'와 '평화의 길'을 중심 으로 (Rev. Sun Myung Moon's Thought of Ideal World and Vision of World Community)." 평화와 종교 3 (2017): 155–85.

Barker, Eileen. "Living the Divine Principle. Inside the Reverend Sun Myung Moon's Unification Church in Britain." *Archives de sciences sociales des religions* 23 (45.1) (Jan.–Mar., 1978): 75–93. http://www.jstor.org/stable/30124308.

Beckford, James A. "Through the Looking-Glass and out the Other Side: Withdrawal from Reverend Moon's Unification Church." *Archives de sciences sociales des religions* 45 (1), (Jan.–Mar. 1978): 95–116. Accessed December 18, 2018. http://www.jstor.org/stable/30124309.

Bletchly, Rachael. "Dark Side of the Moon: How Megalomaniac Moonie Leader Built a Billion-dollar Business Empire Through Sinister cult." *Mirror*, September 4, 2012. Accessed January 15, 2019. https://www.mirror.co.uk/news/Cworld-news/inside-the-sinister-moonie-cult-how-1301689.

Bromley, David G, and Anson D. Shupe Jr. *'Moonies' in America: Cult, Church and Crusade*. London: Sage, 1979.

Campbell, Colin. "Clarifying the Cult." *The British Journal of Sociology* 28, no. 3 (1977): 375–88.

Chryssides, Georg D. *The Advent of Sun Myung Moon: The Origins, Beliefs and Practices of the Unification Church*. Basingstoke: Macmillan, 1991.

Chryssides, George D., and Margaret Z. Wilkins, eds. *A Reader in New Religious Movements: Readings in the Study of New Religious*. London and New York: Continuum, 2006.

Clarke, Peter. *New Religions in Global Perspective*. London in New York: Routledge, 2006.

Detienne, Marcel. *Comparer l'incomparable. Oserexpérimenter et construire*. Paris: Editions du Seuil, 2009.

Family Federation for World Peace and Unification. Accessed January 20, 2019. http://familyfedihq.org/about/.

Hendricks, Tyler O. "Unification Politics in Theory and Practice." *Journal of Unification Studies* 6 (2004–2005): 61–84. https://journals.uts.edu/volume-vi-2004–2005/57-unification-politics-in-theory-and-practice.

Hwang, Po Kun 황보균. "세계평화통일가정연합 복지정책에 관한 연구— 경기북부교구를 중심으로 (A Study on the Welfare Policy of the Family Federation for World Peace and Unification. Centered on North Kyeonggi Region)." 학위논문(박사) PhD Thesis, 경기도 Gyeonggi: 선학UP대학원대학교: 목회학과 Seonhak UP Graduate School, 2017.

International Relief Friendship Foundation. Accessed January 20, 2019. https://www.irff.org/.

International Religious Foundation. Accessed January 27, 2019. https://uia.org/s/or/en/1100039050.

Kang, In Su. "Church Growth through Social Welfare in South Korean Churches: Its Situation and Reformation Plan." PhD Thesis. Lynchburg, Virginia: Liberty Baptist Theological Seminary, 2010.

Kung, Pau Pernghwa. "A Curious Case in Tzu Chi Foundation's Recent Scandal." *Part News* (2015). Accessed May 17, 2019. https://partnews.mit.edu/2015/03/17/a-curious-case-in-tzu-chi-foundations-recent-scandal/.

Lau, Arnold Lindros, and Jayeel Serrano Cornelio. "Tzu Chi and the Philanthropy of Filipino Volunteers." *Asian Journal of Social Science* 43 (2015): 376–99.

Lee, Chengpang, and Han Ling. "Recycling Bodhisattva: The Tzu-Chi Movement's Response to Global Climate Change." *Social Compass* 62, no. 3 (2015): 311–25.

Marsden, Richard. *Democracy's Dharma: Religious Renaissance and Political Development in Taiwan*. Berkeley: University of California Press, 2007.

Melton, Gordon J. "Unification Church." *Encyclopaedia* Britannica, 2017. Accessed December 28, 2019. https://www.britannica.com/topic/Unification-Church.

Merton, Robert K. *Social Theory and Social Structure*. New York: The Free Press, 1957.

Nelson, Geoffrey. *Cults, New Religions and Religious Creativity*. London: Routledge, 1987.

Netting, F. Ellen. "Church-related Agencies and Social Welfare." *Social Service Review* (September 1984): 404–20.

Quebedeaux, Richard, ed. *Lifestyle: Conversations with the Members of Unification Church*. New York: Unification Theological Seminary, 1982.

Parsons, Arthur S. "The Secular Contribution to Religious Innovation: A Case Study of the Unification Church." *Sociological Analysis* 50, no. 3 (1989): 209–27.

Professor World Peace Academy. Accessed January 20, 2019. https://pwpa.org/.

Rev. Sun Myung Moon: His Works. Accessed January 26, 2018. http://www.reverend-sunmyungmoon.org/works_humanitarian.html.

Robbins, Thomas, Dick Anthony, Madeline Doucas and Thomas Curtis. "The Last Civil Religion: Reverend Moon and the Unification Church."*Sociological Analysis* 37, no. 2, (Summer 1976): 111–25.

Rommelspacher, Birgit. "Religion and Welfare." *European Journal of Social Work* 20, no. 6 (2017): 795–800.

Rossi, Marcello. "How Taiwan Has Achived One of the Highest Recycling Rates in the World." *Smithsonian Magazine*. Accessed June 16, 2019. https://www.smithsonianmag.com/innovation/how-taiwan-has-achieved-one-highest-recycling-rates-world-180971150/.

RYS Brochure. 2013. Accessed January 18, 2019. http://www.upf.org/transfer/2013-upf-pr-kit/rys-brochure-1024-11a-vw.pdf.

Stark, Rodney. "Why Religious Movements Succeed or Fail: A Revised General Model. "*Cults and New Religious Movements. A Reader,* edited by Lorne L. Dawson, 259–70. Malden, MA, et al.: Blackwell Publishing, 2003.

Su, Chiaoning. "An Alternative Chronicle of Natural Disaster: Social Justice Journalism in Taiwan." *International Journal of Communication* 13 (2019): 3321–40.

The Women's Federation for World Peace. Accessed January 27, 2019. http://www.wfwp.org/.

Tyndale, Wendy. "Idealism and Practicality: The Role of Religion in Development." *Development* 46, no. 4 (2003): 22–28.

Tzu Chi Organisation, Mission of Humanistic Culture. Accessed June 20, 2019. https://www.tzuchi.org.sg/en/our-missions/humanistic-culture/.

Universal Peace Federation gatefold pamphlet. Accessed January 26, 2018. https://storage.googleapis.com/go1.upf.org/resource/gate-fold/2018-upf-gate-fold-27.85cmx-25.4cm-v0819-press.pdf.

Universal Peace Federation. A global Network of Peacebuilders. Accessed January 18, 2019. http://www.upf.org/.

Unification Church History, Beliefs, and Practices. Accessed January 20, 2019. File://J:/SUn%20Myung%20Moon/Unification%20Church/Unification%20Church%20 2005.pdf.

Yao, Yu-Shuang. *Taiwan's Tzu Chi as Engaged Buddhism*. Leiden: Global Oriental, 2012.

WMSCG 'Home page'. Accessed July 21, 2019. http://zionusa.org/ on.

WMSCG. Accessed July 21, 2019. http://watv. org/.

CHAPTER 6

Park Geun-hye and Tsai Ing-wen

The First Female Presidents of South Korea and Taiwan

Young-Im Lee

1 Introduction

This chapter analyzes the first female presidents of South Korea and Taiwan, Park Geun-hye and Tsai Ing-wen, focusing on each one's biographical background, term as party chairperson, presidential bid, and election results. It is often argued that the candidates' gender is not important in Taiwan's presidential elections but that cross-strait relations are. Sullivan and Lee stated, "that gender hardly featured as an issue in her [Tsai's] election is indicative of a society in Taiwan where 'tradition' is becoming less of a barrier to political participation."[1] Similarly, Park Geun-hye's family ties to the late president Park Chung-hee are often considered more significant than her gender to explain her rise to the presidency. While acknowledging that candidates' gender is not the most decisive factor for the voters, this analysis shows that gender was relevant to how each woman received her party's nomination and framed her campaign.

Women have continually broken the top national executive glass ceiling around the world since 1960, when Sirimavo Bandaranaike became the world's first female prime minister.[2] As of November 2018, 20 women in 14 Asian countries, including Taiwan, have served as presidents or prime ministers, and five are currently in office. They include ten female prime ministers and ten female presidents, and eight have family ties to other leaders.[3] Dr. Tsai

---

1 Jonathan Sullivan and Chun-Yi Lee, "Introduction," in *A New Era in Democratic Taiwan: Trajectories and Turning Points in Politics and Cross-Strait Relations*, ed. Jonathan Sullivan and Chun-Yi Lee (London and New York: Routledge, 2018), 1–9.

2 Melinda Adams, "Women's Executive Leadership in Africa: Ellen Johnson Sirleaf and Broader Patterns of Change," *Politics & Gender* 4, no. 3 (2008), 475–85; Farida Jalalzai, *Shattered, Cracked, or Firmly Intact: Women and the Executive Glass Ceiling Worldwide* (New York, NY: Oxford University Press, 2013).

3 Young-Im Lee and Farida Jalalzai, "President Park Geun-Hye of South Korea: A Woman President without Women?," *Politics & Gender* 13, no. 4 (2017), 597–617; Worldwide Guide to Women in Leadership, "Women Presidential Candidates," 2019, http://www.guide2women-leaders.com/woman_presidential_candidates.htm.

Ing-wen (蔡英文; hereafter, Tsai) joined this wave of women national leaders in January 2016, formally taking office in May 2016. In May 2020, she began her second presidential term after a landslide victory in January 2020. Tsai is the first woman president of Taiwan and one of the few women in Asia to assume the top national executive office without kinship ties to former male political leaders. President Park Geun-hye (hereinafter, Park) is a daughter of former authoritarian president Park Chung-hee and was elected in 2012. However, she did not finish her five-year term, as she was impeached in 2016 and was convicted in the following year.

This chapter compares the political careers and election campaigns of these two leaders, who were elected in societies that share similar trajectories of political and economic development. Both Taiwan and South Korea have dual executive leadership featuring a strong president and a weaker prime minister in terms of constitutionally granted power; the president is elected by a popular vote, and the president appoints the prime minister. Due to the tensions with their non-democratic neighbors, Beijing and Pyongyang, national security and foreign affairs are prominent issues in their presidential elections, which are usually considered "masculine" issues.[4] Taiwan and South Korea achieved rapid economic growth in the 1970s and 1980s and were lauded as two of the Asian Tiger economies. Both were under authoritarian political leadership during this time of economic prosperity; the Taiwanese martial law was lifted in 1987, and South Koreans achieved a democratic transition that same year. Taiwanese and South Korean society exhibit similar levels of women's status, even though Taiwan is slightly less unequal. As of May 2020, 42 percent of the national legislative members (the National Legislative Yuan) in Taiwan were women, whereas only 19 percent of South Korea's national legislators were.[5] The World Values Surveys show that 44 percent of South Korean respondents believe that men make better political leaders, while 35 percent of Taiwanese respondents agreed with that belief in 2012.[6] Regarding labor participation (aged 15 and older, in 2017), 51 percent of Taiwanese women and 67 percent of Taiwanese men are employed, whereas 47 percent of South

4   Leonie Huddy and Nayda Terkildsen, "Gender Stereotypes and the Perception of Male and Female Candidates," *American Journal of Political Science* 37, no. 1 (1993), 119–47.

5   Inter-Parliamentary Union, "Percentage of Women in National Parliaments – Ranking as of May 1, 2020," IPU Parline, 2020, https://data.ipu.org/women-ranking?month=5&year=2020; Taiwan Central Election Commission, "2020 Legislator Election," Taiwan Central Election Commission, 2020, https://www.cec.gov.tw/english/cms/le/32472.

6   World Values Survey, "World Values Survey," 2015, http://www.worldvaluessurvey.org/wvs.jsp, accessed May 1, 2020.

Korean women and 71 percent of Korean men are employed (the OECD average is 61.2 percent).[7]

Despite the social similarities of their backgrounds, the two leaders are quite different, both politically and personally. In addition to differences in their family backgrounds, Park hails from a conservative party, whereas Tsai is part of the Democratic Progressive Party (民進黨, hereafter, DPP), which was organized as part of the *Dangwai* (黨外) movement during the Martial Law in Taiwan. The DPP is a catch-all party that, as its name suggests, embraces social movements; some of its members, such as Yu Mei-nu (尤美女) and Hsiao Bi-khim (蕭美琴), are strong advocates of liberal social issues. Running for the 2016 presidential election, Tsai openly supported marriage equality, making her the first presidential candidate to do so in Taiwan. These differences notwithstanding, Park and Tsai are similar as neither identifies herself as a feminist even though they were both trailblazers in the male-dominated field of politics. Both only reluctantly embraced the slogan of "the first female president" at later stages of their campaigns, and Tsai did not do so in her second presidential bid in 2016. The rest of this chapter will show that the two leaders had to navigate presidential campaigns in similarly gendered terrain.

2   Park Geun-hye: Biographical Background

Since the first presidential election in South Korea in 1948, only 5 of the 63 presidential candidates have been women. Park Geun-hye was the first female candidate from a major party who had a realistic chance of winning the presidency.[8] Park was born in 1952 in Daegu, South Korea, the first daughter of former president Park Chung-hee and Yook Young-soo. The couple had another daughter and a son. Park Geun-hye inherited a controversial political legacy from her father, whose sixteen-year presidency started with a military coup which he led in 1961. Park's family ties are the most prominent factor in

---

7   Organisation for Economic Co-operation and Development, "OECD Data," OECD, 2019; Statistics Korea, "2018 Tonggyero Boneun Yeoseongui Sam (in Korean)," Kostat.go.kr, 2019, http://kostat.go.kr/portal/korea/kor_nw/1/6/1/index.board?bmode=read&aSeq=368636; Foundation for Women's Rights Promotion and Development, "Gender Indicators in Taiwan (姓別指標資訊平臺)," Foundation for Women's Rights Promotion and Development, 2019, http://www.gender-indicators.org.tw, accessed May 6, 2019.

8   Worldwide Guide to Women in Leadership, "Women Presidential Candidates"; Joowon Jin, "Yeokdae Daeseon Wanju Yeoseong Huboneun Gyeou 4myeong (in Korean),'" *Women News*, April 17, 2017, http://www.womennews.co.kr/news/articleView.html?idxno=113273, accessed June 20, 2019.

explaining her political career. Every turn of her personal and political life has been intertwined with her being the daughter of the former president. Even though South Korea experienced rapid industrialization during Park Chung-hee's term, he severely undermined democracy by changing the Constitution to guarantee his lifetime presidency, imposing martial law, and repressing labor movements.[9] The country is still divided as to how to evaluate his presidency. In an annual survey conducted by Gallup Korea, asking who was the "best performing South Korean president," Park Chung-hee was ranked 1st with 44 percent overall support in 2015. Nearly 91 percent of Park Geun-hye's party supporters answered that Park Chung-hee was the best president in South Korean history, and even 48 percent of the Democratic Party supporters did (the main rival party). On the other hand, 72 percent of the respondents also selected dictatorship/martial law/deteriorating democracy as his negative political legacy.[10]

Park Geun-hye served as an acting First Lady after her mother was accidentally killed during a botched assassination targeting her father in 1974. With that capacity, Park appeared at the official government functions and greeted foreign dignitaries. Park capitalized on this role to emphasize her foreign affairs credentials in her autobiography published in 2007.[11] After her father was also assassinated in 1979, she led a private life, mainly focusing on working with memorial foundations for her parents. Then, the ruling Grand National Party (GNP, the *Saenuri* Party's predecessor) recruited her to save Lee Hoi-Chang's faltering presidential campaigns in 1997.[12]

3   Entering Politics after the 1997 Asian Financial Crisis

The existing literature shows that political crises can open up a window of opportunity for political leaders, especially for women,[13] and Park's political

---

9   Young-Im Lee, "From First Daughter to First Lady to First Woman President: Park Geun-Hye's Path to the South Korean Presidency," *Feminist Media Studies* 17, no. 3 (2017), 377–91.

10   Gallup Korea, "Daily Opinion Je 174ho (2015nyeon 8wol 1ju) – Yeokdae Daetongnyeong Pyeonggawa Geu Iyu (in Korean)," Gallup Korea, 2015, http://www.gallup.co.kr/gallupdb/ reportContent.asp?seqNo=676, accessed May 1 2020.

11   Geun-Hye Park, *Jeonmangeun Nareul Danryong Sikigo Huimangeun Nareul Woomjikinda* (in Korean) (Seoul, Korea: Wisdom House, 2007).

12   Lee, "From First Daughter to First Lady to First Woman President: Park Geun-Hye's Path to the South Korean Presidency," 382.

13   Mark Mulcahy and Carol Linehan, "Females and Precarious Board Positions: Further Evidence of the Glass Cliff," *British Journal of Management* 25, no. 3 (July 5, 2014), 425–38; Michelle K. Ryan, S. Alexander Haslam, and Clara Kulich, "Politics and the Glass

entry fits into that pattern. In 1997, the Asian Financial Crisis, which started in Thailand, swept South Korea. The value of the Korean currency halved between June and December 1997. Several chaebols and at least 3000 companies of all sizes went bankrupt or otherwise failed, and finally, South Korea received a 57 billion USD bailout from the International Monetary Fund.[14] As the ruling party of President Kim Young-sam, the GNP was criticized and held responsible for the crisis. South Korea was preparing for the presidential election in December that year. Three weeks before the election, public opinion polls showed Lee Hoi-chang of the GNP trailing behind Kim Dae-jung by a small margin.[15] In addition to the financial crisis, Lee's loss of support was due to bribery charges and his son's avoidance of mandatory military service using his father's influence. To salvage Lee's bleak electoral prospects, the party leaders approached Park Geun-hye to gain support from the voters who were nostalgic for Park Chung-hee's presidency. Park joined the GNP eight days before the election[16] in the party's effort to "rediscover" Park Chung-hee as "a symbol of national identity."[17] The GNP eventually lost the presidential election, but Park was elected to the National Assembly through a by-election in 1998 in her hometown of Daegu. She served as the National Assembly member of the district for four consecutive terms. The core of her popularity lies in her familial ties to Park Chung-hee and Yook Young-Soo. News reports described voters enthusiastically reacting to Park when she went canvassing or gave campaign speeches, with voters crying and bringing lunch boxes for her.[18] In 2000, she was elected as a vice-chair of the GNP, garnering the second-highest number

---

Cliff: Evidence That Women Are Preferentially Selected to Contest Hard-to-Win Seats," *Psychology of Women Quarterly* 34, no. 1 (2010), 56–64; Michelle K. Ryan and S. Alexander Haslam, "The Glass Cliff? Exploring the Dynamics Surrounding the Appointment of Women to Precarious Leadership Positions," *The Academy of Management Review* 32, no. 2 (2007), 549–72.

14   Timothy C. Lim, *Politics in East Asia: Explaining Change&Continuity* (Boulder, CO: Lynne Rienner, 2014).

15   Jaeho Kim, "Yeoronjosa Sunwibakkum Tturyeot (in Korean)," *Donga Ilbo*, November 25, 1997, http://www.donga.com/news/View?gid=7301793&date=19971124, accessed June 10, 2019.

16   Sohyun Kim, "Lee Hoi-Chang Park Geun-Hye, Naega Jeonggye Immunsikyeo Daetongnyeong Doel Jul Mollatda (in Korean),'" *Hankook Kungjae*, August 22, 2017, https://www.hankyung.com/politics/article/2017082277767Y; Kwon-Mo Yang, "Hannara Park Geun-Hye Yoo Dong-Geun Ssi Yeongip Chujin (in Korean)," *Kyonghyang Shinmun*, December 3, 1997.

17   Momoyo Hüstebeck, "Park Geun-Hye: The Eternal Princess?," in *Dynasties and Female Political Leaders in Asia: Gender, Power, and Pedigree*, ed. Claudia Derichs and Mark R. Thompson (Münster, Germany: LIT Verlag, 2013), 356.

18   Jun-Man Kang, "Park Geun-Hye: Abeojireul Wihayeo (in Korean)," *Inmulgwa Sasang*, 1999.

of votes from the party members. Even though there was a reserved vice-chair position for a woman, she insisted on competing for the vice chairpersonship instead of assuming the position reserved for women in an attempt to avoid being labeled as a "quota woman."[19]

4   Becoming the Captain of the Sinking GNP Ship, 2004

As the GNP recruited Park to help them achieve a political victory in 1997, the GNP turned to Park again when it faced two major political crises that threatened its destiny in the legislative election. One was the unpopular move to impeach then-President Roh Moo-hyun, which was led by the GNP starting on March 12, 2004. President Roh was not on collegial terms with the GNP opposition, and the conflict between the two caused gridlock and government conflicts. Roh encouraged voters to support his party members in the 2004 national legislative election so the unified government could get things done. The GNP initiated the impeachment process, charging Roh's pleas to support his party as an impeachable offense, as maintaining political neutrality is required by Chapter 1, Article 7 of the Constitution.

The GNP and the Millennium Democratic Party (from which a pro-Roh faction created the splinter Open Uri Party) proceeded with a motion to impeach President Roh. The impeachment voting process was fraught with fistfights and brawls. The impeachment bill was voted upon with none of the ruling Open Uri Party legislators participating, as they left the floor in protest.[20] This chaotic scene turned the voters off; right after the impeachment, polling showed 70 percent of the public were opposed to the impeachment. Support for the president's Open Uri Party skyrocketed to 34 percent, whereas the GNP's plummeted to 18.2 percent, and the Millennium Democratic Party's sank to 8.5 percent.[21] Eventually, the Constitutional Court found the president not guilty, and he returned to the presidential office.

19   Young-Sik Goo, "Park Geun-Hye Geupbusangui Bimil: Park Chung-hee 3 Kim Heoju Eopgo Chagi Daetongryong Norinda (in Korean)," *Wolganmal*, 2001; Joongang Ilbo, "[2000 Saekttugi] 3. Jeongchi- Park Geun-Hye Buchongjae (in Korean)," *Joongang Ilbo*, December 25, 2000, https://news.joins.com/article/4015286, accessed March 11, 2019.

20   Ji-hye Song, "2004 Roh Moo-hyun vs 2016 Park Geun-Hye Tanhaek Bangjeongsik Bigyohaeboni (in Korean)," *JTBC*, November 24, 2016, http://news.jtbc.joins.com/article/article.aspx?news_id=NB11363644, accessed January 2, 2019.

21   Jeongmin Ryu, "Tanhaekbandae 70 percent Uridang Jijiyul 30%daero Geupdeung (in Korean)," *MediaToday*, March 12, 2004, http://www.mediatoday.co.kr/?mod=news&act=articleView&idxno=26517.

What is worse, the GNP suffered from falling legitimacy due to an ongoing investigation for allegedly receiving illegal campaign contributions from large corporations such as LG.[22] These impending corruption charges, together with the unpopular impeachment of the president in March, tainted the GNP's party image, painting them as the corrupt old-guard. The electoral prospects for the GNP in the upcoming April legislative election in 2004 looked bleak.

The sinking GNP turned to Park again. She became the chairperson about ten days after the impeachment vote. She orchestrated a campaign to appeal to the voters to show the party's commitment to reform and to fight against corruption. The first thing she did was move the party office into a tent structure to show the GNP's commitment to renouncing its material comfort. She held a press conference on March 30, during which she shed tears, saying, "with the heart of a mother whose family is in despair, I plead to voters that they give the GNP just one more chance."[23] These series of actions convinced the voters that the GNP would turn itself around. Moreover, the ruling Open Uri party became mired in controversy. The chairperson of the party mentioned during a press conference that the older voters (who did not usually support his party) did not need to turn out to vote.[24] Amid these controversies, the GNP successfully secured more than 40 percent of the National Assembly seats in 2004 – not a landslide victory, but a surprising result considering that public opinion polls showed lower than 20 percent support for the party after the impeachment.[25]

Interestingly, during the impeachment chaos, both the GNP and the Open Uri Party nominated female party chairs to improve their image in the face of falling popularity among the voters.[26] The female chairs made an emotional appeal to voters, such as Park doing 108 prostrations at a Buddhist temple, making confession at a Catholic cathedral, and attending a service at a Protestant church (thus covering the three major religious groups in South Korea). The

---

22   Gisun Uh, "Daegieobui Angmong, Chattegi Sageoniran (in Korean)," *NewsWatch*, November 15, 2016, http://www.newswatch.kr/news/articleView.html?idxno=8134, accessed March 11, 2019.

23   Daewoong Park, "Park Geun-Hye Tanhaek? Sewolho Chamsa Jiku Miyong Seonghyeong Nollan Gajung (in Korean)," *MK News*, November 21, 2016, https://www.mk.co.kr/news/photo/view/2016/11/808795/, accessed March 11, 2019.

24   Gukgun Song, "Hannaradang Park Geun-Hye Daepyo Dandok Interview Tanhaegi Choeseonui Seontaegeun Anieotda (in Korean),'" *Shindonga*, April 27, 2004, http://shindonga.donga.com/Library/3/06/13/103376/1, accessed March 11, 2019.

25   Jungae Go, "Hannara Cheonmang Dangsa 5junyeon Cheonmang Dwie Sumeun Makjeonmaku (in Korean)," *Joongang Ilbo*, March 24, 2009, https://news.joins.com/article/3542284, accessed March 11, 2019.

26   Hüstebeck, "Park Geun-Hye: The Eternal Princess?," 363.

Open Uri Party's chair, Choo Miae, visited the Honam region (the party's stronghold) and pleaded that "I am here with the heart of Shim Chong who sacrificed her life to open her father's eyes." Shim Chong is an often-invoked symbol of a pious daughter in a Korean folklore story.[27]

Park led her party to electoral victory multiple times after the surprising 2004 election. In 2006, she appeared on a stage to cheer for her party's candidate for the Seoul mayoral election, though an assailant attacked her with a knife which badly cut her face.[28] Amid the chaos, she remained calm, which voters took as a sign of her strong leadership in crisis. It was reported that when she woke up from the surgery, the first thing she asked was how the party did in a city where her party's candidate's support was not strong. She earned nicknames "the queen of the election," and "party savior," due to her appeal to the voters even when things did not look favorable for her party. During her term as the GNP chair, Park Geun-hye was not able or willing to step out from her father's shadow. Her public image became inseparable from her father's military reign.

In a time of major political crisis, her party turned to her to rescue them, which fits into the pattern of women's ascension during a crisis.[29] As argued by Derichs, Fleschenberg, and Hüstebeck, Park was useful to the party in projecting a "progressive, more innovative, and a cleaner image"[30] when all other aspects of the party suggested the contrary. As the "glass cliff" theory suggests, Park became the party leader as the party's last resort, when there were no viable alternatives to turn things around; without these crises, the party leaders might not have given her such a high platform in the party.[31] Park projected the image of an uncompromising leader who stood by her promises and principles. However, these prospects collapsed after she was impeached and, in August

---

27   Jiyoon Lee, "Choo Mi-ae, Honam Minsim Dolligi 3bo1bae: 2bak3il Dongan Gwangju Dosim 15 km Gwantong Yejeong (in Korean)," *Pressian*, April 3, 2004, http://www.pressian.com/ezview/article_main.html?no=44139; Jaehyun Kwon, "Choo Mi-ae Dangsalligi 3bo1bae Ssitgimgut (in Korean)," " *Kyonghyang Shinmun*, April 4, 2004, http://news.khan.co.kr/kh_news/khan_art_view.html?art_id=200404041849331, accessed March 12, 2019.

28   Lee, "From First Daughter to First Lady to First Woman President: Park Geun-Hye's Path to the South Korean Presidency."

29   Ryan and Haslam, "The Glass Cliff? Exploring the Dynamics Surrounding the Appointment of Women to Precarious Leadership Positions."

30   Claudia Derichs, Andrea Fleschenberg, and Momoyo Hüstebeck, "Gendering Moral Capital: Morality as a Political Asset and Strategy of Top Female Politicians in Asia," *Critical Asian Studies* 38, no. 3 (2006), 251–52.

31   Jong-Wook Kim et al., *Park Geun-Hye Hyungsang: Jinbo Nongael Daejoong Sokeui Park Geyn-Hye Rool Haemyong Haha* (in Korean) (Seoul: Wisdom House, 2010), 38.

2018, sentenced to 25 years in prison and fined the equivalent of approximately USD 16 million.[32]

5   "The Well-Prepared Female President": Park's Presidential Bid in 2012

Park's first bid for the presidency, in 2007, failed when she could not win her party's nomination.[33] Four years later, however, Park won the GNP nomination in a landslide, with 86.8 percent of the party members voting for her.[34] Analysis focusing on the South Korean presidential elections shows that when voters evaluate and assess presidential candidates, they rely heavily on the individual candidates' images rather than on the party label. Support for Moon Jae-in and Park was driven by voters' affinity to the candidates more so than by the voters' party loyalty.[35] Despite her 15 years of political experience, voters predominantly associated Park with her father: In one study, 50 percent of the survey respondents stated "Park Chung-hee's daughter" was the first thing came to their mind when they thought of Park Geun-hye.[36]

In the 2012 elections, Park relied on gendered symbols and campaign strategies reflecting "positive" gender stereotypes about women in South Korean society. As Ki-young Shin argued, "Park's construction of her gender identities as a filial daughter of a former national leader committed to the nation successfully portrayed her as the one and only woman destined to be president."[37]

---

32   Sang-hun Choe, "Park Geun-Hye, Ex-South Korean Leader, Gets 25 Years in Prison," *New York Times*, August 24, 2018, https://www.nytimes.com/2018/08/24/world/asia/park-geun-hye-sentenced-south-korea.html, accessed June 10, 2019.

33   Korean National Election Commission, "Je18dae Daetongnyeong Seongeo Chongnam (in Korean)" (Gwachon, Gyonggi-do, 2013), 53.

34   Korean National Election Commission, 67–68.

35   Sang-Sin Lee, "Personalization of Politics and Schematic Assessment of Presidential Candidates: How Korean Voters Perceive the Three Major Candidates for the 2012 Korean Presidential Election (in Korean)," *Hangukjeongchihakoebo* 46, no. 4 (2012), 149–70; Nae-Young Lee and Chong-Ki An, "The 18th Presidential Election and Retrospective Voting: Why Did Negative Retrospective Evaluation on the Ruling Government Did Not Make a Significant Impact on the Outcome of the 18th Presidential Election (in Korean)," *Hangukjeongdanghakoebo* 12, no. 2 (2013): 5–36; Sunghack Lim, "Election Issues' Change and Continuation during the 18th Presidential Election in Korea (in Korean)," *Dongayeongu* 25, no. 2 (2013): 181–201.

36   Lee, "Personalization of Politics and Schematic Assessment of Presidential Candidates: How Korean Voters Perceive the Three Major Candidates for the 2012 Korean Presidential Election (in Korean)," 156.

37   Ki-young Shin, "Gender, Election Campaigns, and the First Female President of South Korea," ジェンダー研究 [*Gender Studies*] 21, no. June (2018): 71–86.

After her unsuccessful slogan, "To Make a Country Where My Dream Comes True," was faced with mockery, her campaign changed gears and stressed the significance of electing a woman as president. She started to use the slogan "The Well-Prepared Female President" on November 18, 2012, approximately one month before election day to appeal to female voters, who were an important support base to mobilize.[38] Park's official campaign pamphlet, featuring the slogan of the first female president, regularly used terms such as change, reform, crisis management, stability, promise, and principles. The pamphlet, which was written in Korean, asserts that electing a female president symbolizes political change and reform, as "even the US has not elected a female president."[39] It argued that female leadership would fight corruption and the old ways of thinking and that Park Geun-hye was married to Korea.[40]

While describing her as an agent of change, Park's campaign underscored her political experience to convince voters that Park, even though she was a woman, could handle the highly masculine position of the presidency. The official campaign pamphlet listed her track record as a problem solver during times of crisis and the turmoil in her party and emphasized that she was trustworthy and had stood by her promises made to voters in the past.[41] Her campaign repeatedly emphasized her fifteen-year political career and indirectly drew attention to her electoral rival's relatively little political experience.[42] Even though Moon Jae-in had worked in the presidential office as a presidential secretary, he had not held any elected position until he was elected to the National Assembly about eight months before the presidential election.[43]

38   Lee, "From First Daughter to First Lady to First Woman President: Park Geun-Hye's Path to the South Korean Presidency"; Young Na, "2012nyeon Daeseonui Yeoseong Hubodeul, Geurigo Kim So-youn gwa Kim Soon-ja (in Korean)," *Journal of Feminist Theories and Practices* 28 (2013): 215–26; Yoo-seok Oh, "An Analysis of Women Policies of the Park Geun-Hye Government (in Korean)," *Minjoo Sahoiwa Jeongchaek Yeongoo* 26 (2014): 201–30.

39   Saenuri Party, "Je 18dae Daetongnyeong Seongeo Chaekjahyeong Seongeo Gongbo: Junbidoen Yeoseong Daetongnyeong Park Geun-Hye [Official Campaign Pamphlet for Park Geun-Hye (in Korean)]" (Gwachon, Gyonggi-do: Korean National Election Commission, 2012), http://nec.go.kr/portal/bbs/view/B0000363/22462.do?menuNo= 200543&scDs=1&sgId=20121219&sgTypecode=2, accessed December 29, 2013.

40   Saenuri Party.

41   Saenuri Party.

42   Jae-Hyuk Choi, "Park, "han Bunya Jeonmoonga Doiryomyon Choisohan 10nyun Naegong Ssaya (in Korean)," *Chosun Ilbo*, September 19, 2012, http://news.chosun.com/site/data/ html_dir/2012/09/19/2012091900241.html, accessed January 6, 2014.

43   Democratic Party, "Sarami Meonjeoda Moon Jae-in (in Korean)," 2012, http://elecinfo.nec. go.kr/neweps/3/1/paper.do, accessed March 12, 2019.

6   The 2012 Presidential Election Result

In the 2012 presidential election, Park won 52 percent of the total votes and became the first female president of Korea. The runner-up, Moon Jae-in, earned 48 percent of the vote.[44] The turnout of women voters was slightly higher than men's voter turnout (76.4 percent versus 74.8 percent) for the first time since 2002.[45] Analyzing the exit poll data, more women voted for Park than for Moon: 48 percent of men voted for Park, and 52 percent of them voted for Moon, whereas 52 percent of women voted for Park, and 47 percent of them voted for Moon. Approximately 66 percent of women voters 50 years and older voted for Park, which made them the most ardent support group. Within each age group, women were more supportive of Park compared to their male counterparts.[46]

Did Park's slogan, "The Well-Prepared Female President," work? In a pre-election public opinion poll, 45 percent of respondents stated that electing the first female president would constitute a reform in politics. In comparison, 48 percent of respondents stated that the slogan, "The Well-Prepared Female President," did not ring true.[47] In a post-election survey, only 14 percent of voters responded that having a female president for the first time was a reason for supporting Park.[48] Voters might not have changed their support away from another candidate to vote for Park to see a female president. Still, the first female president framing appealed to both women and the conservative older generation, who already supported Park and her party. Park could appeal as an icon of change without undermining the symbolic power of her kinship ties – thus continuing the political legacy of her father.[49] Those who experienced rapid economic development under the older Park supported the younger Park almost unconditionally,[50] not because the latter proposed

---

44   Korean National Election Commission, "Je18dae Daetongnyeong Seongeo Chongnam (in Korean)," 141.
45   Korean National Election Commission, "Je18dae Daetongnyeong Seongeo Chongnam (in Korean)."
46   Gallup Korea, *2012 Je 18dae Daetongnyeong Seongeo Tupyo Haengtae [Trial-Heats of the 2012 Presidential Election by Gallup Korea (in Korean)]* (Seoul, Korea: Gallup Korea, 2013).
47   Bong-Gi Kim, "Park, "yeosong Daetongryong Keonan Dui Yoe Jijiyool 4–7% Sangsung (in Korean)," *Chosun Ilbo*, November 22, 2012, http://news.chosun.com/site/data/html_dir/2012/11/22/2012112200200.html. accessed January 6, 2014.
48   Gallup Korea, *2012 2012 Je 18dae Daetongnyeong Seongeo Tupyo Haengtae [Trial-Heats of the 2012 Presidential Election by Gallup Korea (in Korean)*, 86–87.
49   Shin, "Gender, Election Campaigns, and the First Female President of South Korea."
50   Sung Deuk Hahm and Uk Heo, "The First Female President in South Korea: Park Geun-Hye's Leadership and South Korean Democracy," *Journal of Asian and African Studies* 53, no. 5 (2018), 649–65.

an attractive economic development policy but because she was the daughter of Park Chung-hee. For some, Park was the first daughter of the benevolent national mother figure of Yook Young-soo. Some voters were sympathetic to her fate of having lost both parents to the assassination.[51] In contrast, her familial tie to her controversial authoritarian father was the most notable turnoff for the non-supporters. In a post-election survey, 22 percent of respondents stated that her familial ties to the authoritarian Park Chung-hee were the reason they did not support her, and 18 percent questioned her competence. Only 6 percent of those who did not support Park reported that her gender was a problem.[52]

7   Taiwan: The Case of Tsai Ing-wen

On January 16, 2016, Taiwanese voters elected Tsai Ing-wen of the Democratic Progressive Party (DPP) as their first woman president. She won in a landslide victory, gaining 56 percent of the vote, while runner-up Chu Li-luan (朱立倫 or Eric Chu) of the Chinese Nationalist Party (Kuomintang, KMT) attained 31 percent of the votes. Four years previously, Tsai won 46 percent of the vote but lost the presidential bid to the then-incumbent Ma Ying-jeou (馬英九) of the KMT.[53]

Tsai graduated from the National Taiwan University Department of Law, one of the most prestigious educational institutions in Taiwan, and then earned a Master's Degree in Law at Cornell University, and a PhD in Political Science and Law at the London School of Economics. Unlike many other Asian female leaders, Tsai already had a long political career before running for the presidency in 2012 and 2016. Before joining the DPP in 2004, she served as a member of a delegation negotiating the terms with the World Trade Organization during former president Lee Teng-hui's (李登輝) KMT administration in 1998. Many believed that Tsai designed Lee's two-state theory. Later, she joined DPP

51   Eun-Ju Jang et al., "Roundtable: The Meaning of the 18th Presidential Election and the Changes of South Korean Society (in Korean)," *Simingwa Segye* 22 (2013): 74–104; Na, "2012nyeon Daeseonui Yeoseong Hubodeul, Geurigo Kim So-youn gwa Kim Soon-ja (in Korean)."

52   Gallup Korea, *2012 Je 18dae Daetongnyeong Seongeo Tupyo Haengtae [Trial-Heats of the 2012 Presidential Election by Gallup Korea (in Korean)*, 86–87.

53   The International Foundation for Electoral Systems, "Elections – Taiwan – Election for President, Jan 16, 2016," ElectionGuide, 2016, http://www.electionguide.org/elections/id/2735/, accessed March 14, 2018.

President Chen Shui-bian's cabinet as the minister of the Mainland Affairs Council in 2000.[54]

She was born in Pingtung County in 1956 and grew up in Taipei, with a Hakka father and a Hokklo mother. Her paternal grandmother is a Paiwan aborigine, and Tsai is the first president of Taiwan who has claimed indigenous heritage.[55] Tsai's campaign used her ethnic background to reach out to the Hakka voters, who usually vote for the KMT. The KMT tried to undermine her campaign's efforts to attract Hakka voters by calling Tsai a "pseudo-Hakka," pointing out her inability to speak the language. She countered that language proficiency did not define one's ethnic identities and argued that KMT's martial law era rule, which oppressed the use of languages other than Mandarin Chinese, prevented her from learning Hakka and the Paiwan language.[56] In her second presidential campaign, Tsai's campaign tried to reach out to various ethnic groups to counter KMT's accusation that "the DPP was stirring up ethnic tensions and was biased against non-Hokklo ethnic groups."[57] She delivered part of her speech in Hakka, which she had not done in 2012,[58] and her first TV ad featured her speaking Taiwanese, Hakka, and Mandarin. One month before election day, she aired a one-minute ad in which she exclusively talked in Hakka.[59]

She also tried to connect with the indigenous communities during her campaigns. Almost all of the reserved seats for the indigenous people in the National Legislative Yuan since 1972 have been members of the KMT, the People First Party (KMT's splinter party), or independents (though it should be noted that the Legislative Yuan elections were not democratic until 1992).

---

54 Chen Hui-ping and Jonathan Chin, "PROFILE: Tsai's Unexpected Political Journey," *Taipei Times*, January 18, 2016, http://www.taipeitimes.com/News/taiwan/archives/2016/01/18/2003637470/2, accessed June 10, 2019.

55 Chris Wang, "2012 ELECTIONS: ANALYSIS: Multifaceted Tsai Is Different Kind of Candidate," *Taipei Times*, October 28, 2011, http://www.taipeitimes.com/News/taiwan/archives/2011/10/28/2003516876, accessed March 13, 2019.

56 Wang; For KMT's monolingual policy, see Wi-vun Taiffalo Chiung, "Languages under Colonization: The Taiwanese Language Movement," in *Changing Taiwanese Identities*, ed. J. Bruce Jacobs and Peter Kang (London, UK: Routledge, 2017), 39–63.

57 Dafydd Fell, "Taiwan's Political Parties in the Aftermath of the 2016 Elections," in *A New Era in Democratic Taiwan: Trajectories and Turning Points in Politics and Cross-Strait Relations*, ed. Jonathan Sullivan and Chun-Yi Lee (London and New York: Routledge, 2018), 63–82.

58 Lok-sin Loa, "Tsai Pushes for Tolerance, Touts Importance of Hakka," *Taipei Times*, August 3, 2015, http://www.taipeitimes.com/News/taiwan/archives/2015/08/03/2003624526, accessed March 13, 2019.

59 Fell, "Taiwan's Political Parties in the Aftermath of the 2016 Elections."

In 2004, a DPP member was elected to this reserved seat for the first time.[60] During the presidential campaigns in 2012 and 2016, Tsai frequently visited indigenous communities and pledged to issue an official apology to aborigines for the government's past wrongdoing, including political and cultural oppression, as well as for more specific issues, such as the Chiang Ching-kuo administration's secret burial of nuclear waste on Orchid Island, which caused serious health problems for the local Tao (also known as the "Yami") people.[61] After her electoral victory, indigenous children participated in her inauguration ceremony,[62] and Tsai indeed issued the first official apology to the indigenous people on Indigenous Peoples' Day (August 1, 2016). She stated that "the Plains Indigenous Peoples were 'massacred' by the Dutch and the Zheng regimes"[63] and outlined new government policies regarding indigenous peoples.[64]

8   DPP Chairpersonship in 2008

In March 2008, the DPP chairperson and presidential nominee, Hsieh Chang-ting (謝長廷 or Frank Hsieh), lost the presidential election to Ma Ying-jeou, who won a landslide victory with 58.45 percent of the vote. As a result, Hsieh resigned from the chairpersonship to show that he accepted responsibility for the dismal electoral defeat. As with Park Geun-hye, the political crisis opened up opportunities for Tsai to ascend to the party's top leadership position. The DPP needed to transform itself to regain public trust, as it suffered from

---

60   Kharis Templeman, "When Do Electoral Quotas Advance Indigenous Representation?: Evidence from the Taiwanese Legislature," *Ethnopolitics* 17, no. 5 (2018), 461–84.

61   J. Bruce Jacobs, "Evaluating President Tsai's Apology to Indigenous People on Its First Anniversary," Ketagalan Media, 2017, https://www.ketagalanmedia.com/2017/09/11/evaluating-president-tsais-apology-indigenous-people-first-anniversary/; Hui-ping Chen and Jonathan Chin, "Tsai Vows to Issue Apology to Aborigines," *Taipei Times*, September 16, 2015, http://www.taipeitimes.com/News/taiwan/archives/2015/09/16/2003627831, accessed March 13, 2019.

62   J. Bruce Jacobs, "Indigenous Reconciliation? The Case of Taiwan," *Georgetown Journal of Asian Affairs* 3, no. 2 (2017), 31–36.

63   Tsai 2016 cited in J. Bruce Jacobs, "Introduction," in *Changing Taiwanese Identities*, ed. J. Bruce Jacobs and Peter Kang (London, UK: Routledge, 2017), 7.

64   Kharis Templeman, "Indigenous Legislators on Indigenous People's Day," kharistempleman.com, 2016, https://www.kharistempleman.com/blog/indigenous-legislators-on-indigenous-peoples-day; BBC News, "Taiwan President Gives First Apology to Indigenous Groups," August 1, 2016, https://www.bbc.com/news/world-asia-36940243, accessed March 13, 2019.

declining support due to corruption scandals and the party's mounting debt.[65] After the 2008 presidential defeat, the old DPP factions centered around Chen and the *Dangwai*-era figures were weakened, and Tsai emerged as a viable candidate.[66] Her gender, age, and lack of clear factional affiliation could be useful for the DPP's desperately needed change: "The DPP has never had a chairwoman before so it may be a good chance for change."[67] Tsai herself also emphasized that she would lead the party "to become more tolerant of gender, ethnic, class, and ideological issues."[68] Tsai was considered part of a new generation of leaders[69] who could break away from the corruption-tainted old-guard image and start the party image-building with a clean slate.[70] With this heightened expectation of bringing generational change to the DPP,[71] Tsai was elected to the DPP chairpersonship.[72] An editorial in the *Taipei Times* commented that "it would have been very difficult for Tsai to have reached her current position had the DPP won the presidency in 2008."[73] Tsai's lack of clear "factional or ideological baggage" became useful in balancing the factions while navigating her role as the chair.[74]

---

65   Dafydd Fell, *Government and Politics in Taiwan*, 2nd ed. (London and New York: Routledge, 2018); Taipei Times, "EDITORIAL: Tsai Faces a Battle to Reform the DPP," May 19, 2008, http://www.taipeitimes.com/News/editorials/archives/2008/05/19/2003412345, accessed June 10, 2019.

66   Fell, *Government and Politics in Taiwan*.

67   Jimmy Chuang, "DPP Members Discuss Tsai Ing-Wen's Candidacy," *Taipei Times*, April 20, 2008, http://www.taipeitimes.com/News/taiwan/archives/2008/04/20/2003409769; Shu-ling Ko, "Koo Kwang-Ming Expected to Run in DPP Race," *Taipei Times*, April 18, 2008, http://www.taipeitimes.com/News/taiwan/archives/2008/04/18/2003409611/2; Shu-ling Ko, "Tsai Ing-Wen Being Pushed to Stand in DPP Election," *Taipei Times*, April 17, 2008, http://www.taipeitimes.com/News/taiwan/archives/2008/04/17/2003409462, accessed June 10, 2019.

68   Hsiu-chuan Shih, "Tsai Enters DPP Chairmanship Election," *Taipei Times*, April 19, 2008, http://www.taipeitimes.com/News/front/archives/2008/04/19/2003409675, accessed June 10, 2019.

69   Ko, "Tsai Ing-Wen Being Pushed to Stand in DPP Election."

70   Shih, "Tsai Enters DPP Chairmanship Election."

71   Hsiu-chuan Shih, "DPP to Chart New Beginning," *Taipei Times*, April 20, 2008, http://www.taipeitimes.com/News/taiwan/archives/2008/04/20/2003409768, accessed June 10, 2019.

72   Lok-sin Loa, "Tsai Wins Race for DPP Chairmanship," *Taipei Times*, May 19, 2008, http://www.taipeitimes.com/News/front/archives/2008/05/19/2003412357, accessed May 6, 2019.

73   Mao-hsiung Chen, "Challenges Ahead for Tsai Ing-Wen," *Taipei Times*, March 31, 2011, http://www.taipeitimes.com/News/editorials/archives/2011/03/31/2003499524, accessed June 10, 2019.

74   Sullivan and Lee, "Introduction."

After she became chair, the DPP started to see a positive change in the voters' support for the party.[75] Under her leadership, the DPP engaged in organizational reforms, and the DPP won almost all of the 2009 legislative by-elections, a victory dubbed the "Tsai Ing-wen effect."[76] Even though Tsai herself lost her bid for the New Taipei City (新北市) mayoral election in November 2010 to Eric Chu (whom she would beat in the 2016 presidential election), Tsai consolidated her position within the DPP through the chairpersonship,[77] which is similar to what we observed in Park Geun-hye's case.

Another similarity between Tsai and Park was the criticism of Tsai for never having been married or borne children. Because nothing has been known about her romantic relationship, some have questioned whether she is a lesbian. The fact of her being a childless single woman became a target point in campaign attacks against her. During the DPP chairperson election, another contestant in his 80s, Koo Kwang-ming (辜寬敏), said: "the future of the DPP should not be entrusted to an unmarried girl [...] in a traditionally male-dominated society like Taiwan's, positions with great responsibility should be the preserve of men."[78] He apologized later after facing criticism from other party members and at a press conference held by feminists.

9   Presidential Campaigns in 2012

During the primaries for the 2012 presidential election, the conflict between the need for change and the demand for experience resurfaced. Tsai's primary contender, Su Tseng-chang (蘇貞昌), contrasted his political experience with Tsai's.[79] To counter, Tsai emphasized her ability to be an agent of change, expressing her belief that Taiwan needs a "next-generation leader" and "a new

75   Richard Hazeldine, "Tsai Outlines Her Plans to Rebuild DPP," *Taipei Times*, June 28, 2008, http://www.taipeitimes.com/News/taiwan/archives/2008/06/28/2003415958, accessed June 10, 2019.

76   Cho-shui Lin, "'Tsai' Phenomenon Not about Turnout," *Taipei Times*, March 28, 2011, http://www.taipeitimes.com/News/editorials/archives/2011/03/28/2003499286, accessed June 10, 2019.

77   Fell, *Government and Politics in Taiwan*.

78   Shu-ling Ko, "Koo Apologizes for Offensive Remarks," *Taipei Times*, May 8, 2008, http://www.taipeitimes.com/News/taiwan/archives/2008/05/08/2003411329; Taipei Times, "EDITORIAL: When an Apology Isn't Enough," May 8, 2008, http://www.taipeitimes.com/News/editorials/archives/2008/05/08/2003411310, accessed June 10, 2019.

79   Taipei Times, "DPP's Su Tseng-Chang Announces Presidential Bid," March 21, 2011, http://www.taipeitimes.com/News/front/archives/2011/03/21/2003498712, accessed June 10, 2019.

force in politics" to provide the younger generation "a glimpse of their future."[80] At the time, she underscored her achievements as a party chair: "I [Tsai] have proven that the DPP can be reborn from the ashes."[81] Her marital and parental status again became the target of ad hominem attacks. During the primaries, former DPP chairperson Shih Ming-teh called on Tsai, saying that she needed to clarify her sexual orientation because "she needs to be true to herself, her body, in order to be true to her beliefs and her country."[82] This comment drew heavy criticism. Legislators across party lines and activists said sexual orientation is irrelevant to the election and that a presidential hopeful does not need to disclose his or her private matters. Tsai issued a 300-word statement, arguing that "there is nothing wrong with any gender, sexual orientation or marital status. Nobody has the right to question another [on this]."[83] Eventually, Tsai narrowly won the primary against Su (42.5 percent vs. 41.1 percent).[84]

As in her chairperson bids, the fact of her being a woman aroused people's imagination that she could be an agent of change. Tsai did not initiate the association herself; rather, she tried not to attract people's attention to her gender. Her first TV advertisement before the party nomination in March 2011, titled "Reason ... Giving Democracy More Power" did not mention the prospect of Tsai being the first female candidate of the DPP or the possibility of being the first female president. Instead, the ad highlighted her experience as the DPP chairperson, the goal of "winning back the people's confidence," her ability to be a tough leader, and the prospects of bringing "generational change" to the country.[85]

Around June 2011, the narrative of electing a female president as a symbol of democracy and an inevitable global trend started to appear in the op-eds of the *Taipei Times*: "True to its name, the Democratic Progressive Party (DPP) produced a female vice president [Annette Lu] ... It is fairly clear that she [Tsai

80   Vincent Y. Chao, "Tsai Ing-Wen 'Seriously' Considers Bid," *Taipei Times*, March 3, 2011, http://www.taipeitimes.com/News/taiwan/archives/2011/03/03/2003497244, accessed June 10, 2019.

81   Vincent Y. Chao, "Tsai Ing-Wen Officially Launches Presidential Bid," *Taipei Times*, March 12, 2011, http://www.taipeitimes.com/News/front/archives/2011/03/12/2003497974, accessed June 10, 2019.

82   Vincent Y. Chao, "Tsai Takes Stand on Right to Privacy," *Taipei Times*, April 17, 2011, http://www.taipeitimes.com/News/front/archives/2011/04/17/2003500949, accessed June 10, 2019.

83   Chao.

84   Fell, *Government and Politics in Taiwan*.

85   Vincent Y. Chao, "Tsai Unveils Advertisement for Presidential Campaign," *Taipei Times*, March 22, 2011, http://www.taipeitimes.com/News/taiwan/archives/2011/03/22/2003498814, accessed June 10, 2019.

Ing-wen] is not only the best qualified female presidential candidate but simply the best presidential candidate for Taiwan."[86] Numerous women's groups formed the "I Want a Female President Alliance."[87] Even though the possibility of electing the first female president captured people's imagination,[88] Tsai's campaign itself did not emphasize that aspect until the second half of the presidential election.[89] One editorial in the *Taipei Times* in August 2011 argued that "she should make more of her strengths, particularly the possibility of becoming the first-ever female president, to attract women voters."[90] Soon after, starting in late September 2011, Tsai made "Taiwan's first female president" her main campaign slogan.[91]

Tsai said that the "Taiwan's first female president" slogan was adopted "not because it is a 'trendy' or 'fashionable' idea, but because women are often more able to solve problems in a harmonious way through better communication than men"[92] and "can eliminate unfairness and injustice in society."[93] Tsai published her gender policies, entitled "10-Year Policy Guidelines," in August 2011, promising to prioritize women's political participation and promote LGBTQ rights, protect immigrants, and improve gender education in schools.[94] One month later, Ma also published his campaign's gender policies, titled "New

86   Ching-chih Chen, "Taiwan Can Lead Region by Electing a Woman," *Taipei Times*, March 8, 2011, http://www.taipeitimes.com/News/editorials/archives/2011/03/08/2003497638, accessed June 10, 2019.

87   Yu-fang Hsu, "Words Speak Louder than Gender," *Taipei Times*, December 29, 2011, http://taipeitimes.com/News/editorials/archives/2011/12/29/2003521867, accessed June 10, 2019.

88   Taipei Times, "EDITORIAL: Can Tsai Win the Election?," May 9, 2011, http://www.taipeitimes.com/News/editorials/archives/2011/05/09/2003502754, accessed June 10, 2019.

89   Wan-Ying Yang and Kuan-Chen Lee, "Ready for a Female President in Taiwan?," *Journal of Women, Politics & Policy* 37, no. 4 (2016), 464–89.

90   Shih-chung Liu, "Tsai Must Think Nationally to Win," *Taipei Times*, August 30, 2011, http://www.taipeitimes.com/News/editorials/archives/2011/08/30/2003511998, accessed June 10, 2019.

91   Chris Wang, "ANALYSIS: Tsai Is Changing Female Voters' View of the DPP," *Taipei Times*, September 30, 2011, http://www.taipeitimes.com/News/taiwan/archives/2011/09/30/2003514563, accessed June 10, 2019.

92   Chris Wang, "Tsai Ing-Wen Pledges to Promote Sexual Equality," *Taipei Times*, October 25, 2011, http://www.taipeitimes.com/News/taiwan/archives/2011/10/25/2003516632, accessed June 10, 2019.

93   Chris Wang, "2012 ELECTIONS: Tsai Declares 2012 to Be 'Special Year,' " *Taipei Times*, January 1, 2012, http://www.taipeitimes.com/News/taiwan/archives/2012/01/01/2003522130, accessed June 10, 2019.

94   Wang, "Tsai Ing-Wen Pledges to Promote Sexual Equality"; Ching-hui Hu, "Students Voice Support for Tsai's Gay-Friendly Policy," *Taipei Times*, September 3, 2011, http://www.taipeitimes.com/News/taiwan/archives/2011/09/03/2003512347, accessed June 10, 2019.

Visions on Gender Equality Policies." He argued that "we [Ma's administration] are trying to raise the profile of gender equality in society. Carrying out gender equality policies is not enough. We hope that in the future, gender equality will become the basis of every policy."[95]

10   2012 Presidential Election Result—The Gender Affinity Effect?

Tsai's first bid for president was not successful. Nevertheless, Tsai narrowed the losing margin to 6 percentage points from Hsieh's 17 percentage points.[96] Tsai's campaign only half-heartedly embraced the slogan of "the first female president" and did not expect that the slogan would swing the voters to her side. In an interview after the election, Tsai stated that she "felt reservations about making my [her] identity as 'a woman' prominent in my campaign, but I realized that doing so could have the effect of drawing attention to gender issues and triggering forward-thinking ideas."[97] She continued to state that making her gender prominent in her campaign did not bring additional votes. The author's own analysis of the 2012 Taiwan Social Change Survey (Phase 6, Wave 3)[98] also shows little support for the hypothesis that her candidacy mobilized women voters to cross party lines. The party loyalty seemed to be stable in the 2012 elections. Almost 82 percent of the Ma supporters of 2008 maintained their support for him in 2012; only 9 percent of them voted for Tsai in 2012. On the other hand, 91 percent of those who voted for Hsieh in 2008 supported Tsai in 2012, and 4 percent of them chose Ma this time. In analyzing women and men respondents, it appears that men were slightly more likely to support the DPP candidate than the KMT candidate in both 2008 and 2012. From this survey, it is difficult to say whether female voters who had previously voted for Ma instead

---

95   Yan-chih Mo, "President Pledges Push toward Gender Equality," *Taipei Times*, September 3, 2011, http://www.taipeitimes.com/News/taiwan/archives/2011/09/03/2003512346, accessed June 10, 2019.
96   Yang and Lee, "Ready for a Female President in Taiwan?"
97   Taiwan Panorama 2014 cited in Yang and Lee.
98   Institute of Sociology, Academia Sinica, "Taiwan Social Change Survey, Survey 2012, Phase 6, Wave 3, Quetionnaire II Family and Gender," 2012, https://www2.ios.sinica.edu.tw/sc/en/scDownload3.php, accessed July 14, 2019. Data analyzed in this section were collected in the Phase 6, Wave 3, 2012 survey of the research project "Taiwan Social Change Survey." The project was conducted by the Institute of Sociology, Academia Sinica, and sponsored by the Ministry of Science and Technology (formerly known as National Science Council), Republic of China.

TABLE 6.1   Voting patterns in the 2008 and the 2012 presidential elections by voter gender

All Respondents			
	2012 Ma	2012 Tsai	2012 Soong	Total
2008 Ma	725 (81.5%)	76 (8.5%)	24 (2.7%)	890
2008 Hsieh	14 (3.6%)	355 (90.6%)	4 (1%)	392
Total	866 (41.8%)	581 (28%)	52 (2.5%)	2072
Women Respondents			
	2012 Ma	2012 Tsai	2012 Soong	Total
2008 Ma	378 (82.5%)	38 (8.3%)	7 (1.5%)	458
2008 Hsieh	6 (3.6%)	152 (91.6%)	1 (0.6%)	166
Total	458 (45%)	252 (24.8%)	17 (1.7%)	1017
Men Respondents			
	2012 Ma	2012 Tsai	2012 Soong	Total
2008 Ma	347 (80.3%)	38 (8.8%)	17 (3.9%)	432
2008 Hsieh	8 (3.5%)	203 (89.8%)	3 (1.3%)	226
Total	408 (38.7%)	329 (31.2%)	35 (3.3%)	1055

SOURCE: AUTHOR'S ANALYSIS OF THE 2012 TAIWAN SOCIAL CHANGE SURVEY (PHASE 6, WAVE 3)

voted for Tsai because she was a woman. Generally, women voters have tended to vote for the KMT over the DPP in Taiwan,[99] and in this election, the same pattern persisted.

11   Missing "First Woman" Slogan in 2016

Even though Ma was elected with the historically highest level of support in 2008 for his first term, his second term was rocky. Abysmally low satisfaction ratings for Ma led his critics to call him a "9 percent president."[100] In March

---

99   Wang, "ANALYSIS: Tsai Is Changing Female Voters' View of the DPP."
100   Nathan F. Batto, "The KMT Coalition Unravels: The 2016 Elections and Taiwan's New Political Landscape," in *A New Era in Democratic Taiwan: Trajectories and Turning Points in Politics and Cross-Strait Relations*, ed. Jonathan Sullivan and Chun-Yi Lee (London and New York: Routledge, 2018), 10–34.

2014, the student-led Sunflower Movement started as a response to the lack of transparency in a cross-strait service trade agreement made by the Ma administration.[101] Students occupied the Legislative Yuan for 24 days, and more than half the Taiwanese public supported the movement.[102] Among all this turmoil, Tsai was elected as the DPP chair for the second time,[103] and led her party to a sweeping victory in local executive elections the same year.[104] Riding this success, Tsai was nominated as a presidential candidate without a party contest.[105] The KMT nominated Deputy Legislative Speaker Hung Hsiu-chu (洪秀柱) as its presidential candidate.[106] Thus, the two major parties both had women candidates. Public opinion was favorable to Tsai from the early stages of the election campaign,[107] and the gap widened even further as the election advanced. Hung's "ultimate unification with China" stance drew criticism even from her own party members.[108] This, combined with her staggering public opinion poll levels, led to Hung being replaced by Eric Chu, the then KMT chairperson.[109] Chu nominated a former lawyer and self-portrayed advocate of gender equality, Wang Ju-hsuan (王如玄, also known as Jennifer Wang), as

101   Chia-ling Tang and Hsiu-chuan Shih, "Effects of Sunflower Movement to Last," *Taipei Times*, March 18, 2015, http://www.taipeitimes.com/News/taiwan/archives/2015/03/18/2003613823, accessed June 10, 2019.

102   Ming-sho Ho, "The Activist Legacy of Taiwan's Sunflower Movement," Carnegie Endowment for International Peace, 2018, https://carnegieendowment.org/2018/08/02/activist-legacy-of-taiwan-s-sunflower-movement-pub-76966, accessed May 6, 2019.

103   Chris Wang, "Su, Hsieh Drop out of DPP Chair Race," *Taipei Times*, April 15, 2014, http://www.taipeitimes.com/News/front/archives/2014/04/15/2003588056, accessed June 10, 2019.

104   Fell, *Government and Politics in Taiwan*.

105   Lok-sin Loa, "Tsai Picks Chen Chu as Manager for Campaign," *Taipei Times*, August 13, 2015, http://www.taipeitimes.com/News/front/archives/2015/08/13/2003625225, accessed May 6, 2019.

106   Alison Hsiao, "KMT Affirms Hung's Presidential Candidacy," *Taipei Times*, June 18, 2015, http://www.taipeitimes.com/News/front/archives/2015/06/18/2003620960, accessed June 10, 2019.

107   Lok-sin Loa, "Support for Taiwanese Independence, Identity: Think Tank Poll," *Taipei Times*, February 5, 2015, http://www.taipeitimes.com/News/taiwan/archives/2015/02/05/2003610873, accessed June 8, 2020.

108   Hsien-chun Peng and Jonathan Chin, "KMT Politician Demands Review of Hung's Selection," *Taipei Times*, October 4, 2015, http://www.taipeitimes.com/News/front/archives/2015/10/04/2003629216, accessed June 10, 2019; Fell, "Taiwan's Political Parties in the Aftermath of the 2016 Elections."

109   Kuan-long Li, "There Are Reasons to Thank Chu," *Taipei Times*, October 12, 2015, http://www.taipeitimes.com/News/editorials/archives/2015/10/12/2003629832, accessed June 10, 2019.

his vice-presidential running mate.[110] Even though both major parties featured a woman on their tickets, the gender issue, or the first woman framework, did not strongly surface.[111] Tsai's campaign adopted the slogan "Light Up Taiwan" (點亮台灣); her nomination acceptance speech on April 16 did not mention anything explicitly related to women or gender.[112] An address in Kaohsiung on August 16, entitled "Tsai Ing-wen's Five Major Reforms," listed generational justice, executive and legislative reform, transitional justice, and an end to partisanship as major policy goals, but nothing related to gender issues.[113]

12   2016 Presidential Election Result

Eventually, Tsai won a landslide victory, winning 56 percent of the votes, which was 25 percentage points higher than Chu.[114] The DPP won both the presidential and the legislative elections, continuing its electoral victory in the November 2014 local elections.[115] The DPP's vote share increased from 45.6 percent in 2012 to 56.1 percent in 2016, and the KMT earned only 31 percent of the votes, a 20.6 percentage-point decrease from 51.6 percent in 2012.[116] Taiwan's Election and Democratization Study data (TEDS) show that more than 90 percent of those who voted for Tsai in 2012 voted for her again in 2016. In contrast, only 39.6 percent of Ma-Wu voters voted for the Chu-Wang ticket in 2016.[117] The TEDS data show that both men and women supported the DPP at a higher rate than they did the KMT in 2016 compared to four years previously, but men

---

110   Stacy Hsu, "Support for Tsai Passes Critical 50% Mark: Survey," *Taipei Times*, December 9, 2015, http://www.taipeitimes.com/News/front/archives/2015/12/09/2003634366, accessed June 10, 2019.

111   Chao-yuan Tseng and Yi-chien Chen, "Gender Equality Still Unaddressed," *Taipei Times*, December 26, 2015, http://www.taipeitimes.com/News/editorials/archives/2015/12/26/2003635677, accessed May 21, 2020; Abraham Gerber, "ELECTIONS: Stances on Gender Draw Awakening Foundation Critique," *Taipei Times*, January 14, 2016, http://www.taipeitimes.com/News/taiwan/archives/2016/01/14/2003637186, accessed June 10, 2019.

112   Tsai Ing-wen, Chen Chien-jen: Light Up Taiwan, "DPP Nominates Chairperson Tsai Ing-Wen as 2016 Presidential Candidate," 2015, http://iing.tw/en/4, accessed July 14, 2019.

113   Tsai Ing-wen, Chen Chien-jen: Light Up Taiwan, "Tsai Ing-Wen's Five Major Reforms," 2015, http://iing.tw/en/21, accessed July 14, 2019.

114   The International Foundation for Electoral Systems, "Elections – Taiwan – Election for President, Jan 16, 2016."

115   Batto, "The KMT Coalition Unravels: The 2016 Elections and Taiwan's New Political Landscape."

116   Central Elections Commission cited in Batto, 14.

117   TEDS 2016 data cited in Batto, 15.

were still stronger supporters of the DPP than women were.[118] According to the TEDS data, 87 percent of women DPP supporters voted for the Tsai-Chen ticket, and 89 percent of men DPP supporters did so. Only 9 percent of the KMT-identifying women voted for Tsai, whereas 6 percent of KMT-supporting men voted for Tsai. Nathan Batto commented that "at the end of the day, the gender question is decidedly secondary … with every election in Taiwan, [this election] is fundamentally about Taiwan's relationship with China."[119] As in the 2012 elections, the fact that Tsai was a woman did not significantly affect either men or women voters; instead, party affiliation was the more critical voting factor for them than the prospect of having a women president.

13   Conclusion

This chapter has traced the political careers of Park Geun-hye and Tsai Ing-wen. Despite their personal and political differences, both of their trajectories have some striking similarities. The election results data in both Taiwan and South Korea show voters do not support candidates merely because of their shared gender identity with the candidate. However, voters and political leaders are not gender blind. Both Tsai and Park's parties used the "positive" gender stereotypes about women, and the candidates themselves used their gender to curry support when their parties were suffering from declining popularity. For better or worse, the fact that they were women opened up a window of opportunity for them to rise through the ranks in their party when there seemed to be no viable alternatives. They earned credibility and legitimacy by successfully turning things around as their respective party's chair. The fact that both were subject to misogynistic comments and that their campaigns even attempted to use the "first woman" frame to appeal to voters shows that their gender was not invisible.

Interestingly, Park Geun-hye more actively used the "first female president" slogan than Tsai did, even though it took a while for the slogan to take off. Park's track record as a five-term legislator and a party leader did not suggest anything to support that Park would represent women's interests (however they might be defined). Still, her campaign willingly played the gender card when it saw that the slogan could consolidate the already high level of support

---

118   Batto, 21.

119   Austin Ramzy, "Presidential Race Reflects Women's Rise in Politics," *New York Times*, September 10, 2015, https://www.nytimes.com/2015/09/11/world/asia/taiwan-is-poised-to-elect-its-first-woman-as-president.html, accessed May 21, 2020.

for Park among women voters, and the ideal of (or the illusion of?) gender equality could also evoke national pride because it was considered a marker of being an advanced country ("even the US has not elected a female president," Park's pamphlet reads). On the other hand, Tsai's presidential campaign for the 2012 election emphasized the historical significance of her potentially being the first female president only after the media and women's movements initiated such a framing. This evocation was even less noticeable in 2016. The reason for this may be that women tended to vote for the KMT more than for the DPP, so Tsai's campaign did not see that playing the gender card would bring in additional votes – and the 2012 election results supported that premise. The slogan might have consolidated already existing support rather than generating new support.

Will there be future women presidents in South Korea and Taiwan? Regardless of their policy responsiveness or performance, the symbolic importance of these two women being the first female presidents in their respective countries sets South Korea and Taiwan apart from their East Asian neighbors such as the People's Republic of China, North Korea, and even Japan. After Park's impeachment, some political leaders commented that Park's fall was ominous for other women politicians. Park's election as president was initially seen as a breakthrough for gender equality in Korea, but her political demise and impeachment risk raising the bar even higher for future female politicians. Will the national executive glass ceiling be shattered by other female presidents, or will it remain only cracked? Have Park and Tsai marked a new chapter in gender politics in the two societies, or will they rather remain an exception to the rule? We will wait and see.

References

Adams, Melinda. "Women's Executive Leadership in Africa: Ellen Johnson Sirleaf and Broader Patterns of Change." *Politics & Gender* 4, no. 3 (2008): 475–85.

Batto, Nathan F. "The KMT Coalition Unravels: The 2016 Elections and Taiwan's New Political Landscape." In *A New Era in Democratic Taiwan: Trajectories and Turning Points in Politics and Cross-Strait Relations*, edited by Jonathan Sullivan and Chun-Yi Lee, 10–34. London and New York: Routledge, 2018.

BBC News, "Taiwan President Gives First Apology to Indigenous Groups." August 1, 2016. https://www.bbc.com/news/world-asia-36940243, accessed March 13, 2019.

Chao, Vincent Y. "Tsai Ing-Wen Officially Launches Presidential Bid." *Taipei Times*, March 12, 2011. http://www.taipeitimes.com/News/front/archives/2011/03/12/2003497974, accessed June 10, 2019.

Chao, Vincent Y. "Tsai Ing-Wen 'Seriously' Considers Bid." *Taipei Times*, March 3, 2011. http://www.taipeitimes.com/News/taiwan/archives/2011/03/03/2003497244, accessed June 10, 2019.

Chao, Vincent Y. "Tsai Takes Stand on Right to Privacy." *Taipei Times*, April 17, 2011. http://www.taipeitimes.com/News/front/archives/2011/04/17/2003500949, accessed June 10, 2019.

Chao, Vincent Y. "Tsai Unveils Advertisement for Presidential Campaign." *Taipei Times*, March 22, 2011. http://www.taipeitimes.com/News/taiwan/archives/2011/03/22/2003498814, accessed June 10, 2019.

Chen, Ching-chih. "Taiwan Can Lead Region by Electing a Woman." *Taipei Times*, March 8, 2011. http://www.taipeitimes.com/News/editorials/archives/2011/03/08/2003497638, accessed June 10, 2019.

Chen, Hui-ping, and Jonathan Chin. "Tsai Vows to Issue Apology to Aborigines." *Taipei Times*, September 16, 2015. http://www.taipeitimes.com/News/taiwan/archives/2015/09/16/2003627831, accessed March 13, 2019.

Chen, Mao-hsiung. "Challenges Ahead for Tsai Ing-Wen." *Taipei Times*, March 31, 2011. http://www.taipeitimes.com/News/editorials/archives/2011/03/31/2003499524, accessed June 10, 2019.

Chiung, Wi-vun Taiffalo. "Languages under Colonization: The Taiwanese Language Movement." In *Changing Taiwanese Identities*, edited by J. Bruce Jacobs and Peter Kang, 39–63. London, UK: Routledge, 2017.

Choe, Sang-hun. "Park Geun-Hye, Ex-South Korean Leader, Gets 25 Years in Prison." *New York Times*, August 24, 2018. https://www.nytimes.com/2018/08/24/world/asia/park-geun-hye-sentenced-south-korea.html, accessed June 10, 2019.

Choi, Jae-Hyuk. "Park, "han Bunya Jeonmoonga Doiryomyon Choisohan 10nyun Naegong Ssaya [Park Claims That at Least 10 Years' of Experience Is Needed to Be an Expert in a Field (in Korean)]." *Chosun Ilbo*, September 19, 2012. http://news.chosun.com/site/data/html_dir/2012/09/19/2012091900241.html, accessed January 6, 2014.

Chuang, Jimmy. "DPP Members Discuss Tsai Ing-Wen's Candidacy." *Taipei Times*, April 20, 2008. http://www.taipeitimes.com/News/taiwan/archives/2008/04/20/2003409769, accessed accessed June 10, 2019.

Democratic Party. "Sarami Meonjeoda Moon Jae-in (in Korean)," 2012. http://elecinfo.nec.go.kr/neweps/3/1/paper.do, accessed March 12, 2019.

Derichs, Claudia, Andrea Fleschenberg, and Momoyo Hüstebeck. "Gendering Moral Capital: Morality as a Political Asset and Strategy of Top Female Politicians in Asia." *Critical Asian Studies* 38, no. 3 (2006),: 245–70.

Fell, Dafydd. *Government and Politics in Taiwan*. 2nd ed. London and New York: Routledge, 2018.

Fell, Dafydd. "Taiwan's Political Parties in the Aftermath of the 2016 Elections." In *A New Era in Democratic Taiwan: Trajectories and Turning Points in Politics and Cross-Strait*

Relations, edited by Jonathan Sullivan and Chun-Yi Lee, 63–82. London and New York: Routledge, 2018.

Foundation for Women's Rights Promotion and Development. "Gender Indicators in Taiwan (姓別指標資訊平臺)." Foundation for Women's Rights Promotion and Development, 2019. http://www.gender-indicators.org.tw, accessed May 6, 2019.

Gallup Korea. *2012 Je 18dae Daetongnyeong Seongeo Tupyo Haengtae* [*Trial-Heats of the 2012 Presidential Election by Gallup Korea (in Korean)*]. Seoul, Korea: Gallup Korea, 2013.

Gallup Korea. "Daily Opinion Je 174ho (2015nyeon 8wol 1ju) – Yeokdae Daetongnyeong Pyeonggawa Geu Iyu (in Korean)." Gallup Korea, 2015. http://www.gallup.co.kr/gallupdb/reportContent.asp?seqNo=676, accessed May 1, 2020.

Gerber, Abraham. "ELECTIONS: Stances on Gender Draw Awakening Foundation Critique." *Taipei Times*, January 14, 2016. http://www.taipeitimes.com/News/taiwan/archives/2016/01/14/2003637186, accessed June 10, 2019.

Go, Jungae. "Hannara Cheonmang Dangsa 5junyeon Cheonmang Dwie Sumeun Makjeonmaku (in Korean)." *Joongang Ilbo*, March 24, 2009. https://news.joins.com/article/3542284, accessed March 11, 2019.

Goo, Young-Sik. "Park Geun-Hye Geupbusangui Bimil: Park Chung-hee 3 Kim Heoju Eopgo Chagi Daetongryong Norinda (in Korean)." *Wolganmal*, 2001, accessed December 23, 2013.

Hahm, Sung Deuk, and Uk Heo. "The First Female President in South Korea: Park Geun-Hye's Leadership and South Korean Democracy." *Journal of Asian and African Studies* 53, no. 5 (2018): 649–65.

Hazeldine, Richard. "Tsai Outlines Her Plans to Rebuild DPP." *Taipei Times*, June 28, 2008. http://www.taipeitimes.com/News/taiwan/archives/2008/06/28/2003415958, accessed June 10, 2019.

Ho, Ming-sho. "The Activist Legacy of Taiwan's Sunflower Movement." Carnegie Endowment for International Peace, 2018. https://carnegieendowment.org/2018/08/02/activist-legacy-of-taiwan-s-sunflower-movement-pub-76966, accessed May 6, 2019.

Hsiao, Alison. "KMT Affirms Hung's Presidential Candidacy." *Taipei Times*, June 18, 2015. http://www.taipeitimes.com/News/front/archives/2015/06/18/2003620960, accessed June 10, 2019.

Hsu, Stacy. "Support for Tsai Passes Critical 50% Mark: Survey." *Taipei Times*, December 9, 2015. http://www.taipeitimes.com/News/front/archives/2015/12/09/2003634366, accessed June 10, 2019.

Hsu, Yu-fang. "Words Speak Louder than Gender." *Taipei Times*, December 29, 2011. http://taipeitimes.com/News/editorials/archives/2011/12/29/2003521867, accessed June 10, 2019.

Hu, Ching-hui. "Students Voice Support for Tsai's Gay-Friendly Policy." *Taipei Times*, September 3, 2011. http://www.taipeitimes.com/News/taiwan/archives/2011/09/03/2003512347, accessed June 10, 2019.

Huddy, Leonie, and Nayda Terkildsen. "Gender Stereotypes and the Perception of Male and Female Candidates." *American Journal of Political Science* 37, no. 1 (1993): 119–47.

Hui-ping, Chen, and Jonathan Chin. "PROFILE: Tsai's Unexpected Political Journey." *Taipei Times*, January 18, 2016. http://www.taipeitimes.com/News/taiwan/archives/2016/01/18/2003637470/2, accessed June 10, 2019.

Hüstebeck, Momoyo. "Park Geun-Hye: The Eternal Princess?" In *Dynasties and Female Political Leaders in Asia: Gender, Power, and Pedigree*, edited by Claudia Derichs and Mark R. Thompson, 353–79. Münster, Germany: LIT Verlag, 2013.

Institute of Sociology Academia Sinica. "Taiwan Social Change Survey, Survey 2012, Phase 6, Wave 3, Quetionnaire II Family and Gender," 2012. https://www2.ios.sinica.edu.tw/sc/en/scDownload3.php, accessed July 14, 2019.

Inter-Parliamentary Union. "Percentage of Women in National Parliaments – Ranking as of 1st May 2020." IPU Parline, 2020. https://data.ipu.org/women-ranking?month=5&year=2020, accessed May 18, 2020.

Jacobs, J. Bruce. "Evaluating President Tsai's Apology to Indigenous People on Its First Anniversary." Ketagalan Media, 2017. https://www.ketagalanmedia.com/2017/09/11/evaluating-president-tsais-apology-indigenous-people-first-anniversary/, accessed March 13, 2019.

Jacobs, J. Bruce. "Indigenous Reconciliation? The Case of Taiwan." *Georgetown Journal of Asian Affairs* 3, no. 2 (2017): 31–36.

Jacobs, J. Bruce. "Introduction." In *Changing Taiwanese Identities*, edited by J. Bruce Jacobs and Peter Kang, 1–11. London, UK: Routledge, 2017.

Jalalzai, Farida. *Shattered, Cracked, or Firmly Intact: Women and the Executive Glass Ceiling Worldwide*. New York, NY: Oxford University Press, 2013.

Jang, Eun-Ju, Won-Taek Kang, Gui-Young Han, Tae-Ho Lee, Yoon-Cheol Kim, and Joo-Ho Lee. "Roundtable: The Meaning of the 18th Presidential Election and the Changes of South Korean Society (in Korean)]." *Simingwa Segye* 22 (2013): 74–104.

Jin, Joowon. "Yeokdae Daeseon Wanju Yeoseong Huboneun Gyeou 4myeong (in Korean).'" *Women News*, April 17, 2017. http://www.womennews.co.kr/news/articleView.html?idxno=113273, accessed June 20, 2019.

Joongang Ilbo. "[2000 Saekttugi] 3. Jeongchi- Park Geun-Hye Buchongjae (in Korean)." *Joongang Ilbo*, December 25, 2000. https://news.joins.com/article/4015286, accessed March 11, 2019.

Kang, Jun-Man. "Park Geun-Hye: Abeojireul Wihayeo (in Korean)." *Inmulgwa Sasang*, 1999.

Kim, Bong-Gi. "Park, "yeosong Daetongryong Keonan Dui Yoe Jijiyool 4–7% Sangsung [Campaign Slogan, 'Well-Prepared Female Candidate' Increased Female Voters' Support for Park (in Korean)]." *Chosun Ilbo*, November 22, 2012. http://news.chosun.com/site/data/html_dir/2012/11/22/2012112200200.html, accessed January 6, 2014.

Kim, Jaeho. "Yeoronjosa Sunwibakkum Tturyeot (in Korean)." *Donga Ilbo*, November 25, 1997. http://www.donga.com/news/View?gid=7301793&date=19971124, accessed June 10, 2019.

Kim, Jong-Wook, Hun-Tae Kim, Byung-Jin Ahn, Cheol-Hee Lee, and Han-Wool Jeong. *Park Geun-Hye Hyungsang: Jinbo Nongael Daejoong Sokeui Park Geyn-Hye Rool Haemyong Haha.* Seoul: Wisdom House, 2010.

Kim, Sohyun. "Lee Hoi-Chang Park Geun-Hye, Naega Jeonggye Immunsikyeo Daetongnyeong Doel Jul Mollatda (in Korean).'" *Hankook Kungjae*, August 22, 2017. https://www.hankyung.com/politics/article/201708227767Y, accessed March 11, 2019.

Ko, Shu-ling. "Koo Apologizes for Offensive Remarks." *Taipei Times*, May 8, 2008. http://www.taipeitimes.com/News/taiwan/archives/2008/05/08/2003411329, accessed June 10, 2019.

Ko, Shu-ling. "Koo Kwang-Ming Expected to Run in DPP Race." *Taipei Times*, April 18, 2008. http://www.taipeitimes.com/News/taiwan/archives/2008/04/18/2003409611/2, accessed June 10, 2019.

Ko, Shu-ling. "Tsai Ing-Wen Being Pushed to Stand in DPP Election." *Taipei Times*, April 17, 2008. http://www.taipeitimes.com/News/taiwan/archives/2008/04/17/2003409462, accessed June 10, 2019.

Korean National Election Commission. "Je18dae Daetongnyeong Seongeo Chongnam (in Korean)." Gwachon, Gyonggi-do, 2013.

Kwon, Jaehyun. "Choo Mi-ae Dangsalligi 3bo1bae Ssitgimgut (in Korean)" *Kyonghyang Shinmun*, April 4, 2004. http://news.khan.co.kr/kh_news/khan_art_view.html?art_id=200404041849331, accessed March 12, 2019.

Lee, Jiyoon. "Choo Mi-ae, Honam Minsim Dolligi 3bo1bae: 2bak3il Dongan Gwangju Dosim 15 km Gwantong Yejeong (in Korean)." *Pressian*, April 3, 2004. http://www.pressian.com/ezview/article_main.html?no=44139, accessed March 12, 2019.

Lee, Nae-Young, and Chong-Ki An. "The 18th Presidential Election and Retrospective Voting: Why Did Negative Retrospective Evaluation on the Ruling Government Did Not Make a Significant Impact on the Outcome of the 18th Presidential Election (in Korean)." *Hangukjeongdanghakoebo* 12, no. 2 (2013): 5–36.

Lee, Sang-Sin. "Personalization of Politics and Schematic Assessment of Presidential Candidates: How Korean Voters Perceive the Three Major Candidates for the 2012 Korean Presidential Election (Korean)." *Hangukjeongdanghakoebo* 46, no. 4 (2012): 149–70.

Lee, Young-Im. "From First Daughter to First Lady to First Woman President: Park Geun-Hye's Path to the South Korean Presidency." *Feminist Media Studies* 17, no. 3 (2017): 377–91.

Lee, Young-Im, and Farida Jalalzai. "President Park Geun-Hye of South Korea: A Woman President without Women?" *Politics & Gender* 13, no. 4 (2017): 597–617.

Li, Kuan-long. "There Are Reasons to Thank Chu." *Taipei Times*, October 12, 2015. http://www.taipeitimes.com/News/editorials/archives/2015/10/12/2003629832, accessed June 10, 2019.

Lim, Sunghack. "Election Issues" Change and Continuation during the 18th Presidential Election in Korea."'" *Dongayeongu* 25, no. 2 (2013): 181–201.

Lim, Timothy C. *Politics in East Asia: Explaining Change&Continuity*. Boulder, CO: Lynne Rienner, 2014.

Lin, Cho-shui. "'Tsai' Phenomenon Not about Turnout." *Taipei Times*, March 28, 2011. http://www.taipeitimes.com/News/editorials/archives/2011/03/28/2003499286, accessed June 10, 2019.

Liu, Shih-chung. "Tsai Must Think Nationally to Win." *Taipei Times*, August 30, 2011. http://www.taipeitimes.com/News/editorials/archives/2011/08/30/2003511998, accessed June 10, 2019.

Loa, Lok-sin. "Support for Taiwanese Independence, Identity: Think Tank Poll." *Taipei Times*, February 5, 2015. http://www.taipeitimes.com/News/taiwan/archives/2015/02/05/2003610873, accessed June 8, 2020.

Loa, Lok-sin. "Tsai Picks Chen Chu as Manager for Campaign." *Taipei Times*, August 13, 2015. http://www.taipeitimes.com/News/front/archives/2015/08/13/2003625225, accessed May 6, 2019.

Loa, Lok-sin. "Tsai Pushes for Tolerance, Touts Importance of Hakka." *Taipei Times*, August 3, 2015. http://www.taipeitimes.com/News/taiwan/archives/2015/08/03/2003624526, accessed March 13, 2019.

Loa, Lok-sin. "Tsai Wins Race for DPP Chairmanship." *Taipei Times*, May 19, 2008. http://www.taipeitimes.com/News/front/archives/2008/05/19/2003412357, accessed May 6, 2019.

Mo, Yan-chih. "President Pledges Push toward Gender Equality." *Taipei Times*, September 3, 2011. http://www.taipeitimes.com/News/taiwan/archives/2011/09/03/2003512346, accessed June 10, 2019.

Mulcahy, Mark, and Carol Linehan. "Females and Precarious Board Positions: Further Evidence of the Glass Cliff." *British Journal of Management* 25, no. 3 (July 5, 2014): 425–38.

Na, Young. "2012nyeon Daeseonui Yeoseong Hubodeul, Geurigo Kim So-youn gwa Kim Soon-ja (in Korean)." *Journal of Feminist Theories and Practices* 28 (2013): 215–26.

Oh, Yoo-seok. "An Analysis of Women Policies of the Park Geun-Hye Government (in Korean)." *Minjoo Sahoiwa Jeongchaek Yeongoo* 26 (2014): 201–30.

Organisation for Economic Co-operation and Development. "OECD Data." OECD, 2019. https://data.oecd.org/, accessed May 6, 2019.

Park, Daewoong. "Park Geun-Hye Tanhaek? Sewolho Chamsa Jiku Miyong Seonghyeong Nollan Gajung (in Korean)." *MK News*, November 21, 2016. https://www.mk.co.kr/news/photo/view/2016/11/808795/, accessed March 11, 2019.

Park, Geun-Hye. *Jeonmangeun Nareul Danryong Sikigo Huimangeun Nareul Woomjikinda* [*Park Geun-Hye's Autobiography* (*in Korean*)]. Seoul, Korea: Wisdom House, 2007.

Peng, Hsien-chun, and Jonathan Chin. "KMT Politician Demands Review of Hung's Selection." *Taipei Times*, October 4, 2015. http://www.taipeitimes.com/News/front/archives/2015/10/04/2003629216, accessed June 10, 2019.

Ramzy, Austin. "Presidential Race Reflects Women's Rise in Politics." *New York Times*, September 10, 2015. https://www.nytimes.com/2015/09/11/world/asia/taiwan-is-poised-to-elect-its-first-woman-as-president.html, accessed May 21, 2020.

Ryan, Michelle K., and S. Alexander Haslam. "The Glass Cliff? Exploring the Dynamics Surrounding the Appointment of Women to Precarious Leadership Positions." *The Academy of Management Review* 32, no. 2 (2007): 549–72.

Ryan, Michelle K., S. Alexander Haslam, and Clara Kulich. "Politics and the Glass Cliff: Evidence That Women Are Preferentially Selected to Contest Hard-to-Win Seats." *Psychology of Women Quarterly* 34, no. 1 (2010): 56–64.

Ryu, Jeongmin. "Tanhaekbandae 70 percent Uridang Jijiyul 30%daero Geupdeung (in Korean)." *MediaToday*, March 12, 2004. http://www.mediatoday.co.kr/?mod=news&act=articleView&idxno=26517, accessed January 2, 2019.

Saenuri Party. "Je 18dae Daetongnyeong Seongeo Chaekjahyeong Seongeo Gongbo: Junbidoen Yeoseong Daetongnyeong Park Geun-Hye [Official Campaign Pamphlet for Park Geun-Hye]." Gwachon, Gyonggi-do: Korean National Election Commission, 2012. http://nec.go.kr/portal/bbs/view/B0000363/22462.do?menuNo=200543&scDs=1&sgId=20121219&sgTypecode=2, accessed December 29, 2013.

Shih, Hsiu-chuan. "DPP to Chart New Beginning." *Taipei Times*, April 20, 2008. http://www.taipeitimes.com/News/taiwan/archives/2008/04/20/2003409768, accessed June 10, 2019.

Shih, Hsiu-chuan. "Tsai Enters DPP Chairmanship Election." *Taipei Times*, April 19, 2008. http://www.taipeitimes.com/News/front/archives/2008/04/19/2003409675, accessed June 10, 2019.

Shin, Ki-young. "Gender, Election Campaigns, and the First Female President of South Korea." ジェンダー研究 [*Gender Studies*] 21, no. June (2018): 71–86.

Song, Gukgun. "Hannaradang Park Geun-Hye Daepyo Dandok Interview Tanhaegi Choeseonui Seontaegeun Anieotda (in Korean)." *Shindonga*, April 27, 2004. http://shindonga.donga.com/Library/3/06/13/103376/1, accessed March 11, 2019.

Song, Ji-hye. "2004 Roh Moo-hyun vs 2016 Park Geun-Hye Tanhaek Bangjeongsik Bigyohaeboni (in Korean)." *JTBC*, November 24, 2016. http://news.jtbc.joins.com/article/article.aspx?news_id=NB11363644, accessed January 2, 2019.

Statistics Korea. "2018 Tonggyero Boneun Yeoseongui Sam (in Korean)." Kostat.go.kr, 2019. http://kostat.go.kr/portal/korea/kor_nw/1/6/1/index.board?bmode=read&aSeq=368636, accessed May 6, 2019.

Sullivan, Jonathan, and Chun-Yi Lee. "Introduction." In *A New Era in Democratic Taiwan: Trajectories and Turning Points in Politics and Cross-Strait Relations*, edited by Jonathan Sullivan and Chun-Yi Lee, 1–9. London and New York: Routledge, 2018.

Taipei Times. "DPP's Su Tseng-Chang Announces Presidential Bid." March 21, 2011. http://www.taipeitimes.com/News/front/archives/2011/03/21/2003498712, accessed June 10, 2019.

Taipei Times. "EDITORIAL: Can Tsai Win the Election?" May 9, 2011. http://www.taipeitimes.com/News/editorials/archives/2011/05/09/2003502754, accessed June 10, 2019.

Taipei Times. "EDITORIAL: Tsai Faces a Battle to Reform the DPP." May 19, 2008. http://www.taipeitimes.com/News/editorials/archives/2008/05/19/2003412345, accessed June 10, 2019.

Taipei Times. "EDITORIAL: When an Apology Isn't Enough." May 8, 2008. http://www.taipeitimes.com/News/editorials/archives/2008/05/08/2003411310, accessed June 10, 2019.

Taiwan Central Election Commission. "2020 Legislator Election." Taiwan Central Election Commission, 2020. https://www.cec.gov.tw/english/cms/le/32472, accessed May 18, 2020.

Tang, Chia-ling, and Hsiu-chuan Shih. "Effects of Sunflower Movement to Last." *Taipei Times*, March 18, 2015. http://www.taipeitimes.com/News/taiwan/archives/2015/03/18/2003613823, accessed June 10, 2019.

Templeman, Kharis. "Indigenous Legislators on Indigenous People's Day." kharistempleman.com, 2016. https://www.kharistempleman.com/blog/indigenous-legislators-on-indigenous-peoples-day, accessed March 13, 2019.

Templeman, Kharis. "When Do Electoral Quotas Advance Indigenous Representation?: Evidence from the Taiwanese Legislature." *Ethnopolitics* 17, no. 5 (2018): 461–84.

The International Foundation for Electoral Systems. "Elections – Taiwan – Election for President, Jan 16, 2016." ElectionGuide, 2016. http://www.electionguide.org/elections/id/2735/, accessed March 14, 2018.

Tsai Ing-wen, Chen Chien-jen: Light Up Taiwan. "DPP Nominates Chairperson Tsai Ing-Wen as 2016 Presidential Candidate." 2015. http://iing.tw/en/4, accessed July 14, 2019.

Tsai Ing-wen, Chen Chien-jen: Light Up Taiwan. "Tsai Ing-wen's Five Major Reforms." 2015. http://iing.tw/en/21, accessed July 14, 2019.

Tseng, Chao-yuan, and Yi-chien Chen. "Gender Equality Still Unaddressed." *Taipei Times*. December 26, 2015. http://www.taipeitimes.com/News/editorials/archives/2015/12/26/2003635677, accessed May 21, 2020.

Uh, Gisun. "Daegieobui Angmong, Chattegi Sageoniran (in Korean)." *NewsWatch*, November 15, 2016. http://www.newswatch.kr/news/articleView.html?idxno=8134, accessed March 11, 2019.

Wang, Chris. "2012 ELECTIONS: ANALYSIS: Multifaceted Tsai Is Different Kind of Candidate." *Taipei Times*, October 28, 2011. http://www.taipeitimes.com/News/taiwan/archives/2011/10/28/2003516876, accessed March 13, 2019.

Wang, Chris. "2012 ELECTIONS: Tsai Declares 2012 to Be 'Special Year.'" *Taipei Times*, January 1, 2012. http://www.taipeitimes.com/News/taiwan/archives/2012/01/01/2003522130, accessed June 10, 2019.

Wang, Chris. "ANALYSIS: Tsai Is Changing Female Voters' View of the DPP." *Taipei Times*, September 30, 2011. http://www.taipeitimes.com/News/taiwan/archives/2011/09/30/2003514563, accessed June 10, 2019.

Wang, Chris. "Su, Hsieh Drop out of DPP Chair Race." *Taipei Times*, April 15, 2014. http://www.taipeitimes.com/News/front/archives/2014/04/15/2003588056, accessed June 10, 2019.

Wang, Chris. "Tsai Ing-Wen Pledges to Promote Sexual Equality." *Taipei Times*, October 25, 2011. http://www.taipeitimes.com/News/taiwan/archives/2011/10/25/2003516632, accessed June 10, 2019.

World Values Survey. "World Values Survey," 2015. http://www.worldvaluessurvey.org/wvs.jsp, accessed May 1, 2020.

Worldwide Guide to Women in Leadership. "Women Presidential Candidates," 2019. http://www.guide2womenleaders.com/woman_presidential_candidates.htm, accessed June 10, 2019.

Yang, Kwon-Mo. "Hannara Park Geun-Hye Yoo Dong-Geun Ssi Yeongip Chujin [Grand National Party Approaches Park and Yoo]." *Kyonghyang Shinmun*, December 3, 1997.

Yang, Wan-Ying, and Kuan-Chen Lee. "Ready for a Female President in Taiwan?" *Journal of Women, Politics & Policy* 37, no. 4 (2016): 464–89.

CHAPTER 7

East Asian Area Studies Teaching Programs in the United Kingdom

A Comparative Case Study of Korean Studies at the University of Central Lancashire and Taiwan Studies at SOAS, University of London

Dafydd Fell and Sojin Lim

The initial idea of this chapter originated at the International Workshop on the Landscape of Taiwan Studies and Korean Studies held at the University of Central Lancashire (UCLan) in June 2018. The workshop opened with a panel looking at the development of the two fields, with the first author of this paper, Fell, speaking about the experiences of Taiwan Studies teaching at the School of Oriental and African Studies, University of London (SOAS). This was followed by lively debate both in the panel and over the rest of the workshop about the challenges facing both fields. Fell had recently completed a journal paper comparing the experiences of developing Taiwan Studies teaching programs in a UK and a US university.[1] The discussions at the UCLan workshop suggested that it would be equally fruitful to compare Taiwan and Korean Studies teaching programs at two UK universities.

Today's higher education sector in the UK presents a challenging and sometimes hostile environment for niche area studies programs. However, Korean Studies at UCLan and Taiwan Studies at SOAS have managed to expand their teaching programs at a time when many universities have closed or reduced such programs. In this chapter, we examine and compare the development trajectories and operation of these seemingly successful teaching programs. We will also discuss what strategies have proved effective in facilitating program survival but also highlight some of the future challenges to sustainability.

---

1   Dafydd Fell and Sung-sheng Yvonne Chang. "Developing Taiwan Studies Teaching Program in Europe and the United States: the experience of SOAS University of London and University of Texas at Austin." *China Quarterly*, 240 (2019), 1108–1134.

1   Origins and Program Development of Taiwan Studies at SOAS

When the SOAS Taiwan program was established in 1999, Taiwan was largely absent from the university's teaching programs. At most, modules on China's politics or East Asian economics devoted a week to the case of Taiwan. However, this was a time when academic attention to Taiwan and also Taiwan-related publications were on the rise.[2] Taiwan's social, economic and political transformations since the 1980s all contributed to this growing interest in Taiwan.

The development of the SOAS Taiwan teaching program has gone through a number of stages over the last two decades. It started out as a tiny program and over time has become what is now the most extensive range of Taiwan focused modules at any university in Europe or North America. In the initial stage, SOAS created a single year-long postgraduate option entitled Contemporary Taiwan. This was a co-taught interdisciplinary module that included sections on Taiwan's history, society, politics and economics with teachers coming from four different departments. This initial stage ran from 2000–2001 to the 2004–2005 academic year.

The first expansion in the range of modules at SOAS came in the 2005–2006 academic year when the year-long Contemporary Taiwan module was replaced by three term-long modules. These were Government and Politics in Taiwan, Economic Development of Modern Taiwan, and Society and Culture in Taiwan. In addition, another term-long module called Modern Film from Taiwan and the Chinese Diaspora as well as a year-long Elementary Spoken Hokkien option were introduced. While Taiwan classes are often located in East Asia or China Studies departments in many universities, in the SOAS case, many of the new modules were located in disciplinary departments, such as Politics and International Relations as well as Economics. Even though the Taiwan film module was located in the China and Inner Asia Department, it was well integrated into a range of Film Studies degree programs as well.

The Centre of Taiwan Studies was established at the same time and located in the Faculty of Law and Social Sciences. This was partly due to the fact that the lead academics were social scientists; however, the program has tried to be as inclusive as possible in terms of its disciplinary coverage. The Centre has had the task of coordinating the teaching across the various departments, as well as organizing academic events that supplement the teaching program.

2   Shelley Rigger. "Political Science and Taiwan's Domestic Politics: The State of the Field." *Issues and Studies*, 38, no. 4 (2002), 49–92.

The expansion in modules made it possible from 2006–2007 to offer the Master of Arts (MA) Taiwan Studies degree, the first such postgraduate degree in Europe or North America. These MA students were required to take all four of the term-long Taiwan modules, one further year-long optional module and write a 10,000-word dissertation on a topic focused on Taiwan.[3] The second stage lasted from 2005–2006 through to 2009–2010.

The next major turning point came in 2010–2011 and 2011–2012. This was the beginning of the third period of the Taiwan teaching program as once again there was a significant expansion. We can see the overall development of module offerings from 2000 through to the academic year of 2019–2020 in Table 7.1. This reveals that, although there have been some minor adjustments to the teaching program since 2011–2012, we remain in this third period today. Another trend apparent in Table 7.1 is that there has been a high degree of stability in the Taiwan options at SOAS. In other words, once modules have been established, they have run on an annual basis with only a small number of exceptions. This stands in stark contrast to the case of the Taiwan teaching program at the University of Texas at Austin, where though a wider number of modules have been offered, almost none of them operate on a regular basis.[4]

Three major changes marked the start of the third period of the SOAS Taiwan teaching program. First, the term-long Government and Politics in Taiwan was replaced by the year-long Taiwan's Politics and Cross-Strait Relations, allowing much greater depth of coverage for both Taiwan's domestic and external politics. Secondly, SOAS introduced its first undergraduate module, the year-long Taiwan's Politics and International Relations.[5] Thirdly, a year-long module called 'North East Asian Politics: Japan, Korea and Taiwan was introduced. This uses a mix of comparative politics and comparative political economy approaches to examine these three East Asian democracies.[6] Each week a

---

3 Elementary Spoken Hokkien is an optional module on the degree since the establishment of the degree Hokkien has only been taken by a minority of students. Instead, they have tended to either take a Chinese language option or a social science (especially East Asian politics) class. From 2017–2018 SOAS changed its credit framework so that students need to take a further year-long module.

4 Dafydd Fell and Sung-sheng Yvonne Chang. 2019. "Developing Taiwan Studies Teaching Program in Europe and the United States: the experience of SOAS University of London and University of Texas at Austin." *China Quarterly*, 240: 1108–1134.

5 Initially this was titled Taiwan's Political and Economic Development but was redesigned to become a purely political science module after the retirement of the Economics Professor Robert Ash after 2015–2016.

6 The only part of the module that is not comparative is the two weeks looking at North Korean politics.

different political theme is examined by looking comparatively at the three countries and all assessed student work has to be comparative. The changes that have occurred since 2012 to the Taiwan teaching program have been comparatively minor. For instance, after the 2014–2015 academic year, we had to close the Economic Development of Modern Taiwan module due to the retirement of Professor Robert Ash.

Although SOAS introduced an alternative term-long module in 2016–2017 in the Law School entitled Law, Rights and Society in Taiwan, this only ran for two years before being withdrawn. In the academic year of 2018–2019 a new term-long undergraduate Taiwan film module was added. Moreover, in 2019–2020 SOAS introduced an undergraduate version of Culture and Society in Taiwan. This means there will be four Taiwan options available to undergraduates for the first time.

From Table 7.1 we can see a number of features in the way the SOAS Taiwan teaching program has evolved. Most obviously, the number of modules has increased over time and there has been a shift towards more in-depth and disciplinary options. Despite the fact that the Centre is often mistakenly viewed as being social science focused, the teaching has been quite diverse with a similar number of modules in the humanities and languages. Finally, there has also been a gradual attempt to move away from a postgraduate only program by giving a wider set of options to undergraduates.

The patterns of student numbers are also summarized in Table 7.1. We can see how the trends correspond with the three periods and that there has been a growing trend in total numbers over time. Although there was an increase in the total number of students taking Taiwan modules after the first expansion in 2005–2006, at the level of individual modules the picture was often mixed. For instance, in one year (2007–2008) there was only a single student in two modules and the Society and Culture in Taiwan did not run. In the second phase, the Taiwan film module was by far the most popular. The table also shows the positive impact of the expansion in phase three. The undergraduate Taiwan's Politics and International Relations, comparative North East Asian Politics and the new year-long postgraduate module Taiwan's Politics and Cross-Strait Relations have also all proved very popular.

Some readers may feel that the numbers of students on the Taiwan modules look rather low. However, when we compare them to similar regional modules at SOAS the numbers are comparable. For example, the numbers of students on the Taiwan politics or Taiwan film modules tend to be similar to those on the domestic China politics and China film modules. External subsidies were important at SOAS in phases 1 and 2 for some of the modules and even today Taiwan's Ministry of Education partly supports one Taiwan teaching post.

However, in phase 3 (after 2009) the majority of the Taiwan modules have run without external support. This is partly due to the nature of the university as large modules are the exception. Instead, the vast majority of teaching is done on the basis of seminar style classes, especially at the postgraduate level.

Table 7.1 does not of course tell the whole story when it comes to the inclusion of Taiwan into the SOAS teaching program. Many of the modules that do not have Taiwan in their titles also have significant coverage of Taiwan. For example, after the Taiwan Law module was withdrawn, the Chinese Law modules continue to offer a number of weeks looking at Taiwan. This practice of integrating Taiwan into regular disciplinary and regional modules makes it possible to reach a wider number of students and often students that have their first taste of Taiwan in such modules will be inspired to then take a Taiwan specific module later in their studies. For instance, on the Comparative Political Sociology in Asia and Africa module, there are five weeks looking at Taiwan, Korea and Japan and students will often take the Taiwan Politics and International Relations module in their next year.

Readers may also be curious about the nationality of SOAS Taiwan Studies students. These trends are summarized in Table 7.2. Unsurprisingly, students from the UK have been by far the largest group taking Taiwan modules since 2000, accounting for over a third of students. Students from the People's Republic of China (PRC) and Taiwan came second and third respectively. EU countries have also been important, particularly Italy (4th), with Germany and France also coming in the top ten. The other important country sources have been the US (5th), Hong Kong (6th), Japan (7th) and Singapore (10th). While some country's students have proved consistently to select Taiwan modules, there have been some interesting changes over time. There has been a noticeable drop in the proportion of students from Taiwan taking modules in the third phase, falling to the 5th source country after 2010–2011. The most noticeable increase came with the large numbers of students from the PRC, making it by far the most common source of students after those from the UK in phase 3. Another noteworthy rise has been of students from Hong Kong who rose from the 9th source country in phase 2 to fourth in phase 3, even outnumbering students from Taiwan.

One area that has not been covered in the tables is PhD research on Taiwan. Where students wish to conduct PhD research on Taiwan, they do so in the various disciplinary departments rather than getting a PhD in Taiwan Studies. In other words, the Taiwan specialists at SOAS supervise Taiwan research students within their disciplinary departments such as Politics, Anthropology or Law. The Centre supports these PhD students in a variety of ways, such as allowing them to audit Taiwan classes in Year 1, providing platforms for them to present

TABLE 7.1   Student numbers for SOAS Taiwan modules 2005–2020

	2005/ 2006	2006/ 2007	2007/ 2008	2008/ 2009	2009/ 2010	2010/ 2011	2011/ 2012	2012/ 2013	2013/ 2014	2014/ 2015	2015/ 2016	2016/ 2017	2017/ 2018	2018– 2019	2019– 2020
Govt and Politics in Taiwan	6	3	1	4	2	4	7	8	15	11	11	11	19	8	18
Society and Culture	7	3	N/R	6	6	3	4	6	8	7	6	6	8	6	6
Economics	2	3	1	5	3	3	5	5	6	8	Closed				
Film	14	8	6	18	16	10	12	6	5	12	14	15	18	19	17
Hokkien	3	4	N/R	2	12	5	11	8	N/R	N/R	11	8	5	5	N/R
Taiwan's Political and Economic Development (UG)						10	12	16	13	20	11	23	10	10	11
North East Asian Politics: Japan, Korea and Taiwan							5	18	13	16	18	13	15	16	

Taiwan Film (UG)											21		16
Taiwan Law										5	3	Closed	10
Culture and Society (UG)													
MA Taiwan Studies (full degree)	1	2	0	0.5	2.3	3.3	1	4	3	3	5	1	1	3

SOURCE: COMPILED BY FELL

Note 1: In 2010–2011, Government and Politics in Taiwan was closed, and a new year-long module Taiwan's Politics and Cross-Strait Relations was introduced.

Note 2: From 2016–2017, the undergraduate module was redesigned and renamed Taiwan's Politics and International Relations.

Note 3: The numbers for the single Contemporary Taiwan modules were: 2000–2001 (12), 2001–2002 (9), 2002–2003 (5), 2003–2004 (4), 2004–2005 (6).

Note 4: N/R means Not Run.

TABLE 7.2   Most common nationalities taking SOAS Taiwan modules

Ranking	2000–2005 (40)	2005–2010 (122)	2010–2018 (460)	2000–2018 (622)
1	Taiwan: 11	UK: 30	UK: 135	UK: 173
2	UK: 8	Taiwan: 22	China: 83	China: 93
3	HK: 4	Italy: 20	USA: 32	Taiwan: 61
4	Japan: 4	France: 9	HK: 29	Italy: 45
5	USA: 3	China: 9	Taiwan: 28	USA: 43
6	Germany: 3	USA: 8	Italy: 26	HK: 36
7	Thailand: 2	Japan: 5	Japan: 21	Japan: 30
8		Germany: 4	Singapore: 17	Germany: 20
9		HK: 3	Germany: 13	France: 18
10		Singapore/ Canada: 3	Korea: 9	Singapore: 20

SOURCE: COMPILED BY FELL

Note: Data does not include Hokkien module.

their research design and later results, as well as offering some limited funding support. However, perhaps the most important contribution the Centre can make towards PhD students is through the academic events program that provides a Taiwan Studies study environment quite unlike any other university.

2   Origins and Program Development of Korean Studies at UCLan

The development of Korean Studies at UCLan shows a pattern similar to the gradual expansion of SOAS Taiwan Studies. However, while SOAS Taiwan Studies initially focused on the postgraduate level, UCLan has a higher number of students at the undergraduate level. At UCLan, taught courses in the field of Asian Studies were dominated by Chinese and Japanese Studies until 2012. However, since Korean Studies was introduced in the 2013–2014 academic year, it has become the largest group in terms of the number of students. The Korean Studies teaching program at the undergraduate level is called 'Korean subject or pathway' since it has not yet been validated at the degree level, but instead is embedded under the following three degrees: BA (Hons) Asia Pacific Studies (APS); BA (Hons) Teaching English to Speakers of Other Languages

(TESOL); and BA (Hons) Modern Languages (MOLA). Like the SOAS case, the BA Korean subject at UCLan also started with a small number of students in 2014, but within five years, it has increased more than six times as shown in Figure 7.1. The number of students in the Korean Studies BA program at UCLan has become one of the largest in the UK and Europe.

The expansion in the range of modules at UCLan happened at the same time as the launch of the International Institute of Korean Studies (also known as IKSU) in 2014. Similarly, after establishing the MA North Korean Studies (NKS) in May 2015, UCLan also began to design and expand non-language modules at the BA level in the social sciences and humanities. For example, in the 2014–2015 academic year, UCLan began to run two modules related to history (Background to Korea) and society and culture (Contemporary Korean Society and Culture) alongside Ab Initio Korean language modules. From the 2016–2017 academic year, UCLan began to run a module on South-North Korea relations (Divided Korea), which was intended to link to its MA NKS program. The MA NKS is the only MA degree program in North Korean Studies outside the Korean Peninsula for both teaching and research programs.

The Korean Studies teaching program at UCLan started with a strong emphasis on language training, but recent trends show some changes. For example, from the academic year of 2019–2020, MA NKS does not have any language modules at all, but runs as a social science program under the area studies field of study. Students will still be able to take language classes, not from regular degree modules, but from the certificate language program. However, there has been a more mixed picture in the structure at the under-graduate level. From the 2019–2020 academic year, the existing Contemporary Korean Society and Culture module is no longer offered but is replaced by a new module which contains both language as well as society and culture (Ab Initio Korean Language and Society 2).

While SOAS Taiwan Studies has existed for over two decades, the history of Korean Studies at UCLan is relatively short–only less than ten years. In this sense, it does not have such distinct 'phases' of development in its teaching program. However, as its MA program was re-launched in the 2018–2019 aca-demic year, this can be perceived as the beginning of its second phase. In its initial launch in the 2015–2016 academic year, UCLan received one applicant for its research-based master program (MRes). Unfortunately, there were no more applicants for the following two years as the program was not officially advertised. However, with a new leadership at the International Institute of Korean Studies in August 2017 and with increasing interests in the Korean Peninsula, especially in North Korea, the University decided to re-open the MA NKS degree with more active marketing. The re-opened MA NKS has now

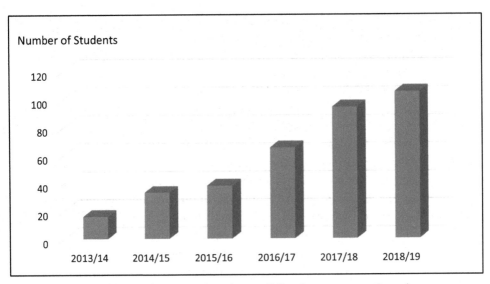

FIGURE 7.1   Number of BA students in Korean subject at UCLan (2013–2014 to 2018–2019)

been interwoven with the MA Asia Pacific Studies (APS), which was validated in November 2017.

The MA NKS and MA APS degrees are closely linked as they share some of the same modules. For example, modules in MA NKS are optional modules for MA APS, while modules in MA APS are optional modules for MA NKS. The logic behind this structure is that MA NKS students need to understand a wider spectrum of dynamics in the Asia Pacific region, including international relations with non-APS countries, such as the United States (US), in order to become experts on North Korea. Of course, they also need to build an in-depth understanding and knowledge of North Korea.

At the same time, we can see signs of a second phase in the Korean Studies teaching in the structural change to the postgraduate program. From its inception, MA NKS was designed in a similar style to the undergraduate level with a mix of language and non-language modules. It had three pathways (the Social Science pathway, the Korean Language pathway, and the combined Social Science/Korean Language pathway). However, UCLan decided to remove the language component from its MA NKS program in order to focus more on social science modules so that students can develop a deeper country knowledge base within the one-year program. As postgraduate degrees in the UK generally run only for one year, it is not practically efficient for students to take both social science and language modules. Instead with more Korean social science and humanities modules they can build up sufficient country and region-specific

TABLE 7.3   UCLan BA Korean subject modules (as of 2019–2020)

Code	Module title	Year
KO1000	Background to Korea (year long)	Year 1
KO1001	Ab Initio Korean (year long)	Year 1
KO2001	Ab Initio Korean Language and Society 1 (semester long)	Year 2
KO2002	Structure, Variation and Change in the Korean Language (semester long)	Year 2
KO2003	Ab Initio Korean Language and Society 2 (semester long)	Year 2
KO3001	Korean Language (semester long)	Year 4 (after study abroad)
KO3002	Korea Language and Studies (semester long)	Year 3 (who did not take study abroad year)
KO3003	Korean Language for Academic Purposes (year long)	Year 3/4
KO3008	Divided Korea (semester long)	Year 3/4

SOURCE: COMPILED BY LIM

knowledge. The Korean Studies modules available in 2019–2020 at both post-graduate and undergraduate levels are listed in Tables 7.3 and 7.4.

One key thing that distinguishes SOAS and UCLan is that most of the students enrolled in the UCLan Korean pathway at the undergraduate level can take their third year as study abroad in Korea before they proceed to their final year. On average, about 87 percent of students take study abroad for their third year. Until 2018–2019, UCLan used to have 11 partner universities in South Korea for its study abroad program, but due to the increasing number of students who are expected to go to Korea for their study abroad year, six new partners joined in 2018, and students had 17 universities in Korea for their study abroad as of 2018–2019. A further two more universities in Korea will be added in the 2020–2021 academic year. The list of partner universities in Korea is available in Table 7.5.

The picture is quite different at SOAS as the majority of undergraduates taking Taiwan courses are not enrolled in Chinese language degree programs and do not have the option of a year or even a semester in Taiwan. Even for those

TABLE 7.4   UCLan MA North Korean studies modules (as of 2019–2020)

Code	Module title (semester-long modules)	Credit (180 credits to be completed)
Compulsory		
KO4900	Dissertation in North Korean Studies	60
Optional		
KO4010	Explaining Inter-Korean Relations	20
KO4011	North Korea: History, Politics and International Relations	20
KO4012	North Korea: Economics and Society	20
KO4013	Development in Fragile States and Accountable Institution	20
KO4014	Divided Nations: Disputes, Violence, and Conflict	20
AI4101	China-Japan-Korea Trilateral Relations	20
AI4102	Globalization and Economic Development in the Asia Pacific	20
AI4103	Historical Transformation in the Asia Pacific	20
AI4104	Political Changes and Social Movements in the Asia Pacific	20
AI4106	East Asian Philosophy and Thought	20
AI4107	Critical East Asian Cinema Studies	20
TR4002	Theory of Interpreting and Translation	20
TR4008	Professional Business Skills	20
TR4071	Diplomatic Service & International Organizations	20

SOURCE: COMPILED BY LIM

on Chinese language degrees at SOAS, they currently can only choose one university in the People's Republic of China (PRC) for their year abroad (taken in the second year). At the same time, while SOAS tends to have a wide range of nationalities for its students, the majority of UCLan Korean Studies students are UK home students with a small group of European students.

TABLE 7.5   UCLan BA Korean subject study abroad partners in South Korea (as of 2019-2020)

1. Ajou University
2. Busan University of Foreign Studies
3. Chonbuk National University
4. Chung Ang University
5. Dongguk University
6. Ewha Womans University
7. Hankuk University of Foreign Studies
8. Inje University
9. Jeju National University
10. Keimyung University
11. Kyungpook National University
12. Pusan National University
13. Sejong University
14. Sogang University
15. Sookmyung Women's University
16. Soongsil University
17. Sungkyunkwan University

SOURCE: COMPILED BY LIM

The doctoral program in Korean Studies at UCLan began to receive applications in 2014, and the first PhD candidate was recruited in October 2014. In May 2015, two more PhD candidates were recruited in Korean Studies. During this period, UCLan provided one fully funded PhD scholarship and another partially funded PhD scholarship for its Korean Studies doctoral program. As of 2019–2020, a new PhD candidate starts her Korean Studies program at UCLan based on the second author's (Lim's) expertise, development cooperation in North Korea.

Throughout the BA, MA and PhD programs in Korean Studies at UCLan, the majority of students have tended to select dissertation themes in international relations, although some have written their dissertations on culture and society issues. It is very unlikely that students write their dissertations on Korean language or linguistics topics. Recently, at the PhD level, there has been growing interest in North Korea and the Korean Peninsula in the context of international development cooperation, which is the second author's (Lim) research area. In contrast, at SOAS, dissertations on Taiwanese domestic and international politics have been popular and the topics and disciplines covered have been very diverse. Other topics that have proved popular for recent dissertations have included social movements, education policy, film studies, literature, tourism, music and modern history.

3 Rationales for Studying in Korean and Taiwan Studies: Student Surveys

In order to analyze the main reasons why students want to take Korean subjects, UCLan conducted a survey among students in Korean language modules in 2018–2019 (1st year, 2nd year, and final year students). Language modules are mandatory for all Korean pathway students. 164 out of a total of 229 students, 72 percent, responded.

In general, there were six main reasons why students selected the Korean pathway including language, culture, history, non-language modules, general interest in Korea, and the study links to their career plan. Among students who responded to 'language', we found an interest in languages in general, specific interest in the Korean language, and an interest in Asian languages. For those with a specific interest in the Korean language, students tended to take the Korean pathway because they want to learn Korean or to develop their existing Korean proficiency to a more professional level. The latter mentioned that they had studied Korean on their own and wanted to continue to learn. Cultural interests can also be divided into three categories including general interests in culture, specific interest in Korean culture, and interests in Asian cultures more broadly. In history, students had general historical interests, specific interests in Korean history, and interests in broader Asian history.

An interesting result from the survey is that not many respondents mentioned K-Pop or K-Drama as the reasons they chose the Korean pathway. We had initially assumed that the main reason why there has been an increasing number of students in the Korean pathway is due to the recent global trends in popular culture, especially with K-Pop and K-Drama. Only 12 percent of respondents mentioned that they became interested in Korean language or Korean culture due to K-Pop, while 5 percent of respondents mentioned K-Drama. Most respondents stated that they are interested in Korean language and culture as it is different from European languages and culture.

At the MA level, it seems that having dedicated a MA in North Korean Studies is a strong reason for students to choose UCLan for the MA NKS degree. At the same time, the fact that there are specialized academics in the field tends to attract students to enroll in this course as those aspects make the modules and the course itself appealing. For example, one applicant mentioned that he could not find any other academics in the UK, but the one at UCLan, who is working on development cooperation in North Korea with hands-on experience at the aid agency. In the case of the PhD program, candidates joined UCLan Korean Studies PhD program due to the expertise of academics. However, it was also revealed that scholarship opportunities played an important role for some of the candidates when they joined the PhD program at UCLan in Korean Studies.

SOAS has conducted two student surveys for those taking a Taiwan module as well. The first surveyed those who had taken a module between 2000 and 2015 and a second for those studying between 2015–2016 and 2016–2017. We did not include an item on why students selected a Taiwan course, but we can comment on some of the common explanations given by students over the years.

As we saw in the UCLan survey of the MA NKS degree, many SOAS students wanted to take advantage of being able to take modules that were not available at any other university. For instance, many who had graduated from Chinese Studies undergraduate programs had learned a little about Taiwan but wanted to take advantage of the more in-depth Taiwan modules at SOAS. Another similarity was in the importance of popular culture. While Korean culture was a partial source of attraction for Korean Studies, it has been the success of Taiwanese cinema in winning major international awards and critical acclaim that helps explain the popularity of our Taiwan film modules. Although some students did first become interested in Taiwan as a result of its Mando-pop, the proportion was lower than those selecting Korean Studies due to K-Pop.

One major difference in our two cases concerns the importance of language learning, which was the dominant factor for UCLan Korean Studies. In contrast, this was rarely cited as important at SOAS. One of the reasons is that most of the SOAS students who do a language year abroad currently only go to universities in the PRC. Nevertheless, this should not be entirely discounted, as many of our students did visit Taiwan during their year in China and became fascinated with the differences they found. Moreover, others had previously received scholarships to study Chinese in Taiwan prior to coming to SOAS and wanted to learn more about its politics, society and history. In addition, SOAS was attractive to some students, being the only university that offers a year long Hokkien (Taiwanese) language course.

Partly because many of the SOAS students are postgraduates, many had previous experiences of visiting Taiwan for travel or study or even working in Taiwan. A number of the growing group of PRC students had also been to Taiwan as exchange students. Other students had worked in Taiwan, often as language teachers, as was the case for the first author (Fell) of this paper. Another link that has attracted students to Taiwan modules has been through family ties. A number of our students are second or third-generation overseas Taiwanese living in Europe or North America.

Generally, the most important reason for taking SOAS Taiwan modules has been academic related. In other words, students wanted to take a Taiwan politics or film module to give them an overall regional coverage from a disciplinary perspective. In fact, the vast majority of SOAS students are only taking a single Taiwan option in their degree program rather than specializing solely on Taiwan. For instance, though area studies students on programs such as MA Chinese Studies still make up a significant proportion of Taiwan module students, the overall trend has been towards students on disciplinary degrees such as Master of Science (MSc) Politics of China or MSc International Politics.

Overall SOAS had positive survey findings about students' experience of its teaching program. In the first survey, 75 percent (88 percent in the second survey) were very satisfied with their Taiwan modules, with a further 23.1 percent somewhat satisfied. In addition, 65.4 percent (80 percent in the second survey) percent of respondents stated that they had used what they learned in their Taiwan modules in subsequent work or studies. Over 80 percent of respondents stated they still follow the Centre of Taiwan Studies developments after graduating either on social media or by continuing to join events after graduating. One of the most pleasing trends from the perspective of teachers at SOAS has been seeing a number of students continue their Taiwan research at the doctoral level. Many have later returned to SOAS to give academic talks and published their work on Taiwan.

4   Strategies for Success

Before the Korean pathway was created at UCLan, the APS course (Hons) was established in order to embrace all of the Chinese, Japanese and Korean subjects under a regional Asian Studies theme. This strategy has worked out well since the APS degree program has the largest number of students enrolled in comparison with other degrees within the school, and within the APS program, the largest number of students are taking Korean subjects. At the beginning, it was the Japanese pathway which had the highest number but, more recently, Korean Studies is the most popular subject. The situation is similar in TESOL and MOLA courses as well. This can be observed from our survey — about 39 percent of respondents answered that they chose UCLan as they were attracted by the chance to incorporate Korean subjects into their degree program.

Another strategy for Korean Studies is to diversify its subject coverage. In other words, Korean Studies does not stay within one School (or Department at other universities) but operates in conjunction with other Schools at UCLan. For example, students enrolled in the degree of English Language and Linguistics BA (Hons) in the School of Humanities and Social Sciences can take the Korean pathway in the School of Language and Global Studies. In this way, UCLan has successfully increased the number of students enrolled in the Korean pathway. UCLan is currently developing a 'Game Design and Korean' pathway involving the School of Journalism, Media and Performance and the School of Language and Global Studies. We expect that more students will be able to study Korean Studies across a wider range of disciplines.

At SOAS, the modules do not belong to the Centre of Taiwan Studies but are located in either disciplinary departments (such as Politics and International Studies) or area studies departments (especially East Asian Studies). Although SOAS has its unique MA Taiwan Studies, where students take multiple Taiwan related modules, these only make up a minority of the students enrolled in Taiwan-related modules. Most students are only taking a single Taiwan option as part of an area studies or disciplinary degree. Therefore, a key challenge to Taiwan Studies sustainability has been raising awareness of the various Taiwan modules and also making them available in a wide range of degree programs. In the early phases, the Taiwan modules were highly reliant on students from area studies degrees. This led to variation in student numbers due to the very diverse range of options on such programs and because the numbers of students on area studies have often been unstable. Over time, awareness of Taiwan modules has increased and similarly, more of them have become either core or compulsory modules.

One of the reasons for the popularity of the North East Asian Politics module at SOAS is that it is well integrated into the Korean Studies, Japanese Studies and Asian Politics degree programs. Similarly, the Taiwan Politics and Cross-Strait Relations module has benefitted from becoming a core compulsory module of the MSc Politics of China. In the same way, the Taiwan film modules have benefitted from being well integrated into a range of film-related degree programs. In contrast, where Taiwan modules were not well integrated into programs or the home departments were not overly supportive, certain modules proved less popular and ultimately were withdrawn. The fate of both the Taiwan economics and Taiwan law modules fit this pattern. In short, in both universities, a key reason for the viability of our specialist modules has been better integration into a wide range of both area studies and disciplinary degree programs.

At the postgraduate level, as discussed above, having a unique degree in the field of study has worked well strategically for MA NKS at UCLan. At the same time, the Divided Korea module at the undergraduate level seems to attract students interested in North Korea, and thus, encourages students to continue their studies in this discipline. SOAS holds an advantage similar to UCLan's MA NKS. The SOAS MA Taiwan Studies offers a unique set of modules not available elsewhere. Originally, the Centre of Taiwan Studies had also hoped that there could be more students starting to study Taiwan at the undergraduate level and moving on to study at greater depth at the MA Taiwan Studies level. However, this has not been common as there is too much overlap in the postgraduate and undergraduate module content. For instance, the Taiwan Film module has a shared lecture for undergraduate and postgraduate students. Instead, where students do become interested in Taiwan at the undergraduate level and stay on to postgraduate study, they will take a single postgraduate Taiwan module or focus on Taiwan for their postgraduate dissertation research.

As the MA NKS degree is situated in area studies, UCLan has developed a strategy to develop dual/double degree programs with other area studies departments in Taiwan, South Korea and Japan. As students enrolled in UCLan MA NKS program are mostly from the UK and Europe, it is intended to bring more dynamics in nationalities and different cultural backgrounds of students in the classroom by inviting students through dual/double degree programs from the above-mentioned countries. While the UK MA degrees are designed for one year of study, UCLan MA NKS students spend one year at UCLan, and continue to study another year at a partner institution in order to obtain dual/double degrees. In this way, students can graduate with MA NKS at UCLan, along with another degree in, for instance, MA International Relations, MA International Studies or MA Korean Studies from partner universities in Korea and Taiwan. As this program is about to start from the academic year of 2019–2020, UCLan does not know direct impact of this strategy, but it is likely that this strategy will strengthen the MA NKS program at UCLan.

Unlike UCLan, SOAS has not been able to develop dual/double degree programs with a Taiwan Studies focus. A key reason for this is that the majority of postgraduate students are on one-year master programs and so even short visits to Taiwan would not fit into an already intensive program. There is more scope for a Taiwan language year option or study abroad option. The main barrier to this has long been that SOAS Chinese language year abroad students have only had the option of the PRC. It is hoped that the option of a Taiwan language year could be added in the future. Given that SOAS has now started a dual degree program with a Japanese university, this is something that SOAS Taiwan Studies will be considering for the future.

One major feature that makes the SOAS teaching program stand out is the related Taiwan events program organized by the Centre of Taiwan Studies. In recent years, the schedule has included 60–75 public events per year. The design of the events program closely complements the teaching program. Thus, events relevant to Taiwan's politics, film, modern history, sociology, and popular culture reinforce the Taiwan teaching program. Students soon realize at the start of the academic year that they are likely to meet many of the authors from their Taiwan module reading lists during their time at SOAS.

There are a few events that are especially important in creating a unique study environment for students of Taiwan Studies. Firstly, the Centre of Taiwan Studies holds regular events throughout the two main teaching terms, and these are generally held on the same day as the main Taiwan classes. It is hoped that these will allow students to have the confidence to join the events and be equipped to ask challenging questions to the speakers. Similarly, such events often will become the topic of class debate in the subsequent weeks. Secondly, the Centre of Taiwan Studies has held a popular screening series called Understanding Taiwan through Film and Documentary since 2013. In addition to film screenings these usually also include Q&A sessions with either the film director or a film scholar. A highlight of this program is the annual Taiwan Film Week, usually held in February.

As with the regular events program, the films selected tend to be ones that deal with topics such as political and social issues or Taiwan's modern history. In other words, the event is designed with the hope that the screening will provoke lively debate and discussion and again to supplement the more academic readings on the modules. Probably the most popular annual event is the SOAS Taiwan Summer School that is usually held in late June or early July. This is a free four to five-day event that looks at a different set of themes each year. However, the themes are often chosen on the basis of topics about which the students are especially interested in. For instance, in recent years, a common theme has been Taiwan's vibrant civil society and social movements, a subject many students have been working on in their dissertation research.

One of the most important parts of the Summer School is that students have the chance to give brief presentations on their dissertation projects and receive feedback from both the teaching team and their peers. In addition, students are encouraged to join other postgraduate conferences to gain feedback on their dissertation research, particularly the European Association of Taiwan Studies and British Postgraduate Chinese Studies Conferences. The final type of noteworthy event has been sessions with politicians. Each year the Centre of Taiwan Studies hosts a number of politicians to give public talks or sometimes non-public dialogue events. In recent years the Centre of Taiwan Studies has hosted Taiwanese presidential candidates, serving cabinet ministers, former foreign ministers and even former premiers. Often these kinds of events are cited as the most memorable for students during their time at SOAS. Allowing the students to engage with cultural and political practitioners strengthens their understanding of subjects in a way that cannot be achieved solely through academic readings and talks.

In the case of UCLan, at the undergraduate level, Korean Studies under the Korean pathway is highly focused on language; however, there has been an increasing level of requests from students to introduce more modules about politics, economics, and international relations of both Koreas. Therefore, the International Institute of Korean Studies, as a multidisciplinary hub of research, teaching and public policy in the study of contemporary Korea at UCLan, has helped to fill this gap. For example, the International Institute of Korean Studies has provided not only cultural activities for students to participate in, but also academic guest talk series and conferences so that students can explore various aspects of Korean Studies. In addition, the International Institute of Korean Studies plays its role as the face of Korean Studies at UCLan. As mentioned above, the Korean pathway does not represent Korea Studies itself at UCLan, but rather stays as a subject area under the three main courses. Based on this, the International Institute of Korean Studies was strategically established as a body representing Korean Studies at UCLan.

At the postgraduate level, the International Institute of Korean Studies works as a platform for both the MA and PhD programs in Korean Studies at UCLan. In other words, while the BA Korean pathway is run under the APS, TESOL and MOLA umbrellas, the (North) Korean Studies MA and PhD programs are more closely attached to the International Institute of Korean Studies activities in a way to provide an independent study environment for students. For example, the School has funded the 'Postgraduate student-led Guest Talk Series'. Experts in North Korean Studies have been invited by students, which has successfully gained more attention among students. In doing so, the International Institute of Korean Studies has played its role as a scholarly networking platform which students can benefit from. This link between the School and the Institute has worked positively in order to provide a strong academic environment at the postgraduate level.

5   Challenges Ahead

As seen above, Korean Studies at UCLan started with language teaching; however, the institution has gradually increased its non-language modules. Despite this, there is an increasing level of requests from students to introduce more modules that address such topics as politics, economics, and the international relations of both Koreas. The reason why the Korean pathway at UCLan tends to focus more on language is partly because it does not offer post-A-Level Korean language modules. A-Level in the UK is equivalent to the high school education system in other countries, and currently, both Japanese and Chinese are run based on the post-A-Level curriculum, as both languages are included in the secondary education in the UK, while Korean is not. Accordingly, Korean language modules at UCLan remain at Ab Initio levels, which means, students cannot gain high proficiency when graduating with their BA. In order to overcome a "language-academy"-like system, language modules need to be developed as post-A-Level, which means students' language proficiency after graduation becomes a lot higher. Converting the current curriculum level to post-A-Level requires the introduction of Korean language as one of the language subjects at GCSE and A-Level. Once the post-A-Level curriculum is introduced at BA level, more non-language modules will need to be designed.

There are three major challenges at the postgraduate level facing UCLan Korean Studies. First, one of the prominent challenges facing our postgraduate teaching in Korean Studies can be found in the lack of scholarship opportunities. As mentioned above, scholarships are important for PhD candidates to have a better-quality environment for their research. However, this not only applies for PhDs, but MA students are also seeking scholarship opportunities, especially international students. In order to create a better-quality postgraduate environment, achieving external funding for PhDs, and even for MAs, is crucial. Second, external funding for academic activities at the International Institute of Korean Studies, which can contribute to high quality development of Korean Studies, needs to be guaranteed at a sustainable level. Finally, from the discussions over dual/double degree programs with partner institutions, it turns out that, in comparison, UCLan lacks module options. Unlike the structure in many East Asian countries, UCLan tends to have a minimum number of modules and, thus, students are forced to choose among a small number of modules. In order to provide a wider scope of knowledge development, we must consider expanding module options covering a broader disciplinary spectrum within Korean Studies. In the end, the future of Korean Studies lies in building on its multidisciplinary and interdisciplinary bases which includes various fields of study.

At SOAS, the Taiwan teaching program faces similar challenges. Like at UCLan, scholarships are a challenge, especially for MA students. One of the long-term goals has been to establish a MA Taiwan Studies scholarship that replicates what is available for Japanese, Korean and Chinese Studies students. In contrast, students doing PhDs on Taiwan have found funding easier to obtain. One of the constant challenges is how to resist the calls to cut smaller niche modules at a time when the UK universities are under financial pressure. Since SOAS has had to close a couple of Taiwan modules over the last few years, there have been many discussions over what kind of new modules to introduce and how to make sure such options are sustainable. A further challenge has been related to external funding. Since one SOAS Taiwan Studies teaching post is supported by a Taiwan Ministry of Education Teaching grant, there is always some risk that if external funding is cut or removed, then some of the Taiwan modules would come under threat. A further challenge is administrative. The extensive events program puts quite heavy administrative pressure on teaching staff and the Centre of Taiwan Studies has only managed to gain limited part-time administrative support. As at UCLan, SOAS staff often have a difficult act balancing the disparate demands of administration, research, and teaching.

6   Conclusions

In this chapter, we have compared two unique area studies programs – Taiwan Studies at SOAS and Korean Studies at UCLan. Area studies is interdisciplinary and, thus, humanities, linguistics and social sciences have all been integrated into both Taiwan and Korean Studies. SOAS Taiwan Studies has had a humanities and social science centered approach, with languages (especially Hokkien) a secondary component. In contrast, UCLan started its Korean Studies program with a heavy focus on language, but recently more non-language modules have been introduced, especially with its postgraduate program. Both programs are attempting to offer a more comprehensive coverage of their relevant countries for their students. After two decades of Taiwan Studies at SOAS, its teaching program is an important case supporting the argument that we are experiencing a Golden Age in international Taiwan Studies.[7] In comparison,

---

7   Fell, Dafydd. "FORUM: The State of the Field of Global Taiwan Studies Institutions: A Time for Optimism or Pessimism." *International Journal of Taiwan Studies*, 1, no. 2 (2018), 371–394.

Korean Studies at UCLan has started much more recently and is expected to develop further in the future.

Both SOAS Taiwan Studies and UCLan Korean Studies teaching programs have expanded successfully. While SOAS Taiwan Studies has been more focused at the postgraduate level, UCLan Korean Studies was initially based on its BA program. However, although beginning from different starting points, both are developing a greater degree of balance between their undergraduate and postgraduate programs. Both universities believe in the advantage of offering a unique set of country specific modules that are not available at competing universities. At the same time, Korean culture and Taiwanese culture have been very good starting points for students to engage in both studies. While both SOAS and UCLan share many similarities in their Taiwan and Korean teaching programs, one of the most noteworthy differences can be found in UCLan's MA dual/double degree strategy. Both universities offer study abroad for language development at the undergraduate level, but so far it is only UCLan which provides dual/double degree programs at the MA level.

While both the SOAS and UCLan programs are well-integrated in their university structures, both the Centre of Taiwan Studies and the International Institute of Korean Studies face similar challenges such as securing external funding and scholarship opportunities. In order to provide continuous academic activities which can contribute to teaching programs, and retain quality students, external funding is essential. At the same time, academics need to focus more on teaching-related research activities rather than administrative burdens. In order to provide quality teaching and research environments for both students and academics, both universities will require innovative strategies as well as strong engagement with relevant funders.

References

Fell, Dafydd. "FORUM: The State of the Field of Global Taiwan Studies Institutions: A Time for Optimism or Pessimism." *International Journal of Taiwan Studies*, 1, no. 2 (2018): 371–394.

Fell, Dafydd and Sung-sheng Yvonne Chang. "Developing Taiwan Studies Teaching Program in Europe and the United States: the experience of SOAS University of London and University of Texas at Austin." *China Quarterly*, 240 (2019): 1108–1134.

Rigger, Shelley. "Political Science and Taiwan's Domestic Politics: The State of the Field." *Issues and Studies*, 38, no. 4 (2002): 49–92.

Index